Ed Su-

THE GOOD RAIN

THE GOOD RAIN

Across Time and Terrain
in the Pacific Northwest

Timothy Egan

 ALFRED A. KNOPF   NEW YORK   1990

THIS IS A BORZOI BOOK
PUBLISHED BY ALFRED A. KNOPF, INC.

Copyright © 1990 by Timothy Egan
Maps copyright © 1990 by George Colbert

All rights reserved under International and Pan-American Copyright
Conventions. Published in the United States by Alfred A. Knopf, Inc.,
New York, and simultaneously in Canada by Random House of Can-
ada Limited, Toronto. Distributed by Random House, Inc., New York.

Library of Congress Cataloging-in-Publication Data
Egan, Timothy.
The good rain: across time and terrain in the Pacific Northwest /
Timothy Egan.
p.   cm.
ISBN 0-394-57724-8
1. Northwest, Pacific—Description and travel.   2. Northwest, Pa-
cific—History.   3. Landscape—Northwest, Pacific.   I. Title.
F851.E28   1990
979.5—dc20   89-43288   CIP

Manufactured in the United States of America
Published June 5, 1990
Second Printing, August 1990

To my mother,
who always said, Stay West,
and then showed me why

The flora and fauna grew or died, flourished or failed, in complete disregard for man and his aims. A Man Can Make His Mark, did they tell me? Lies, lies. Before God I tell you: a man might struggle and labor his livelong life and make no mark! None! No permanent mark at all! I say it is true.

KEN KESEY, Sometimes a Great Notion

Contents

Acknowledgments

Writing may be a solitary pursuit, but building a book is collaborative. Support, both inspirational and informational, came from Joni Balter, Wallace Turner and Joel Connelly in Seattle. Through their writings, Bruce Brown, Bill Dwyer, Murray Morgan, Emmett Watson and the late William O. Douglas helped to point me in the right direction. I'm grateful to Carol Mann in New York for her superb job of editorial matchmaking. I would also like to thank my editors at the *New York Times*, particularly Soma Golden and Jon Landman, for allowing me the time to try and get it right. Finally, I owe my biggest debt to Ash Green at Knopf.

T.E.

THE GOOD RAIN

Introduction

FINISHING UP WITH GRANDPA

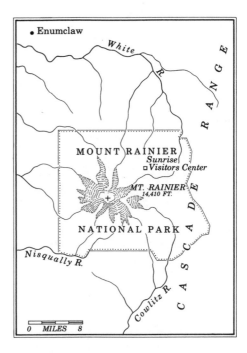

All summer long Grandpa remains in the basement, two pounds of cremated ash in a plain cardboard cylinder. I can't get used to the idea of this odorless beige powder as the guy who taught me how to land brook trout with a hand-tied fly, the son of a Montana mineral chaser, the teller of campfire tales about hiding from the Jesuits with his schoolboy chum, a jug-eared kid named Bing Crosby. He had smoked himself to death, and near the end Grandpa couldn't even take a pee without falling down and gasping for breath. He'd be lying on the bathroom floor of his house in Seattle, a plastic-tipped cigar clenched between his teeth, all that loose skin draped over a shrinking body. Fifty years of two packs a day, that's what did it. Finally, the emphysema literally asphyxiated him. He was as old as the twentieth century when he died.

My job is to bury him. Something appropriate, my Granny

3

says, handing me the cylinder after the funeral. "Just throw him off the ferry or dump him into the Yakima River," she says. "Whatever you think is best."

This sends me to the map. He'd fished every stream of substance on both sides of the Cascade Mountains, and when the Winnebagos and ghetto blasters began to invade the trout haunts close to home, he went north to British Columbia in search of the adrenal surge that came every time a foot-long native cutthroat rose from the glacial chill to snap one of his tricolored nymphs. With his hip-waders, history books and flasks of Murphy's, he wandered from the crest of the Canadian Rockies to the mean edge of the Pacific, following fish. As I think about what to do with him now, a river seems a logical last home. Like the chinook salmon that swim eight thousand miles from the Siberian shore to mate and then die in the same Cascade Mountain stream in which they were born, he needs to return, full cycle. But where, exactly?

Stumped for the time being, I set Grandpa on a stool in the basement of this tired house we are renting near Lake Washington. Joni and I live upstairs, but we have to pass through the basement in order to get outside. This means the what-to-do-with-Grandpa question is at least a twice-a-day nuisance. As the summer dries out and the pink glow off the western glaciers of Mount Baker disappears earlier and earlier, I begin to feel like a spiritual delinquent, holding up a long-planned reunion of body and soul.

Mid-fall now, the leaves of the red maple out front are clinging to a thread of memory, and we know he has to go. A winter with Gramps in the basement will not do. On a Sunday in late October, one of those weekends when the jet stream is lacerating southeast Alaska but leaving this corner of continental America alone, we put Grandpa in the car and drive south, heading for Mount Rainier. I decide to take him to the apex of the Northwest, the blue hulk which has shadowed over both of us for so long. The volcano of Rainier, I conclude, is where he belongs.

The road follows the water, beginning in Seattle, where Lake Washington is fed by the Cedar River, a point which used to be the favorite summer camp for the salmon-fat Duwamish Indians. Now, it's covered with Boeing barns stuffed with generic-green 737s and 757s. In his time, Grandpa could still fish the Cedar as it snaked toward the lake; he could take a ferry for a Sunday picnic in the park of Mercer Island; he could climb up the hills just east of the lake, the first swelling of the Cascades, and maybe see a cougar, or at least a few elk among the stands of hemlock and spruce. It's all highway and cul-de-sac now: the Cedar River straightened in parts by those orthodontists of nature, the Army Corps of Engineers; Mercer Island cut by ribbons of the most expensive freeway ever built and bridged by two of the world's longest floating spans; and the hills shaved and shorn of their five-hundred-year-old trees to make way for the waves of California exiles seeking a slice of paradise in a metropolis where insider-trading is not yet required in order to afford a first mortgage.

We follow the Cedar for twenty miles or more, until Rainier comes into sudden view, rising nearly three vertical miles above the dairy farms of Enumclaw. Here the valley is wide and oddly level, as if the Corps has been here earlier, correcting some quirk of nature which didn't match an Army engineer's blueprint. The flat valley is Rainier's own doing, the result of the largest mudflow ever known, a slide which eventually took with it the top two thousand feet of the mountain and spread a swath of broken basalt and clay for forty-five miles down the valley.

Past Enumclaw the road begins to climb, winding through fresh-shaved forest land, denuded in the modern style of the timber industry, and then picks up along the milky way of the White River. "Glacial piss" is what some fishermen call the White River—colder than a football trainer's icepack, the color of thin milk. Into this river Grandpa will go, or pass through; its source, like most of the water in these parts, is high up on Rainier, locked in another molecular form.

An hour's drive from Seattle we enter the national park, nearly 250 square miles of protected scenery, thanks in large part to those twin demons of turn-of-the-century timber barons, Theodore Roosevelt and John Muir. Roosevelt helped stir up populist sentiment, thundering against land-grabbers and tree-shavers; in turn, they named an elk after him. The prolific Muir, a naturalist who could massage a phrase as very few scientists can, provided the push from the pen. Muir's name is attached to the 10,000-foot-high camp on the most popular climbing route to Rainier's 14,410-foot summit. On summer weekends, Camp Muir is not unlike a small mining town on a roll, full of climbers laden with gear and seeking glory in higher ground. Old Man Muir, dragging around a beard that went past his navel, had a sense of humor not always evident among some of his modern-day followers. But he would most likely disapprove of the odd distinction the camp named after him has gained: it is the site of the world's most expensive outhouse, a $50,000 solar shitter which uses high-altitude ultraviolet rays to cook and compost climbers' waste.

My intention is to toss Grandpa's remains on the east side of the mountain, away from Camp Muir, so the ashes will scoot with Rainier's runoff until they blend with the trout streams below. First, though, I have to get him to the high point of the White River, where the drip of glacier melt and gravity conspire to form a common flow. We park the car at Sunrise Lodge, 6,400 feet above sea level, just below timberline, facing a crest of the Cascades where William O. Douglas roamed as a boy. The late Supreme Court Justice, a thin-haired noodle of a man who favored lonely alpine meadows and young wives, was that rare breed from another time, the Renaissance Man of the American West: lawyer, author, outdoorsman, lover. He was equally at home under a dripping canvas pup tent or in the halls of New York's Museum of Modern Art. In his later years, the sage of Goose Prairie, a hamlet just over the crest, was quite worn down; paranoid in the Nixon era, he feared that the FBI would grow marijuana plants on his Cascade Mountain ranch in an effort to trap him. In fitting tribute, a large tract of wild country that surrounds Goose Prairie is now the William O. Douglas Wilderness. The growing season is too short, the winds too harsh, for pot, something the FBI or a good defense lawyer would soon have learned.

The old visitors center at Sunrise is closed for the season. The grass nearby has the stiff, brown look of vegetation which has felt the sting of first frost. We find a trail leading up to the headwaters of the White River, Grandpa in the pack on my back, Joni carrying a bottle of a local Chardonnay. The day, by midmorning, is as bright as a calendar page. The huckleberry bushes are aflame, low red borders holding berries sweetened by the chill set against subalpine spruce. The cold nights have not been enough to freeze up the tarns and small lakes filling scooped-out bowls along the way. Here and there, deer poke around the edges.

After a thousand feet or so of elevation gain, the 12,307-foot summit of Mount Adams first appears to the southeast, in and out of view as we scale the ridges, its ice crown shining like a bald man doing chin-ups in the morning sun. Adams, in most other parts of the world, would be revered, a national park at least; here, in an area once said to have enough mountain scenery to fill a half-dozen Switzerlands, it is a seldom-visited sentinel in a ravaged land. Weyerhaeuser, the world's biggest lumberjack, owns most of the land between here and Mount Adams, at least that which is not ice or rock. They've left their usual calling cards, stumps and clearcuts.

We are breathing heavily now, taking in the chill air and exhaling exuberance. I kiss Joni, a native of Pittsburgh, where the rivers struggle to hold some hint of natural life. With every step upward, I feel a deeper attachment to this land. The trail peters out, disappearing among rock and wind-blown moraine dust. A few bony tufts of tree, polished skeletons at the edge of the alpine zone, protrude from the hard ground. At glacier's edge, several thousand feet above the White River valley, nothing grows or lives. In just over an hour, we have passed from full-throttled vegetation of the lower forest to the dead zone. We half-step our way to a rocky edge worn and wrinkled by the persistent moisture. Below, the valley drops steeply; a shout takes several seconds to land, and then bounces away.

"Here," I say to Joni. "This is the place." We laugh, both realizing the echo of Brigham Young, multiple wives and a caravan of zealots in tow, when he crossed the Wasatch Range and used those same words, now immortalized on the statue in the center of Salt Lake City.

I take out my map, the sweat atop my forehead dripping, and follow the glacier fingers down the summit. We are close to the Emmons Glacier, the longest ice mass in continental America, four miles of frozen precip, at its core as deep as the Seattle Kingdome from playing field to roof. I trace the glacier on the map and see that it is not the Emmons which feeds the White River. A lesser glacier, the Winthrop, appears to be the source.

I take Grandpa out of the pack and set him next to a rock. No wind. From below comes a marmot whistle, a high pierce. I think: Winthrop. What is an old Puritan's name doing up here, on the frozen side of a mountain that wasn't even spotted by white men until after the Revolutionary War? What cartographer's trick, or cheap flattery, placed the name Winthrop here, a country of noble Indian names—Tacoma, the original word for this mountain; Sluiskin Falls, named for the native who first led whites to the demon-dwelling pit of fire at the summit; Ohanapecosh, where the rivers meet below. Most of the English names were coined by syphilitic prospectors and timber beasts—the Frying Pan Glacier, Old Scab Mountain, Anvil Rock, Panhandle Gap. Why Winthrop? It's too genteel for this massive chunk of glacial anarchy, like an Eskimo in an Izod.

I will investigate later. Now, I'm shivering, the sweat turning cold on my skin. I put on a vest while Joni opens the wine. We sip, and soak in the scenery, seeking the rhythm of late October at eight thousand feet, the countryside slow to close down for the winter. I eat some smoked salmon, bread, an apple, drink more wine, all products of this land.

When he died, Grandpa was almost fifty years older than I, and I now wonder about my life at full term. This country of misted forests and untouched islands, of living volcanoes and a tidal shoreline that would stretch from Seattle to New York and back if laid out, has changed so

7

much in the course of his lifetime. Holding Grandpa, his eighty years reduced to these ashes in a cylinder, I realize we have gone from the canoe to the hydrofoil, from cedar longhouse to thousand-foot-high sky-scraper, in slightly more than the span of his life. Despite the material insulation in which we wrap ourselves, these tousled forests and ocean currents pushing through inland passages still determine how we live; the landscape overwhelms. We are not that removed—yet—from the arms of the land.

I do not live in the Northwest, nor did he, out of habit, although that is part of it. There are just under 12 million people in Washington, Oregon, Idaho and British Columbia, a bit more than the population of Sweden, and most of them live within one hour of the mountains. In the last light of day we can look up, from the low point of urban stress, and see the high point of outdoor relief—the natural neon of alpenglow. Is that the connective link from his generation to mine?

The wind has picked up some. A cloud cap, one of Rainier's mood halos, hustles over the summit. Joni is shivering. My ears are numb. It's time to finish up with Grandpa. I open the cylinder and stand. We say nothing, although she smiles. Solemnity does not fit either of us for long; like an itchy sweater, it is soon discarded. I tiptoe out to the edge of the rock. The wine, at this elevation after hard work, has made my head light and my feet slow to react. I swing back all the way and toss the ashes out. They shoot up and then curve down in a grand arc, a sepia-toned rainbow, stretching from this glacial edge to the dawning trickle of the White River, a thousand feet or more below. We watch until all the ashes have scattered from view. And then we say Goodbye.

In Seattle, I go to the library and look for something about Winthrop. I will face queries from family members, and I want to know as much as possible about this source of the White River. The Winthrop Glacier, says a thick, valuable book called *Place Names of Washington*, was so named by Theodore Winthrop during his summer visit to the Pacific Northwest in 1853. It must've been nice to be a tourist in those days: instead of returning home with a credit-card debt and a suitcase full of "I'm With Stupid" T-shirts, you left a legacy—peaks and rivers and glaciers named on whim. Theodore Winthrop was the great-great-great-grandson of John Winthrop, first governor of the Massachusetts Bay Colony, the original Puritan. A stuffed shirt, a humorless Yankee, I presume, out to manifest his destiny in a still-unspoiled part of the frontier.

Further investigation leads me to the *The Canoe and the Saddle*, Winthrop's account of the three months he spent in the Northwest that summer. At the time, he was twenty-five years old, well traveled and looking for fresh adventure, a Yale graduate who called himself a writer, and a humorist at that—he had yet to shake a tag as the family gadfly. I go to the oldest bookstore in Seattle, Shorey's, and ask about *The Canoe and the Saddle*. The clerk looks up from a written ledger (there is nothing even remotely late-twentieth-century about this bookstore) and smiles broadly. That book, he tells me, is not only one of the first ever written about the Pacific Northwest, but one of the best, to this day.

Three weeks later I go back to Shorey's and pick up my copy, on special order. In the meantime, I've learned a little more about Winthrop. He was a frustrated novelist, and it was only after his highly publicized death that his books—five works of fiction, all of which had been initially rejected by publishers, and *The Canoe and the Saddle*—became a sensation. As the first American officer killed in the Civil War, he was profiled and praised by virtually every paper in the northern states.

Like the legions of 1960s kids who took to the West in Volkswagen vans, he came to this corner of the country on a lark, looking for a new way of life and some high times and a clear fount of writerly inspiration. He found all of that, and more. His book was a song to the infant Northwest, and it was prophetic.

Winthrop arrived in the Oregon Territory in the early summer and quickly caught smallpox, the scourge of the native population. While convalescing in a fort above the Columbia River, he fell in love with the land. He felt as if he were living in a painting, one of those rich, pre-Impressionist oil renderings that had so gloried the Hudson River Valley. Stricken with the pox, he missed an early caravan back east. Rather than brood, he decided on a quick adventure—north of the Columbia. Late in the summer of 1853, he sailed to Victoria, then a handful of homes and a trading post on the large island which the British were trying to remake into an outpost of old England and had named for George Vancouver, a chubby, iron-willed explorer whose cartographic legacy is everywhere in these parts. It was on the southern tip of Vancouver Island that Winthrop began his journey back south and then east. That adventure is the story of *The Canoe and the Saddle*.

The trip of 320 miles took him by canoe down Puget Sound, by horseback around the north and east flanks of Mount Rainier, across the Cascades into the dry, fertile valley country around Yakima and then down to The Dalles, a desert cleave in the Cascades where the Columbia

River has carved out the magnificent gorge. At the time, there were less than four thousand whites living north of the river, in what is now Washington State and British Columbia, visited annually by 20 million people. Today, they come to see what Winthrop saw: the ice cone of Mount Baker rising off the horizon of the San Juan Islands; the whales playing in clear water surrounding the islands; the unbelievable bulk of Rainier, with its thirty-five square miles of eternal ice; the thousand-year-old evergreens thriving on Pacific storms that pummel the wet side of the Cascades; the desert flowers growing in rain shadow east of the crest, now orchard and wine country; the Columbia River, last great hope for a Northwest Passage, called the River of the West; the snowfields of Mount Hood, the juniper-tree high country surrounding Oregon's sawed-off volcanoes, and the sublime violence of that state's coastline.

Opening his book, I find that Winthrop, contrary to my perception of his Puritan breeding, is a renegade with the language—an unhoned Twain set loose in a country where no one can challenge him. His writing is undisciplined, given to flowery flights of description and sweeping racial denigration of the Coastal Salish Indians, who were then fast dying from the smallpox epidemic. He has little time for the characters he meets, hardscrabble prospectors, drunken explorers and natives who stink of body odor and campfires; he prefers the company of forests and creekbeds and durable horses.

Even so, he makes a few good points that are still pertinent nearly a century and a half later. Near the end of his journey, he concludes that a new human order can rise in the wilderness, a civilization ennobled by the wild, leaving behind the rusted thought and social patterns of the East, which he views as an America not yet a hundred years old but already showing signs of enfeeblement. In the Northwest, where the mountains meet the Pacific, Winthrop prophesied that a special breed would predominate, one infused with the spirit of the land; he hoped that the American character would mature at last in the far corner of the country.

He wrote:

> Our race has never yet come into contact with great mountains as companions of daily life, nor felt that daily development of the finer and more comprehensive senses which these signal facts of nature compel. That is an influence of the future. These Oregon people, in a climate where being is bliss—where every breath is a draught of vivid life—these Oregon people, carrying to a newer

> and grander New England of the West a full growth of the Amer-
> ican Idea . . . will elaborate new systems of thought and life.

New systems of thought and life—is that what's clogging the freeways
of the Puget Sound megalopolis, the Willamette Valley and the urban
forest above the Fraser River? After setting Winthrop aside for several
years, I resolve to follow his footsteps and look at what's developed in the
presence of a countryside "strong, savage and majestic." Forget the
boundary of Canada and America at the 49th Parallel; the Northwest is
united by landscape, not divided by latitude lines. The regional icons—
salmon and trees and mountains and water—spring from the elements.
If people here become too far removed from those basic sources of life,
then they lose the bond to a better world.

Winthrop completed his trip in fourteen days, a virtual sprint by horse
and canoe. I will take a year, attempting to follow the Yankee from Oregon
desert to green-smothered rain forest, from storm-battered ocean edge to
the inland waters, from the new cities of the Northwest to the homesteads
of the Columbia Plateau, to see what a century can produce from scratch,
and maybe . . . come to some understanding of why Grandpa belonged
in the wellspring of the White River, as do I.

Chapter 1

THE CONTINENTAL HEAVE

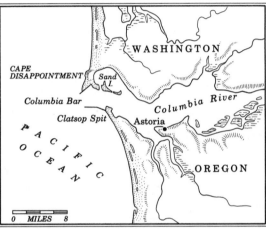

During the last month of the driest winter in a hundred years, I go to the wettest spot in continental America, looking for truth from the sky and the sea. The moisture is predatory in this part of the world, and no element, be it stone or wood or tin or steel, lasts very long without losing some part of its composition to the nag of precipitation. Lewis and Clark, the moonwalkers of the early nineteenth century, spent four miserable months here, the winter of 1805–06, in a spongy spruce forest about two miles from the beach on the Oregon side of the Columbia River. Of all the real estate which Jefferson wanted to have a look at, none was wetter or more wild than the country here at land's end. Sick of eating fish and crazed by toe-rot, they recorded only a dozen days without rain.

Now, in late winter, everybody is talking drought, as if the earth were in the midst of a prolonged snit. In the churches they call it ungodly and whisper in apocalyptic overtones, for this is not Jimmy Swaggart shake-and-shout country, but heavily Scandinavian and emotion-tamed. In the bars they call it unmanly. Sunshine? That's for people who think salmon sprout from bagel factories in Iowa and come with little umbrellas. Here in the seaport of Astoria, the oldest permanent American settlement west of the Rockies, cars wear coats of third-generation rust and wrinkled bumper stickers with the warning "We Ain't Quaint."

The sun is villainous: it warms the river, spooks the salmon, browns the evergreens, wilts the winter wheat, dries up the mushrooms, cracks the skin, befuddles the fish, the sea lions and the birds—they don't know when it's time to go home. About eighty miles north of here, beyond the hamlet of Humptulips at the headwaters of Washington's Wynoochee River, it rains nearly two hundred inches annually, wettest spot in the Lower 48. Most of it comes in the winter, which can be like a season of living in a leaky basement. This year, January brought less rain than usually falls in July, and February passed without a gully-washer. Suicides are down, the camellias are blossoming, the tulips are at the gate. Must be a tear in the ozone, people say, or the jet stream has jumped track. Maybe the preacher's finally going to get it right.

Except for the coastal strip from northern California on up, most of the American West is a desert, flat-bottomed and mountainous, kept alive by two arteries: the Colorado and the Columbia, both of them overworked. "A land of little rainfall and big consequences," as Wallace Stegner said. The culture and population centers of the Southwest are built around the sun; in the Northwest, life flourishes under a cloud cover. Water shocks color and movement into even the most sedentary of life forms. The intrusion of brown in this land of green sets off alarms. A drought causes fear, then wild speculation, and finally panic as once-familiar land becomes a stranger.

In Astoria, as elsewhere in the Northwest, they are tired of this planetary prank, and waste no time taking drastic measures. In Seattle a few months earlier, the city had created the water police, a hydro-sniffing platoon on the prowl for car-washers and violators of the three-minute limit for showers. The mayor, pointing to pictures of water reservoirs at one-tenth of the normal level, encouraged neighbor to snitch on neighbor. The governor created the position of water czar and then told the 4.6 million residents of Washington to put bricks in their toilets. A flush spared is a fish saved. For several months, there was a run on bricks. Along the waterfront of Astoria, a middle-aged woman at the market said that thirty-seven straight days had passed without rain last summer. She said it as if her son had cancer: *thirty-seven days, and I've tried to live a good life.*

Astoria's sense of self is wrapped up in the elements; rain and raging sea must be constant companions. Life is flat, sterile, and entirely too comfortable without storm or tidal tantrum. For two centuries, the consensus here has been that what happens indoors is of little consequence compared to what happens Out There. Mysteries of current and tide, of gravitational pull and spring runoff, of moonlit gillnetting and dark-season tree-felling, are vital secrets, not easily learned or shared. The history of the Northwest begins, and to some extent is still influenced by, the daily struggle just west of here, where the Columbia River, mightiest of Western waterways, meets the Pacific, the bully of oceans.

The wandering Theodore Winthrop, twenty-five years old as he entered the Northwest following a three-week sail up the Pacific Coast from San Francisco, was much impressed by the Columbia Bar. He was no geographical ingénue, having spent his years after Yale traveling through Europe, South America, Central America and up the California coast. In 1853, the year of his Northwest visit, Congress funded the first West Coast lighthouse, to be planted at Cape Disappointment, a mound of sea-pounded rock above the bar. The bark *Oriole*, loaded down with supplies and engineers to build the beacon, sank on the shoals offshore of the cape, a cruel joke appreciated by no one except a few Chinook Indians whose ancestors have plied the vertical waters of the bar for centuries in cedar dugouts. On a spring day young Winthrop took a look at this sumo match of gravity and tide, and wrote, in the opening lines of *The Canoe and the Saddle*:

> A wall of terrible breakers marks the mouth of the Columbia, Achilles of rivers. Other mighty streams may swim feebly away seaward, may sink into foul marshes, may trickle through ditches of an oozy delta, may scatter among sandbars the currents that once moved majestic and united. But to this heroic flood was destined a short life and a glorious one—a life all one strong, victorious struggle, from the mountains to the sea.

The struggle from mountains to sea is considerably more indirect now, with hurdles of concrete at every big bend and more than 130 dams of all sizes on the tributaries of the river. But the incorrigible breakers of the Columbia Bar hold clues to the character of this country, and into the mouth of the ancient guardian of the Pacific Northwest I must go to find a taste of the ages.

"If you fall in the water, the first thing you want to do is pull the flare out from your life vest and point it at a forty-five-degree angle. Whatever you do, don't point it back at you—it'll take your face off."

And if a wave knocks the flare out of my hand?

"Then you want to reach into the other vest pocket and pull out this beeper, so we have a chance of finding you through the signal."

Should I tread water?

"No. You lose body heat faster that way. It only takes twenty minutes in these waters for hypothermia to set in. What you want to do is curl up your legs in a sort of ball, to preserve whatever heat you can."

When's the last time you lost somebody?

"We lose about ten people a year off this bar, sometimes twelve or more. Most of 'em drown before we can get to them."

Lt. Michael Monteith is taking me to the Columbia Bar on a boat that's supposed to be sink-proof, designed to roll 360 degrees if necessary. It is a forty-foot barrel cut in half and sealed tight, essentially, and bobs like one heading for the cliff of Niagara. Not very fast. The basic rescue boat. Naval types come from all over the world to see how the Americans master this bar with this boat. I'm on a training run, midmorning, dressed in orange body suit, waterproof except for a slight opening around the neck. A former schoolteacher from South Carolina, Monteith runs the station at Cape Disappointment, considered the most hazardous Coast Guard operation in the Lower 48, with one rescue mission a day, on average. He's thirty-seven, looks twenty-two—his face preserved by the unrelenting moisture. Most of his underlings are teenagers, kids with faint mustaches, easy jokes. The base doesn't seem like the military; more like the fire department at sea, where the gang waits in summer for the inevitable call to pull some cokehead out of the surf off Peacock Spit, and in winter to collect fishermen from the froth.

When the waves crash over the bow and into my face, which they do with increased frequency as we move closer to the bar, the water spills down my neck and stomach. Cold. But I'm not worried about the chill. I want to look inside the throat of this beast, the river bar Lewis and Clark labeled "the bare ribs of the continent, that seven-shouldered horror." Though muscle-bound and flood-trained for most of its length, the Columbia comes to a crashing finale here, the end of a 1,243-mile ride

that drains 250,000 square miles and then collides head-on with Pacific breakers. Were it not for this stretch of profound turbulence, the American Northwest would probably belong to England, or Spain, or Russia, or it might even be its own nation-state united with British Columbia. For two centuries, the best mariners in the world, flying the flag and carrying the cross, couldn't find this river with its four-mile-wide mouth. Fools, schemers, liars, incompetents, connivers—every name in the book was thrown at them when they returned, unable to locate the Northwest Passage.

Every bit of water falling on all of France, channeled into one drainpipe—that's similar to what goes into the Columbia, or at least a shallow part of it. The river's source is a glacial drip 2,619 feet above sea level in the foothills of the Canadian Purcells; by its midway point in a high desert, the Columbia has a depth several hundred feet below the ocean plane. The only river to smash through the Cascades, the Columbia carved an eighty-five-mile gorge through the basalt spine of a mountain range with little fat. Snowmelt from the Cascades, the Rockies, the Selkirks, the Monashees, the Bitterroots, and every ounce of pine sweat and heather dew west of the Continental Divide from lower British Columbia to parts of Utah, Wyoming, Montana, Idaho, Nevada, Oregon and Washington muscle their way into the Columbia. In the Western Hemisphere, no river empties more water into the Pacific.

And yet, most of the modern Columbia is flaccid, pinched by fourteen big dams, which back up fourteen big lakes. Upriver, where once there was violence and froth, now there is order and glass. In the scablands where the Snake River meets the Columbia, engineers operating out of a government nuclear reservation half the size of Rhode Island water-ski atop the surface of a river that used to dump settlers into hellish whirlpools. This river may have been shaped by God, or glaciers, or the remnants of the inland sea, or gravity or a combination of all, but the Army Corps of Engineers controls it now. The Columbia rises and falls, not by the dictates of tide or rainfall, but by a computer-activated, legally-arbitrated, federally-allocated schedule that changes only when significant litigation is concluded, or a United States Senator nears election time. In that sense, it is reliable.

This dog on a leash occasionally bites back. Just after World War II, though freshly harnessed by the completion of the Grand Coulee Dam, the Columbia rose up with spring rain and snowmelt and wiped out a city of forty thousand on the Oregon shore north of Portland. Without warning, the war-born town of Vanport was gone, insta-shacks crushed and neat little streets swooshed away. Most of the residents were working at the time, smelting bauxite into aluminum at Henry Kaiser's factory. Buried under the surge, Vanport was never rebuilt.

I'm in Astoria this month, at a time when winter storms usually chew at the coastline like a rabid hound tearing at a couch, to get a sense of what is left of this power, to ride the same river stretch that Winthrop rode during his introduction to the Northwest in the nineteenth century—if it can be found. The thrust of Winthrop's prophecy, that the land in this last unspoiled corner of continental America would have a wonderful influence on its future inhabitants, requires the prophet-checker to first inspect the foundation. Is the natural world intact? Winthrop began his journey here in 1853, crossing the Columbia Bar in order to see the land hidden behind the surf, a passage of will that has frightened even the most sea-scarred. Captain John Wilkes, the naval officer sent by the White House in 1841 to circumnavigate the globe and, on the way back, to see whether any of the Oregon Country was worth fighting the British over, took a look at the Columbia River Bar after three years at sea and reached for his thesaurus. "Mere description can give little idea of the terrors of the Bar," he wrote. "It is one of the most fearful sights that can possibly meet the eye."

The oldtimers here, the men with ocean-polished faces who still speak with thick accents and congregate at the Sons of Norway Hall for secret rituals and snorts of chilled vodka with their vile-tasting *lutefisk,* refer to this area by its historical tag: the Graveyard of the Pacific. Justifiably, such talk makes them feel more alive. The Columbia River Bar has swallowed more ships, about 2,100 at last count, than any other location on the Pacific north of Mexico. "Graveyard of the Pacific" is not some desperate booster slogan seized upon after all the canneries closed down and the money left town. The Chamber of Commerce hates it when locals bring up shipwrecks. They don't want to scare people. It's all under control now, they say.

As we move out beyond the rock walls of Cape Disappointment and into the ocean, my stomach softens to mush. The sealed half-barrel seems as helpless as a twig in a whirlpool. Now the roar of the surf is too loud for conversation; Lt. Monteith communicates with hand signals and eyebrow pushups. Looking back toward the river entrance, I see nothing but a wall of breakers. The Columbia . . . disappears! Then, to the front—more breakers. The River of the West, which first began showing up on maps as early as 1709—eighty-three years before it was officially discovered—where'd it go? The Northwest Passage? I'm sorry. There is no river into the continent from the west, your majesty. It's a phantom, this Northwest Passage. Now I have some understanding of why it took so long for Europeans to find this waterway: it has been protected by natural camouflage. Just as a porcupine throws quills at intruders and a cactus guards its moisture with stinging lances, the land here has its own front line of defense in the violent surf. But, in an age when most of the river-wrestling is done by government workers sitting behind green computer screens in underground rooms, does this old guardian of the Northwest still mean anything?

Still dazed by a ride through the spin-dry cycle of the bar, I walk the ancient streets of Astoria. Surrounded by fresh-cut logs stacked for export to Japan and studded with old hotels where a seasonal worker can still rent a room for sixty dollars a week, Astoria is among the last of the West's true Resource Towns. They used to be everywhere in this part of the world—Monte Cristo, Washington; Bonanza City, Idaho; Goldcreek, Montana; Barkerville, British Columbia. Somebody would strike gold, or find a vein of coal, or build a planked skid road to scoot the timber downhill, or set up a fishwheel, and people would swarm in. Overnight, the towns sprouted hotels, whorehouses and hiring camps, and just as easily shed them when all the timber was cut or the silver mined or the fish netted. Theodore Winthrop's song to the scenery was seldom heard above the growl of all the primitive machines used to attack the object of his flattery. Not to the Resource Towns of the Northwest was the New England model of village-platting and orderly agricultural communities applied. In the hamlets notched from mountain sides and scratched into river valleys, it was grab and guzzle.

Most of those towns have been used up, and the honest outdoor laborer is an endangered species. Even though timber and fish are selling at record high prices, the towns built near the source of these basic products of the Pacific Northwest are sick. Some say it's the revenge of the land. The Resource Towns that are healthy, like Bend, in the high desert of central Oregon, or Coeur d'Alene, in the Idaho Panhandle, have put in tanning salons and River-Vue Estates. Others have gone Cute, packaging a savage past in theme-park sanitation. Astoria? In the center of this town is a section of a Douglas fir, a slice of botanical history from a six-hundred-year-old tree that once stood 230 feet high and provided enough wood to build a dozen homes. It's a museum piece, the kind of stump you see in every spent timber town of the Northwest. Once, the waterfront here was cluttered with thirty-nine salmon canneries, wobbly warehouses built on piers over the Columbia, a sight which astonished Rudyard Kipling when he got off the boat. But no more—every cannery in Astoria has closed. The Columbia River chinook run, once the greatest wild salmon run on the planet, was nearly wiped out by overfishing and dams. For a while, there was talk of declaring the fish that is synonymous with this land an endangered species.

For the time being, there are enough trees around Astoria still to cut, mostly scrawny second-growth from the timber farms, and enough fish still to catch, mostly dim salmon from the fish hatcheries, to keep this seaport from joining the ranks of the Resource Towns that have gone Cute. But this is a tough year to hold on to the land and the sea as a source of livelihood. Not since the Dust Bowl days, when Woody Guthrie wrote a populist anthem about how the great River of the West would turn "our darkness to dawn," has the Columbia been so low.

However, even in low-water years, the river still has a considerable amount of punch left at Astoria. I'm drawn to one such casualty of the capricious Columbia, the wreck of the *Peter Iredale*, a four-masted British sailing vessel that went aground in the fall of 1906 off Clatsop Spit, just south of the bar. The fully barnacled skeleton of this relic lies half-buried in soft sand. I step around the rusted ribs, late sun tinting the frame to cinnamon. The waves are gentle at Clatsop, no hint of the horror just around the corner, where it looks as if dynamite is blasting the sea at the location of the bar. And at night, there's fresh evidence that the Columbia lives: when I return to Astoria, I hear news of a shipwreck.

Just past sunrise this morning, during the opening week of a brief commercial fishing season, the frenzied bar crushed a salmon boat and dumped the crew into the swirling mouth. It's all very ho-hum around Astoria, where tragedies at sea provide a steady business. Not by accident was the first millionaire on the Columbia a pilgrim who set up a bar pilot service, guiding the frightened through hell for a stiff fee. The fishermen whose boat went down this morning were chasing the first returning salmon of the year, the big spring chinook. Following the rough outline of the old Siberian land bridge, then down along the Continental Shelf, the chinooks may swim eight thousand miles sniffing for clues to direct them back to the natal homeland. The Columbia carries so much water to the Pacific that the salmon sense some dilution three hundred miles from the river mouth. After picking up the hint, they start to make the left turn home. Ten thousand years or more of Indian prayers have been directed at the left turn.

Before the dams, some chinook would swim as far inland as the Continental Divide, deep in Idaho, Montana and British Columbia, before committing the final act of fornication, a very proper squirt before death. Like British sex, it is dignified and oddly ritualistic, following a strict set of biological rules, most of which seem to make no sense at first glance. From a seasonal perspective, the year really begins now, at the start of the first salmon run. Up and down the length of the Columbia and along the coast and into the interior, all things slowly come to life with the start of the left turn. The rain forest quakes, giant fern stems coiled for release; the fifth-generation anglophiles in Victoria prune their roses and mow their lawns for the first time since October; the skiers on the volcano of Mount Baker wax their K2s for corn snow; the tavern owners of Seattle's Pioneer Square hold a week-long drunk outdoors in the drizzle, set to music, on the site of the original Skid Road; the overbundled eco-activists shed their sweaters and hold their first howl for the wolves; the vintners in the Yakima Valley crack inaugural bottles from last year's crush; Indians shore up faulty wood platforms for dipnet fishing and pray to a variety of gods that the Army Corps of Engineers will not go ahead with a plan to dredge the last free-flowing stretch of the Columbia. All life, pulsing in late winter to begin the new year, craves the clouds that ride across the Pacific on the warm Japan Current and then collide with the Olympic and Cascade mountains.

This morning, the white commercial fishermen, most of whom seem to hate the Indian fishermen, are finding a decent number of chinook who've reached the Columbia. Migrating salmon do not eat once they enter the river. The Indians have traditionally caught them by spear or dipnets attached to the end of twenty-foot-long poles. The whites set up nets that snag the fish in their gills. Approaching the bar where the fish funnel into the Columbia, the boats navigate through a tide that courses at up to ten knots and an equally powerful river current pushing the other way. In places outside the narrow channel of the bar, a boat can ground on sand, and is then quickly crushed by the fist of the surf. Nobody ever really masters it. Today the crew of the ill-fated twenty-eight-foot boat are thrown into the froth, but manage to find their way to Sand Island, an ever-shifting oasis of silt and sediment which has been to shipwrecked sailors what the Heartbreak Hotel is for broken lovers. Nobody lives there; the island is too windswept, too waterswept, too unconnected. But it's something to hold on to. Both Washington and Oregon used to claim Sand Island, a dispute that led to gunfights between gill-netters and purse-seiners, each armed with different state fishing laws.

The salmon wars of Sand Island lasted until the United States Supreme Court awarded the island to Oregon. Washington now begins at Cape Disappointment.

The Snake, the Pend Oreille, the Spokane, the Clearwater, the Owyhee, the Deschutes—all of these rivers used to carry salmon to the desert, a twice-yearly occurrence surely as miraculous as the irrigation which brought golden wheat and plump fruit to the treeless hills above the central Columbia. Now the desert east of here is full of Corps of Engineers trucks; the salmon travel the interstate, or die. Most of the young fish don't do well on the highway. A maze of ladders, locks, lifts, channels and portages is used to help the dying older chinooks reach their spawning grounds upstream. When their eggs hatch and the young fry start to head downstream, they run smack into the hydroelectric turbines. Many are sliced and diced in these massive blenders. Others die of the bends, tossed to such depths and then pushed up so quickly that their respiratory systems can't adjust in time. More than half of all the young salmon which head downstream, seeking the ocean and three or four years of wandering, expire before they get past the first few hurdles.

Under pressure, the Corps started trucking some of the young fish downstream several years ago. In early spring, Interstate 84, which follows the Columbia River Gorge from desert to rain forest, is full of these silver government trucks. This particular year, Congress directed the Corps to spend $9 million to help the young salmon get around the turbines of the government dams. But the Corps is balking. They are willing to spend $60 million on a proposal to dredge Grays Harbor to make easier the foreign exploitation of raw logs from the forests nearby, but they have nothing for the native salmon. And it gets stranger yet. While one arm of the government is serving Columbia River salmon at the state dinner for Russian President Mikhail Gorbachev—the fish is a national treasure, the White House chef says—another arm is trying to kill off the remaining wild stock of that salmon.

When asked about all of this, Corps officials point out that their mandate is to dam, dredge and direct rivers. Fish belong to Fisheries. River-bottom-scraping and rapid-taming and lock-building have made Lewiston, Idaho, an ocean port. Everything gets through but the salmon. But at what price? The loss of a regional right. The Pacific Northwest is simply this: wherever the salmon can get to. Rivers without salmon have lost the life source of the area. I will stick to that yardstick, following the historical fish arteries from the continental crest to the ocean, and consider the dams a false boundary marker.

I wonder now, staring at one of the last bucking stretches of the Columbia, whether the river will soon become just another quaint background object, the tame centerpiece of the next Western theme park. While Seattle, Portland and Vancouver gleam and prosper with their glass monoliths to match the mountains, virtually every town along the river and up and down the coast has double-digit unemployment. Several of the river villages are officially bankrupt and have had to close their police and fire departments, the last vestiges of government. In the grocery stores of these towns, king salmon sells for eight and nine dollars a pound. Timber, with the Japanese demand, is at an all-time high; a ten-foot cedar two-by-four sells for twelve dollars in Astoria. Both are out of reach for the person who helped bring them to market.

And where have all the jobs gone? In the last decade, more timber was cleared from the Northwest than ever before, by the fewest amount of loggers ever employed for such volume. Like the big trees themselves, romance and heroism are fast fading from the lumberjack trade. Today, evergreens are cut with giant snippers attached to bulldozer-like vehicles, and mills are slouching toward full automation. Nearly a century and a half after Winthrop sailed up the Columbia, saying no amount of avarice or technology could control or deplete this bounty, salmon and trees are in short supply, owned by companies whose fortunes are traded on Wall Street, three thousand miles from this colony, and sold in a fashion similar to the exporting behavior of Third World countries. From the damp timber village of Raymond to the oyster-rich ghost towns on Willapa Bay, the working stiff hears the refrain: give up the land and sea. Here, among the last of America's outdoor warriors, fishermen and gyppo loggers are told they must become waiters who say, Hello, my name is Bud.

Walking along Astoria's waterfront, I pass another car with the "We Ain't Quaint" bumper sticker. There seems to be some kind of revolt under way. This has always been a working waterfront. Bar pilots. Tugboats. Gillnetters. Hookers with orange hair. Seasonal marketplaces. Windowless taverns facing the water. Astoria still sweats, but only in spurts. The bar pilots are housed atop a rotting pier, perforated and mushed by the moisture, the wood washed to Pacific gray. Inside, everybody is chainsmoking and black-coffee-slurping. Captain James McAvoy takes off the bright orange coat he wears when he's inside his small ship that looks like a drainpipe, and he talks about the latest problem he's having with captains trying to cross the bar—they don't speak English. They come in for wood, from Japan or Korea or Taiwan or China, five-hundred-foot vessels looking for a load of raw logs from the Northwest colony. McAvoy was trying to lead one over the bar a few days ago, barking directions to make sure the ship found the fifty-five-foot-deep channel which would allow it to enter the continent. He said, "Turn to starboard three degrees." They thought he said, "Have a nice day."

At its worst, the collision of river and sea can create waves of up to a hundred feet at a point in the river that is so shallow from sediment that few ships can get through without expert guiding. Captain McAvoy, bearded and with blue eyes buried by overhanging brow, is the head of the Bar Pilots Association of Astoria. A chain smoker who knows how to use an active verb, he ain't quaint. He says the bar is like "two giant hammers smashing into each other."

What's it like inside his ship, which was built to take the biggest hit the bar could deliver?

"You seen a steel pipe before. Imagine one that can hold three guys, then roll it downhill. That's my ship on the bar."

He bought his boat from the German Coast Guard years ago; it looks like a submarine, painted orange, fully sealed, ugly as hell. He calls it the *Peacock*, after the ship Captain Charles Wilkes lost in 1841 when he tried to enter the bar. McAvoy's *Peacock* is designed to take the pressure of a hundred tons of water banging up against the skin of the hull. Twenty years after he started escorting ships into the Columbia, McAvoy still is scared to death of the bar. Any ship, any size, can get tossed. Earlier this year, while he was leading a container ship twice the length of a football field through the mouth, the current turned the Korean vessel around when it lost power temporarily. For more than an hour, the big boat was helpless, caught in the vise of river current and angry Pacific breakers. If it broke up, well, some of the beach-dwellers still count on a good wreck every now and then to get by. Oldtimers who live on Long Beach, the twenty-eight-mile-long Washington peninsula formed over the years by Columbia River sediment, say they used to pray for this manna from the sea, the charity of shipwrecks. It was God's way of redistributing wealth. A hundred years ago, the *Queen of the Pacific* was caught in the usual bind; three hundred tons of merchandise had to be thrown overboard, including pianos, fancy new clothes, hats, barrels of liquor. The whiskey ended up in the hands of some Sand Island fishermen, who threw a party that lasted a week. Stetson hats, plucked from the beach, were worn around the mouth of the Columbia for years.

These days, the big ships from Pacific Rim countries have autopilot and sonar and fathometers which warn of approaching shallow water; they come with fax machines printing out the latest from weather satellites above, and video channel charts. A lot of their captains don't want to use some old-fart bar pilot in an orange coat, approaching them in an orange ship that looks like a pipe. But the high-tech stuff—it doesn't mean shit here, says McAvoy.

"This river is like a snake," he says. "You gotta know when to turn and when to jump. All the gadgetry behind the wheel won't help you decipher local currents. We're talking a quarter-million-odd cubic feet a second out there, a ten-knot current, sometimes. I've seen floating lighthouses go down."

Does McAvoy feel like he's part of a dying profession, the last of a breed. "Dying?" he says, lighting a new cigarette with his old one. "What d'ya mean by that?"

"The trends don't look good. Ever thought of opening a tanning salon?"

"Hell—everybody's dying."

Early the next morning, still no sign of the low clouds that permanently park themselves over these parts in winter. I go up to the top of Coxcomb Hill, the highest point in Astoria, where a faded column frieze commemorates the two centuries of white history here. Firmly anchored to the north slope of the hill, Astoria could've been San Francisco but for the abusive storms of the dark season. Astoria is crafted to the peculiarities of this hill, washed by the rain and sculpted by the Pacific wind. The town seems a place of brooding resignation, where hope and commerce peaked long ago. The population, stalled at ten thousand for half a century, still makes Astoria one of the most populous towns on the Pacific Coast north of San Francisco.

In many parts of the American West, anything older than a mobile home is sometimes considered historic. Not so for Astoria, which seems built up beyond its purpose, like an accountant with bulging forearms and a tattoo on his ass. The British took it during the War of 1812, the Confederacy roamed offshore in the Civil War, and the Japanese fired a few rounds from a submarine during World War II. This was to be the "New York of the West," capital of a fur empire founded by John Jacob Astor of Manhattan. He never saw the city named for him; the owners of most Resource Towns seldom got out among the muck that brought them all their money. The New York monicker, and similar names transplanted from the East, have been dropped on locations all over the Northwest, as if they could bestow some instant sophistication on the stumpland settlements. Seattle's first name was New York–Alki, the last word a bit of Chinook jargon meaning "eventually." When the city expanded north across Lake Union, David Denny named the new part of town Brooklyn. Farther up Puget Sound the city of Everett, in a moment of profound sycophancy, was named for the toddler son of a New York Resource Baron who was supposed to build an empire on the mudflats of Port Gardner; its first name was Lowell, after the Massachusetts town. Trying to flatter the New York capitalist at a dinner in Manhattan, the North-westerners offered the name of his boy, who was crawling around at their feet. Oregon has Albany, but most of the state's cities are named for Bay State locations—Salem, Medford, Springfield. Boston lost out to Portland in a coin toss.

Up the 164 steps of the Astoria Column's circular stairway I go. Atop the promontory, the wind is fierce, the sky scrubbed clean and salty. The big river snakes the last few miles and then empties into the horizon. I look in every direction, but I'm drawn to the kicking bar.

Lieutenant Monteith's face is grim. The killer breakers are about three hundred yards away, off a tongue of sand called Peacock Spit. He tells me to hold on tight to the rail of our boat while a smaller ship, a thirty-foot wave-slicer, pulls up. This other boat is faster, a bullet used to get in and out of Peacock in a hurry. If you really want to butt heads with the bar, the bullet is the way to go, he says. The smaller vessel, called a surf rescue boat, coasts to within three feet of our craft, which is riding six-foot swells.

"When I give you the word, jump over to the other boat," Monteith says.

"What?"

"Jump! Now!"

On board the thirty-foot bullet are two men in helmets, face visors and orange-sealed body suits; they look like hornets. They pull me up on deck and strap me into the boat with two cables, so that I'm completely tethered to the deck. Coxswain Randy Lewis tells me to hold on to the bars up front, and forget about the laws of gravity and the notion of balance. The bullet is fast, with a top speed of twenty-seven knots, and can handle just about anything except stopping. Inert, it dies, a passive cork on an angry sea. If it slows to a certain speed, the breakers will toss it. We head for Peacock Spit, where no ships of any size or purpose are supposed to go, a mile or so northwest of the bar. Yet, three days out of five, this is where Lewis gets called in for rescues, steering the bullet up close enough to the shipwreck so his partner can lean over and grab the poor bastard.

Low clouds start to shove the high pressure ridge off the coast. Just the smell of rain has everybody excited. Piloting the bullet scares Lewis— it always has—but he's hooked on the thrill. There is nothing else like it on land or sea. As he says, "You've got to be good in order to be lucky out here. And you can't be lucky unless you're good." Now, the waves are on either side of us, building—fifteen feet, twenty—cutting off everything else on the horizon. I'm afraid. It's like being stuck in a grave and watching dirt shoveled down from above. There is no order to the breakers, no rows of successive curls. They come from port and starboard, bow and stern. At all times, Lewis moves his head back and forth, dodging and ducking—radar the old-fashioned way.

"Back there!" He points. "Where'd that one come from?" Another curled wall crashes over the bow and into our faces. When my eyes clear, Lewis looks down at me and smiles.

"Look back at the Cape," he yells. "See the inlet, just below the rock. That's Deadman's Cove, where all the bodies wash up. When somebody's missing, that's the first place we look."

Seeking the Northwest Passage, Francis Drake, the reformed pirate of the late sixteenth century, sailed as far north as the coast of Oregon and then turned back because of the weather. "The most vile, thicke and stinking fogges," he wrote, in the first description of the Northwest by a Western writer. A land of "congealed rain." A Greek, Apostolos Valerianos, sailing under his Spanish alias of Juan de Fuca, thought he'd hit paydirt in 1592. Instead, what he apparently found was the passage to Puget Sound, a strait that would bear his assumed name forevermore. He never went inside to investigate. He was said to be a gifted liar, an invaluable asset for any mariner in the company of benefactors and historians. The English captain James Cook, his reputation on the line, tried three times to find the bloody river, the last attempt coming in 1778 when he poked around the mouth of the Umpqua River on the southern coast of Oregon, then missed both the Columbia and the Strait of Juan de Fuca. While eating human arms at Nootka Sound, a culinary gift of the Vancouver Island tribe, he agonized about his place in history, which as matters turned out would have more to do with his death in Hawaii than with his failures off the Northwest Coast. With him was a young midshipman, George Vancouver, who would return.

Captain John Meares, a British trader, came next, following Cook's maps and the recent chartings of a Spaniard, Bruno Heceta. Meares saw the discolored water, the pounding surf, and tried to find an entry point. There had to be a river here. It was July, the best weather month of the year, and still he could not get beyond the wall of breakers to see if anything was on the other side. He concluded that the River of the West was a fiction: "Disappointment continues to accompany us," Meares wrote in his journal on July 6, 1788. "We can now safely assert that no such River exists."

Meares left a name: Cape Disappointment.

George Vancouver returned in the spring of 1792, himself the captain now, with three Royal Navy ships under his command. A dour man of Dutch descent, still young at thirty-four, Vancouver was determined to find the River of the West or die in disgrace. His mission was to fill out the rest of the map of the north coast of the continent. There was still no such thing as Puget Sound on this map, no 250-mile-long island severed from the mainland of British Columbia, no Fraser River, no Mount Rainier, no Mount Baker, no Mount St. Helens, no Mount Hood, no Cascade Range. But there was a River of the West, labeled as such, a drawing based on optimism and little else, showing a waterway that began in the Midwest, drained out of Lake Superior and emptied into the Pacific. Of course, there were no Rocky Mountains.

At the same time, some Boston merchants had sent off an American, Robert Gray, and loaded his 212-ton sloop with cheap trading goods. Eighteen months out of New England, in the spring, Gray met Vancouver off the Pacific shore. Cautiously they exchanged information, deleting a channel here and a landmark there, embellishing certain discoveries; but neither claimed to have seen the River of the West. Vancouver had unknowingly sailed past the Columbia's mouth on April 27. "The sea," he wrote, "had now changed from its natural to river-coloured water, the probable consequence of some streams falling into the bay. Not considering this opening worthy of more attention, I continued our pursuit to the northwest."

A few weeks later, on May 11, 1792, three hundred years after Columbus laid eyes on the New World, Gray's ship, the *Columbia Rediva*, passed through the barricade of the sea and found, at north latitude 46 degrees and west longitude 122 degrees, The River. He noted it in his journal, a dry, technical description, considering what he'd discovered. Gray seemed more fascinated by the Chinook natives just inside the mouth, stark naked, their noses perforated, their foreheads oddly flat. They seemed to have not a care in the world, but their secret—and the secret of this land hidden behind the bar—was now out. Upon meeting the Chinooks, the "Boston men," as the natives called them, traded one nail for two salmon. This set a trading pattern, and soon Gray had picked up three hundred beaver skins for two nails per skin. The beaver-skin hat was all the rage among fashionable men of Europe and the fledgling states of America. Problem was, beaver was becoming scarce. Here in sponge-land, beavers were everywhere.

Gray, on a mission of commerce before nationalism, only ventured fifteen miles upriver, far enough to gather more than three thousand sea otter pelts. These silky mammals, up to five feet in length and with the disposition of a toddler just after a long nap, were easily clubbed, smiling right up until the moment their skulls were smashed. In China, on the way back to Boston, Gray made a fortune on the otter furs, selling them to mandarin lords for about $100 apiece. From here on out, the Columbia would be on every nautical route that went anywhere near the North Pacific.

Back at sea, Gray met Vancouver a second time and told him of his discovery. Vancouver acted as though he hadn't heard him; he later claimed the Columbia as the property of Great Britain after his ship, the *Chatham*, commanded by Lieutenant William Broughton, sailed over the bar in the fall of 1792. Vancouver had spent the late spring in Puget Sound, which he discovered for Europeans, charted, and named. In the Columbia, the *Chatham* went a hundred miles upstream, within naming distance of Mount Hood, tagged for Lord Samuel Hood, a British naval officer who had been second in command of the English fleet during the Revolutionary War. Two of the biggest volcanoes in the Northwest, Hood and Rainier, are named for wartime enemies of America.

All the otter and beaver profiteering caused a considerable amount of excitement among eastern capitalists. John Jacob Astor thought the way to monopolize the beaver and otter trade in the far Northwest was to build a fort at the mouth of the Columbia. Nobody would get in or out without passing by the watchful eye of his American Fur Company outpost. Astor, a millionaire who was once called the richest man in America, sent out one of maritime history's great megalomaniacs, Captain Jonathan Thorn, to found the settlement. Thorn arrived in his 290-ton ship, the *Tonquin*, with ten mounted guns on board. He came around the tip of

South America, then stopped in Hawaii, where he picked up some natives to use as cheap labor. He arrived at the Columbia entrance in March of 1811, loaded down with livestock, potatoes, a near-mutinous crew, and the Hawaiians. Facing the guardian breakers at the mouth of the river, Thorn backed off. Unable to get the *Tonquin* near Peacock Spit, he ordered his first mate, Ebenezer Fox, and three companions into a small boat and told them to find a channel through the bar. They were never seen again.

Thorn tried a second time. He sent a dinghy off, at ebb tide, and the boat capsized. Two Hawaiians and one Boston man drowned. The bar had now claimed seven men from a crew that was supposed to furnish the first American settlers in the West. It was as if the land itself were resisting these newcomers. Eventually, several crewmen got through, and the fort of Astoria was built in the spring of 1811. Shortly thereafter, Captain Thorn was butchered and the *Tonquin* torched off Vancouver Island by the much-offended natives of Nootka Sound, who were angered when he rubbed a pelt in their chief's face.

Fort Astoria lasted all of one year in American hands. During the War of 1812, with the British sloop *Raccoon* fast approaching, Astor's representative sold the whole settlement to the Montreal-based Northwest Company, which later merged with the Gentlemen Adventurers of England Trading into Hudson's Bay—the boys of the HBCo, an amalgam of French-Canadian, English and Indians who knew better than to rub a pelt into the face of a trading partner. After the war, Astoria went back under American jurisdiction, though there were few Boston men to be found at the post. When the Florentine silk hat was introduced at a Paris fashion show in 1825, the beaver hat was doomed. The Hudson's Bay Company moved upriver, to Fort Vancouver, headquarters of a trading and agricultural network that stretched from Fort Umpqua in the south, to Fort Thompson in northern British Columbia, from Fort Colville on the upper Columbia to Fort Boise on the lower Snake. Ostensibly, the area was under the joint occupancy of America and England; in truth, it was governed by the HBCo.

The Columbia River Bar continued to swallow big ships at the rate of one a year. The *William and Ann* sank in 1829, killing forty-six people who were on board. The *Isabella*, a Hudson's Bay Company trading vessel, went down in 1830 and wasn't discovered until 1987. When the American exploring party led by Charles Wilkes lost the *Peacock* here, and all the scientific material which had been gathered in three years of exploring the distant points of the planet went under, the sinking so incensed

Wilkes that he concluded Americans should not settle for the northern border of the Columbia River. He raged against the river bar, declaring it too hazardous to serve as the northwestern entrance of America. The American property should include Puget Sound, with its calm water and safe harbors, Wilkes argued.

Off Peacock Spit, we climb a twenty-foot wave, chugging like a truck straining to make the crest of a hill, and then slide down the other side. Gumby-legged, I'm standing on the deck, soaked to the bone, trembling with cold, my stomach puréed, my sense of balance shot. Then, without warning—*Swooooosh.* I'm blinded, buried, and swept off the boat, my feet and hands knocked loose, water down the front of the suit. For a few seconds, I have no sense of up or down. Everywhere, water. The cables hold me to the top of the boat, but my feet flutter somewhere at the edge of a breaker. I spit icy salt water out, coughing to regain a full breath. When at last I can breathe again, Lewis tries to tell me something else about Deadman's Cove, but I've had enough. I pull myself back up, trying to stand. I catch a glimpse of the southern end of the Willapa Hills to the northeast, clouds crawling all over the deforested summits. A storm is brewing. It's time to chase the rain, to follow the moisture to the heart of the Wet Zone. Forward then, north by northeast, to the rain, the darkness, the mud—the real country. After tossing around on either side of this bar, I'm convinced: at this gateway to the continent, the river is still in charge.

We pass two jetties, five miles in total length, designed to channel the force of two tons per square foot into some sort of orderly outflow. The channel is continuously dredged by the Corps of Engineers. They scrape and dig, the river pushes and refills, a struggle repeated in varying degrees of ferocity throughout the length of the Columbia; only here does the river win. Now, a light rain is falling. Has the jet stream come home? Will there be no withered cedars after all, no frustrated salmon flopping around arid spawning beds? Approaching landfall, I look toward shore: the spruce forest blurs against the rock of Cape Disappointment. I see nothing through the drizzle but green and gray, deep colors here, and true. As long as they remain the tint of this land, the Columbia River will never be quaint.

Chapter 2

ENCHANTED

VALLEY

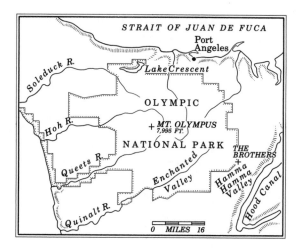

For the next nine weeks the sky drops low to the ground and empties rain onto the Pacific shore every day until the forest canopy is weepy and the ground is mush and the little woman inside the ranger station at the end of the road next to the Quinault River is happy. Spring has come to the western valleys of the Olympic Mountains: nearly six feet of rain in two months.

"It's a start," she says, looking up at the swollen heads of her rhododendrons. Towering plants, vaguely domesticated, giving off a light of their own when in blossom, they look as if they escaped from the nursery long ago and settled into lawless residence here where the sun is not supposed to shine. She lives on the edge of a freak land, a place unlike any other on this earth, where ferns grow taller than Magic Johnson and cedars live for centuries on nothing more than the rotting carcasses of other logs. Reality checks are needed hourly: that hemlock with the trunk as wide as a garage door, it's pure science fiction; that moss draping the bigleaf maples, a cotton-candy spin of filament-thin fiber, it seems to be growing on air; those elk coming down the draw, they're so big and barrel-chested they look steroid-pumped. The air is heavy with the basic lubricant of life. Rain doesn't fall inside this forest; it blends with the moss and then floats downward in webs of tinted moisture. Six feet of rain in two months. On the Olympic Peninsula, a porkchop of land as big as Massachusetts bordered by the sea on three sides, it's almost invisible. No cloudbursts. No storms. It seldom freezes, seldom sizzles in continental America's only temperate rain forest. Just . . . the reliable drip, drip, drip.

European and American explorers feared the rain forest as they did no other part of the New World. It was too dark, too green, too impenetrable, a place of death and danger, home for cannibals, hell with a cloud cover. Left alone, the land went crazy: trees grew to sizes unheard of anywhere else; eleven plants and seven species of wildlife flourished here and no-place else; and the prodigious salmon runs filled gravel beds with such numbers as to create a white noise of their own. Naturalist Roger Tory Peterson has calculated that the Olympic Rain Forest is weighted down with more living matter than any other place on earth. And yet, this is not some distant land in a far-off corner. A straight line from Seattle to the Olympics, across Puget Sound and Hood Canal, marks a distance of about 40 miles. Three million people crowd the Puget Sound basin, but 40 miles and 120 additional inches of rain away, there is almost nobody— a million acres of ice and elk and evergreens and sea-washed rock and devil's club and sword ferns and salmonberry and water and wildflower and ocean, all bunched up at the western edge of the continent.

I shoulder my pack and enter the outer edge of the Quinault River valley on a day when the sky is supposed to clear up. I don't know. In some places, it looks like the rain flows up, leaping off the chin-high vegetation of the forest floor. Forget the gentleman's club of normal plant growth; here, the curled ferns lengthen by the hour. Twenty miles inland from the Pacific, the rain forest welcomes. I don't want to worry about anything except how I'm going to slow-cook dinner and how that Jack Daniels is going to taste when I sip it while listening to the drip, drip, drip, soothed by the massage of moisture. The poison of excessive sun will kill thousands, victims of malignant melanoma. No one has ever died of too much drizzle.

Gridlock and cocaine gang wars rule the valley in the city where I live. Once it was full of small farmers and family merchants, a long, tree-lined boulevard with views straight up to the north spine of Mount Rainier. Now the farmers are all gone, and many Seattle merchants operate from behind bullet-proof windows, and the walls are spray-painted with the slogans of young men who kill one another because somebody is wearing the wrong-colored hat. The towers of downtown prosperity are five minutes from the desperate gulch, with no connection between the two. I drive through the valley to get to my home; sometimes, stuck in traffic, I daydream off Rainier's distant glaciers. Other times, I'm an urban warrior, adrenalin-primed for combat, even if the only battle is one to beat a yellow light.

A few weeks before this rain forest trip, I was driving home one evening when I saw something that chilled me for a long time. Stopped at a crosslight, I witnessed a little girl get clipped by a speeding car. She was dirty-faced and shoeless, no more than sixty pounds, with soiled brown hair tied in pigtails. She was clutching a toddler when I first spotted her, eyeing the flood of traffic. Protecting the smaller child, she waited until three of the four lanes had stopped, and only then ventured across Rainier Avenue in the dim twilight. I was in the inside lane, stopped. As they walked in front of me, I glanced at the rear-view mirror: the lane to my outside was open, and a car was screaming toward the kids. I honked my horn, jumped out of the car. Too late. Without ever slowing down, a big car smashed into the little girl, sending her flying off the hood. The toddler was spared, somehow, but her sister lay crumpled and crushed on the sidewalk, spitting up blood and teeth, her leg badly mangled, her stomach heaving in and out.

The driver of the car walked toward his victim—two faces pulled from the urban stream, both in shock.

"I never even saw her," he said when the ambulance arrived. "Never even saw her."

My first hour in the rain forest I can't shake the caved-in face of the little girl, the spindly legs, the look of horror from her sister. I'm here, in part, to put some distance between the city and me, to seek shelter from the daily storm of civilization. Maybe such a thing is impossible in the late twentieth century. I wonder what happened to that valley in the city? The land has not changed too much: trees will still grow, the moisture will still be there, Rainier will still loom. The climate is the same. But the laws of nature are irrelevant in that valley. The urban beast is king of that jungle. In less than a hundred years, the roles have reversed: the valley in my city is dark, dangerous, a place where humans don't belong. And this valley in the rain forest is life-giving, a sanctuary for old trees and wounded urban refugees. Now I walk under a cathedral of conifers, pleasantly daydreaming, pumping no adrenalin. I'm not on alert.

The rain forest could have gone the same way as the valley in my city. Near the turn of the century, a white homesteader named John Huelsdonk entered the Hoh River valley, a few miles north of here, determined to conquer. The Hoh contained more fish, more elk, more deer, more berries, more cedar bark than any tribe of Coastal Salish Indians could ever hope to give away in the most elaborate of potlatches. But the rain forest had never experienced a person quite like Huelsdonk; his nickname was the Iron Man of the Hoh. He entered the valley carrying a woodstove on his back, proceeded to clear part of the forest, punch in a primitive road and set up a home. In the next few years, Huelsdonk boasted of killing three hundred cougars and an equal number of bears. By eliminating the chief predators of the tree-nibbling elk herds, he single-handedly disrupted an ecosystem that had existed for several millennia without change. However, few whites followed Huelsdonk into the Hoh to crowd the land and drain the air of green. Most of the valley is now part of Olympic National Park, saved by the drip, drip, drip.

What kept the resource armies away, at first, was the basic freakiness of the place. A hundred years ago, after the completion of the transcontinental railroads caused Washington's population to triple in ten years to 350,000 people, the Olympic Mountains still remained essentially un-mapped. The new residents of Puget Sound knew the land buckled to cloud-snagging heights across the water. They knew a dozen or so loud rivers poured out from the glacial heart of the mountains. But no white man had ever walked all the way through the place, even though the valley floors are gentle, the rain always soft, and the mountains relatively low. In an age when nature existed only to be corraled—Cotton Mather preached that wilderness was an insult to the Lord—the land was useless, a wild, overgrown child of the West, the one that got away. By 1890, when the American frontier was officially pronounced closed, Washington's governor wrote of the heart of darkness forty miles across the Sound, this land of mystery, and called it "terra incognita."

The rain has not been a total shield. Approaching the Olympic park border by car from the south, I pass the 190,000-acre reservation of the

Quinault Indians. Decimated by smallpox and alcoholism, this once prosperous tribe dwindled to practically nothing just after Washington became a state in 1889. Under the management of the Bureau of Indian Affairs, the reservation's timber has been sold off, tract by tract, to the worst kind of cut-and-run loggers, who leveled the forest. In most cases, there was no reforestation. Just rip and roar, slash and grab, and get the hell outta this freaking mudhole, leaving behind as much as two hundred tons of debris per acre. A ravaged stumpland, it looks now like a junkyard finished off by vandals. Half-burned slash. Spindly alder. Muddy roads leading to nowhere. The green is all gone, replaced by black and brown, the colors of decay and erosion. Now, day after day, no matter what season, the mist of early morning peels away to reveal the same sight, the untended casualties of Western man's war with the rain forest.

As a consequence, the sockeye salmon run fell from nearly a million fish a year in the Quinault River to a few thousand. Without shade, the river warms; without trees, the soils shed nutrients and dilute the spawning beds. The Quinault natives, who worshipped cedar as a gift from God and salmon as an edible icon of even higher rank, knew as much. But the Bureau of Indian Affairs, based in a windowless office in Washington, D.C., did not. So a big part of mainland America's only temperate rain forest is gone, impossible to duplicate by even the most advanced of tree farm schemes and a platoon of biologists. Something which has lived longer than most of Western civilization was wiped out in a few years.

I stop for water at a place where the trail crosses a planked bridge over the gorge of the Quinault River. Swollen by runoff and the recent rains, the Quinault here is so deep and fast, so clear, it seems a continent away from the naked land downstream, outside the park boundary. My destination is the Enchanted Valley, thirteen miles into the heart of the Olympics, at the river's source. There is supposed to be a wide, flat valley and an enormous glacier and an old chalet inside the Enchanted Valley, a place resonant with adjectives from previous visitors. The rain forest I walk through now is protected from further predations of chain saws and bureaucrats; never touched, a national park for half a century, it has since been recognized by the United Nations as a world-heritage site, joining the pyramids of Egypt and the Grand Canyon as places on this earth worthy of saving for the generations that will live in an overcrowded greenhouse warmed by the loss of forests and the negligence of governments. Even with the protection, timber companies are talking again about the need to "open up" the national park and get at these small valley corridors of ancient natural history, the last true remnants of a much bigger rain forest that once covered most of the Northwest Coast.

The river roar here is just right, a pleasant numbing. Overhead, shafts of light pierce the canopy, illuminating the many shades of green, a color full of moods. I have little in common with the Quinault Indians and won't try to act like I'm their nature buddy. I'm Irish Catholic, but feel closer to this wet land than that wet land across the Atlantic. I was born in this country because the land in Ireland went tired and thin, unable to keep the inhabitants alive. Quinault country was just the opposite, a frenzied bounty. However, I do share something with the natives of the rain forest: a family ghost with a permanent address in the Olympics. I lost my Uncle Hank in the cold waters of Lake Crescent, a deep mountain lake on the north side of the Olympic park. He and his wife raised a truckload of kids on a small plot of land surrounded by thick woods. One day in the early spring Hank and Virginia went for a canoe ride on the lake; caught in a squall, the canoe tipped. Hank was not a good swimmer. He clung to the canoe while Virginia swam for help. She crawled up out of the bank, looked across the way at Hank, and told him to hold on. By the time she flagged a passing car, Hank was gone. Although they dragged the lake, his body was never found. A few years later, my mother put me on a bus, and I rode the ferry with strangers across Puget Sound and then over the winding roads on the north side of the Olympic Peninsula until Virginia, a friendly woman with sad eyes and lots of lipstick, picked me up for a summer on the farm. I was eight years old, and I learned how to ride a cow and jump-start a tractor and sneak up on a deer and make a whistling sound with a blade of grass between my thumbs and fish without a pole and say words like "piss" and "pecker-head." We talked a lot about how Hank was always just lurking in the woods somewhere, their pop, my uncle, this ghost. Kept us out of serious trouble.

Halfway to the Enchanted Valley, I come upon an open section bordered by oddly muscled maples past their prime. In this part of the valley, the forest opens up enough to let you look at the glacier peaks upriver and the green tunnel downriver, so I decide to put up camp here. My feet are blistered and my back's whining, but I feel just fine inside the nest of the rain forest. I slump down against one of the maples and go for a sip of Jack Daniels to take the edge off the blisters. Slowly, the forest reveals itself; the truth of a place is never found on first glance, or even third glance. Here among the ancients, tree roots spread out in all directions searching for soil in a place where the earthen floor is not easily found. In one small patch of the forest, a big hemlock has taken over like a brother-in-law who's moved into the guest room, glomming onto anything of value, its two-foot-thick tendril roots clambering over boulders to find sources of nourishment. A monument to adaptive creativity, the tree must be close to a thousand years old.

I slip out of the boots and put on leather tennis shoes, bedroom slippers for this country. It's time to take a closer look, get lost in the green air and the drip, drip, drip. All around me are evergreens in varying stages of the struggle with gravity. One tree lies on the ground, over the trail, with a swath cut through the middle to allow passage. I try to count the rings, but I get bored after three-hundred-and-something. Another tree is snagged in the branches of a giant, stuck at a forty-five-degree angle. In the rain forest, few opportunities are lost; a host of young alders, some as tall as ten feet, have taken root in the slow-dying flank of the snagged tree—a "nurse log," in the terminology of biologists. The seedlings are nurtured on the moss of the nurse log, sucking, searching, probing until gradually the old tree is compost and the new tree is king. Only one of a thousand small trees ever lives to maturity. But when they finally settle in, they're here for centuries. The Quinault, a classic U-shaped valley carved by a retreating glacier, offers protection from most natural disasters. The upper reaches of the mountain walls on either side of the river snare all the lightning bolts and take the brunt of forest-leveling avalanches. The valley is too wet for fires. The only threats to these trees are chain saws and an occasional superstorm.

The Douglas firs here grow two hundred feet or more, straight as a carpenter's plumb line, adding as much as three feet a year in the hunt for sunlight. On the bark of these trees, growing sideways, are ferns and fungi. The bigleaf maples are the spookiest, their hardwood branches draped with sleeves of moss and lichen, a Gothic gown.

I can see why the first Spanish sailors who came ashore to the rain forest thought they had landed on another planet. Most of them were up from California and Mexico, brown land, cactus country, where three inches of annual rainfall produces the geek of New World plant life, the Joshua tree, a skeletal oddity that looks as if it has been electrocuted. A party of Spaniards landed in 1775—apparently the first whites to set foot in the Northwest—and were promptly killed by a group of natives near the mouth of the Hoh River. They were looking for water. Twelve years later a British sea otter ship landed near the same spot, and its crew was likewise slaughtered. Some of their body parts turned up in a feast offered British traders at Vancouver Island. These two clashes did not sit well with the travel writers of their time, the mariners whose journals were widely read throughout Europe. The Olympic Peninsula therefore remained unmapped and deeply disparaged, as if it had a poison label on the outside. By the time the Spaniards, led by Manuel Quimper, tried to take formal possession of the peninsula in 1790, they were quite wary of the place. Quimper, adding to the area's reputation as a land of death and mystery, wrote that the natives "decorated the beach with the impaled heads of their enemies." Taking no chances, Quimper approached landfall waving a large cross and firing twenty-one shots from the cannon of his ship. The next year Spain tried to build a settlement at Neah Bay, in the extreme northwest corner of the peninsula, heart of Makah Indian country. They purchased twenty slaves for a price of thirty-three sheets of copper, then built a fort and ten log cabins. New Spain in the Pacific Northwest lasted all of four months—the four driest months of the year, at that. Even during the summer, what chased the whites away was the drip, drip, drip.

The Pacific shore here looks about the same now as it did to the first, unfortunate European visitors; a sixty-one-mile stretch of beach, from south of the Hoh to just below the northwest tip of the state, is the longest wilderness coast in continental America. Winter storms are legendary. During one such convulsion, the surf threw a 135-pound rock more than a hundred feet through the air and into the wall of a lighthouse. Wind-shaped, spare-limbed Sitka spruce hold to sand at the vegetation line, the visual embodiment of Japanese haiku. Sea stacks, with curled evergreens sprouting from their rock sides like hair growing from the ears of a hermit, are planted offshore, the crumbs of a mountain range that used to be underwater. Marine fossils have been found atop the highest summits of the Olympics, which are young—formed just 30 million years ago—and still growing. Entirely roadless, without any hint of man, the edge of the continent is thick with life: one cubic foot of tidepool can support more than four thousand living things. The nine coastal tribes that lived on the peninsula were pudgy from clams and crab and salmon and whale blubber. The first Europeans to visit nearly starved to death.

After the Spanish settlement collapsed, no whites set foot near the rain forest for another sixteen years, till 1808, when a boatful of Russians went off course in a storm and was shipwrecked at the mouth of the Hoh, the same place where the British had ended up as a dining delicacy. The stranded Russians, lucky enough to have made it onshore, were chased up and down the Hoh, finally caught, and held until they were ransomed two years later. The only European who seems to have had a pleasant experience was one who stayed offshore, Captain John Meares, the fur trader who had missed the mouth of the Columbia and left the name Cape Disappointment. Sitting in his ship off the rugged coast at sunset on a warm summer night in 1788, Meares took pen to hand and named the highest peak, a pink-hued glacial mass just under eight thousand feet. He wrote: "If that not be the home wherein dwell the Gods, it is beautiful enough to be, and I therefore call it Mount Olympus."

So the area remained, ice-draped on top, rain-smothered in the valleys, unsettled and unmapped, the home of the gods and some contented salmon-eaters on the coast. A pandering attempt was made in 1849 to call the mountains the Presidents Range, and to rename Olympus as Mount Van Buren, a stillborn idea. When Winthrop canoed off the eastern shore of the peninsula in his summer of 1853, whites had yet to try transplanting New England near the rain forest. Winthrop looked at the mountains as a cushion for the soul, a respite. Cannibals? Darkness? No, of course not, he said—the Olympics are a masterpiece of nature's art. His view was an oddball one. Nature, at least in the West, was treated like a disease awaiting the cure that had yet to cross the Rockies. Gliding down Puget Sound in a canoe, Winthrop turned his gaze to the west and found instant comfort.

"The noble group of the Olympian Mountains became visible—a grand family of vigorous growth, worthy of more perfect knowledge," he wrote. "On the highest pinnacles of this sierra, glimmers of perpetual snow in sheltered dells and crevices gave me pleasant, chilly thought in that hot August day." Then he added, "The calming influence of these azure, luminous peaks, their blue slashed with silver, was transcendent."

The idea that mountains, especially ones with such an evil reputation, could be . . . transcendent . . . was visionary. During the very summer that Winthrop felt calmed by the Olympics, a group of fellow New Englanders, having exhausted the timber of the state of Maine, were making plans to begin leveling the Olympic rain forest. Possibly Winthrop, the rebel who had to lug around five generations of Puritan baggage, was influenced by Ralph Waldo Emerson, the poet and philosopher who thought reality was best experienced through a soul in tune with the rhythms of the earth. In the description of his Pacific Northwest journey, a few pages after crowing about the Olympics, Winthrop skewers the old view while accurately predicting his own place in history: "Poet comes long after pioneer. Mountains have been waiting, even in ancient worlds, for cycles, while mankind looked upon them as high, cold, dreary, crushing, as resorts for demons and homes of desolating storms." Instead, he says, mountains should be "our noblest friends, our most exalting and inspiring comrades, our grandest emblems of divine power and divine peace."

As it turned out, a handful of poets came to the Olympics before pioneers. The great naturalist John Muir, tromping through the ancient forests here in 1889, found a scattering of Winthrop-type characters a full generation after the Yankee's prophecy. Muir wrote: "In these Washington wilds, living alone, all sorts of men may perchance be found— poets, philosophers, even full-blown transcendentalists, though you may go far to find them."

What came of these poets is not recorded. But one year after Muir's visit, the prose was considerably less flattering when the Seattle *Press* organized an expedition of well-armed explorers to penetrate the interior of the Olympics. This was the so-called Press Expedition, put together as a newspaper promotional stunt to satisfy the forty thousand citizens of Seattle who in 1890 still had no idea what lurked behind those blue and green walls forty miles across the Sound. The first group photo shows a mean-faced crew clutching rifles, with bullet belts slung over their shoulders. They look like mercenaries on leave from the barbershop quartet. Loaded down with tons of food, boxes of whiskey, carpenter's tools and enough ammunition to wrest Vancouver Island from the British, the Press Expedition took four weeks just to leave the outskirts of civilization on the northern peninsula. By then, "our supply of whiskey was well-nigh exhausted," one member told the paper in a dispatch.

The ultimate boys camp-out quickly soured. Two months into the trip, they had completed construction of a flat-bottomed barge, which moved upstream at a slug's pace and had to be portaged most of the way because the rapids of the Elwha River were too shallow. Bereft of whiskey, the group leader, James Christie, gave some insight into the ordeal in midwinter. "An extraordinary amount of rain—water falling in sheets," he wrote. "There has scarcely been a single hour for the last week without a shower bath that went straight to the skin. Oil clothing seems to be of no use and we have discarded it as useless." In a bid for wider readership, they named dozens of mountains after dozens of newspaper editors, most of whom had never been west of their city rooms. George Childs, owner of the Philadelphia *Ledger*, was given a mountain; Joseph Pulitzer of the New York *World* was offered Mount Pulitzer; a competitor, James Gordon

Bennett of the New York *Herald*, had his Mount Bennett, and another
Manhattan rival, George F. Jones of the New York *Times*, could sleep
easier knowing he had an Olympic peak to call his own; Mount Hearst
was named for William Randolph Hearst of the San Francisco *Examiner*;
and of course a city editor at the Seattle *Press*, a gentleman by the name
of John G. Egan (no relation), was immortalized with Mount Egan. On
my map today, I cannot find a single one of their names.

In the late spring, with snow on the mountainsides twenty-five feet
deep, the expedition neared its destination. Desperate for animal fat after
months of living on salmon and pancakes, they killed a bear one spring
day, devoured the animal's liver and drank the meat grease as if it were
fresh-squeezed orange juice. At last they reached the Quinault River and
were hailed as conquering, but somewhat slow-moving, heroes. It took
them six months to travel forty-nine miles. No mountains were climbed.
Essentially, it was a valley walk, one which today can be done on national
park trails in three days, maybe four if you're burdened with extra
whiskey.

The white-tipped ridge ahead of me is hidden by cloud cover again; the
peek-a-boo views through slits in the forest are replaced by puffs of gray
and an increase in the tempo of drip, drip, drip. Everything is greener
and darker. No light directly overhead. The canopy has hogged it all; the
low-level vegetation must compete for the afterlight. Midday, and I can't
shoot a picture in here without boosting the film speed. I'm not sure
exactly where I am—somewhere in the valley—but I can still hear the
distant river, my tether. Now, I hear a clomping sound, branches breaking
underfoot. I look up and see elk, black-chested beasts, about a thousand
pounds each. I count six, eight, ten, and then to the other side, six more.
A herd of Roosevelt elk. I feel tiny and two-legged. In the salad bar of
the rain forest, they are pruning shrubs and chomping brush. Their coat
of fur is reddish, except for the black-vested chest. Some have antlers.
Their legs, muscled and taut, are long and graceful. I watch them eat,
they watch me watch. After a few minutes, somebody gets a bad scent,
they crash and clomp up the steep side of the valley and disappear.

President Teddy Roosevelt, alarmed by the dwindling coastal elk herds
and the fast-approaching loggers, made much of the Olympic Peninsula
a protected National Monument in 1909, shortly before he left office.
Hunters were slaughtering the elk to get at their teeth, which were sold
as watch fobs to Elks Club members around the country. Nearly thirty

years later, Teddy's cousin, Franklin Delano Roosevelt, the cripple who could not walk, toured the perimeter of the peninsula by car. Though it drizzled off and on, the President was enchanted. One night at Lake Quinault, timber industrialists and their allies in the Forest Service argued against a park in the Olympics, saying the rain forest should not be protected. Roosevelt got up early the next morning, looked east across the lake to the sun rising over the iced peaks above the thousand-year-old evergreen trees, and made up his mind. The Olympics, he said, "must be a national park." This at the depths of the Depression. Score one for Winthrop; the poet's spirit had lingered in the mist of the rain forest.

In ardent defense of the Olympics, Harold Ickes, Roosevelt's Interior Secretary, said, "If the exploiters are permitted to have their way with the Olympic Peninsula, all that will be left will be the outraged squeal of future generations over the loss of another national treasure." The mountain range and narrow corridors along the lowland western valleys of the rain forest were set aside as a national park in 1938. Nature has since repaid the family: the largest Roosevelt elk herd in the world roams the Olympic Peninsula.

Had Roosevelt gone the other way, and opened the Olympics to deforestation and pell-mell settlement, much of the peninsula might well look like the area around Forks, an abused timber town west of the national park. Surrounded by thick stumps, burned-over land and eroded hillsides, Forks is to the Olympic Peninsula what a butt rash is to Venus. The logging company officials who work out of this town still look at the park covetously; in their braver moods, they speak of getting at the protected timber.

Once, most of the country was covered with trees; now the American jungle has shrunk to this strip at the edge of the continent. The natives who lived on the Olympic Peninsula for thousands of years left only a few fingerprints. In the brief run of Western Man's attachment to this place, the Olympics have nearly been exhausted of fish and trees, the two sources of native prosperity. Instead of cutting on an even rotation, the timber industry turned to automation and export, tearing down as much of the ancient forest as the law would allow, and they now demand the last of the old trees. The town of Forks, painful to see, its social ills heartbreaking to hear of, is their monument.

At dinnertime, I decide to cook sausage, fresh tomatoes, mushrooms, and oregano and pour it all over spaghetti noodles. I take my time, adding a dash of wine from a plastic container, and letting everybody get to know each other over the low heat of my camp stove. Soon I've got company, a doe and her fawn, wobbling on new legs. When I stand up, the deer makes a defiant scrape of the ground with her hoof, something I've never seen before. The fawn is toy-store cute, a Bambi look-alike, and would not do well to get a taste of Italian cooking at her age. The doe steers her away. I eat while sitting on a log next to the roaring Quinault, watching the river flow. So hypnotic, this surge of deep, clear water, bouncing out of the mountains and sprinting toward the Pacific. Later, inside my tent, I find sleep comes easy, aided by the drip, drip, drip and the white noise of the Quinault. I dream of traveling geologists (like traveling salesmen) who come by the campsite with tips on how to comprehend the mystery that surrounds me: Have you considered the influence of the Cordilleran Ice Sheet, the late movements of the Pleistocene Epoch, the relative youth of these mountains?

In the morning there is sunlight—sunlight! The drip is gone. I stick my head out and see a woodpecker drilling into a dying fir that looks completely different from what it did ten hours ago; the striations of advanced age are fully visible in this light. I get some idea of why a woodpecker pecks: he drills for sap, knowing it will draw bugs. Later, it's easy pickings. For me, breakfast is much simpler, instant oatmeal and coffee. I break camp in a hurry. Sunlight, who knows how long it'll stick around? On the trail, my blisters hurt, but the scenery is diverting. The Enchanted Valley is six miles upriver, and I'm told to expect a place that lives up to its name. Even with the sun, the forest is dark most of the way, and becomes greener still with each mile closer. Where the valley walls steepen, there are more casualties among the giant trees. After living the long life on shallow topsoil gouged by the glacier, they are felled by exhaustion. I pass several uprooted monsters, their trunks at root level fanning out in a starburst pattern. The valley is about a thousand feet above sea level here, and the river is so swollen and hurried it appears to have come from an outlet of some grand lake.

After passing through the darkest, greenest, thickest, wettest and most sweet-scented part of the valley, I find the air lightens, the canopy opens up and the trees change somewhat. There is something big and white straight ahead, shining through the trees. The valley widens, until it is flat and open and grassy, a perfect park with a wall of glaciers at the head. Ice Age and temperate jungle commingle. The first thing I notice about the Enchanted Valley is the wildflowers, great bursts of color against a green backdrop. The waterfalls—to the north, the south and up ahead in the cirque of the valley—plunge down rock walls, falling hundreds of feet to shock life into the infant Quinault. Like movements of a symphony, they each contribute to the sound of the valley—a rumble, a splash, a rhythmic slapping of water on rock, water on snow, water on moss.

On the floor of the Enchanted Valley is a three-story chalet, made of wood, cedar-shingled on top, with large windows, a nice porch, a stone fireplace. Very storybook, something like a retirement home for Hansel and Gretel. Once a hotel whose guests were hauled up the valley trail on horseback, the chalet is National Park Service property now, a fact the government makes instantly clear. In search of human companionship, I go to the chalet and find it locked. I peer through the window: inside is a well-cleaned, well-kept residence, home of some lucky park ranger. Outside, in bold letters, is this sign: WARNING: THIS STRUCTURE IS U.S. GOVERNMENT PROPERTY AND MUST NOT BE MOLESTED. Molested?

Fresh coffee is brewing somewhere. I follow the scent to a bright-orange-domed tent, occupied by a man and a woman from Maine. We swap exclamations, talking about the strange and wonderful things happening within this fortress of green. The man from Maine says he's come to the valley to look at the biggest hemlock tree in the world. It's somewhere in the Quinault, but unmarked. I tell him he can go into the Queets River rain forest, one valley over, and look for the biggest Douglas fir in the world, which is marked. Or he can look for the biggest Sitka spruce in the world, which is also in this neighborhood. He likes trees better than just about anything and had to come all across the country and wait out several weeks of rain and then some to find them. He started in Oregon, where the temperate rain forest begins, extending in a coastal strip all the way north to the Alaskan panhandle. But nowhere do the trees grow so big, so fast, in such a protected setting as in the Olympics, where the garden of conifers is watered by glacier melt and Pacific storms.

I ask him and his girlfriend if they mind the drip, drip, drip, and they say not at all, because in Maine the drip falls as snow, and the land doesn't come alive until late in the spring. I look up at the Anderson Glacier, which leans down from a pass at the head of the valley, and get to thinking about doing some climbing while the weather is just right. I ask the people from Maine if they want to come along, through snow up to Anderson Pass, and they say no, they want to read their books and lie in the grass.

While I'm traveling over the snow, the wind is chill and fresh. The giant trees are gone, and the land becomes white except for the rock and the tops of dwarfed firs which poke through the snow. My heart is racing, but not from the exertion. Something the man from Maine said sets off an internal palaver. In New York City, there is a tree from the Olympic Rain Forest inside a glass cage in the basement of the Museum of Natural History, as frozen as a stuffed moose head. I remember seeing the trunk of that tree, and a little stuffed deer nearby, and some salal bushes and grass and ferns and other plants from the forest inside this window display. In the explanatory museum text, they got it just about right: the story of a single drop of rain that comes from a Pacific wind that feeds on the moisture of the warm sea, sweeps into the land, is forced up the mountains, then falls and becomes part of the ice or snow that will eventually return to the earth. It's a fine story, as nature tales go. Lots of conflict and resolution. But I'd hate to learn about this place from a glass cage.

A few years out of college, I traveled a lot, working just long enough to get a big wad of money to spend on some exotic trip, looking for places ever more remote and foreign and new. When I arrived at these places halfway around the globe, I had an attitude of, Okay, I'm here, now surprise me. Only now am I starting to learn that this place across Puget Sound, forty miles from my home in Seattle, contains enough secrets to last a lifetime.

In the valley of the Hamma Hamma River, the woods are not as thick. This is the eastern drainage of the Olympics, over the ridge from the Quinault Valley, no longer rain forest but still overgrown and evergreen. I'm trying to climb The Brothers, a twin-peaked mountain of just under seven thousand feet which rises between the Duckabush and the Hamma Hamma valleys. I come up through the Hamma Hamma, which means "stinky stinky" in native parlance. The river does not smell, but it used to be so full of salmon that their rotting, spawned-out carcasses filled the shallow riverbed in early fall. Not now. Most of the drainage is outside the national park boundary, and logging has shaved many of the low-elevation hillsides dry. In a short trip from the salt water of Hood Canal, a natural arm of Puget Sound, to the head of the Hamma Hamma, the salmon pass through several war zones.

After the Press Expedition of 1890, it didn't take long for the new residents of Puget Sound to get over their fear of the Olympics and get on with the business of making something of the newly mapped place. The old-growth forests around the new cities were fast disappearing. The Olympics were virgin. However, it was still tough to get in and get out with the monster trees. World War I changed all that. When a Serbian nationalist assassinated Austrian Archduke Francis Ferdinand, he set in motion a series of events that remade the national boundaries of Europe— and the landscape of America's only rain forest. By the time the United States entered the war, many of the crucial battles were being fought in the air by planes made of spruce, a wood that is both light and sturdy. The best spruce in the world is grown in the Olympics. Overnight, the forests that started rising when gunpowder was first invented a thousand years ago were leveled to help fight an incomprehensible war across the Atlantic.

The most abundant spruce forests were in the northern part of the Olympics near Lake Crescent, the site of my Uncle Hank's disappearance, thick with ocean mist. Boeing was then still a garage operation run out of a red barn on Seattle's Lake Union. But the factories of Europe, and later America, couldn't get their hands on enough Olympic Peninsula spruce to fight the war. An Army Signal Corps detachment, eight thousand men strong, began work on a spruce-hauling railroad on the north side of the peninsula. The United States Spruce Production Division worked at a frenzied pace for more than a year, clearing the forest and blasting two tunnels to lay out forty miles of track from Port Angeles on the Strait of Juan de Fuca to the woods. They finished on November 30, 1918—nineteen days after the war ended. A private timber company bought the railroad and, having hooked the world on Olympic spruce, proceeded to drain much of the area of its trees.

From an elevation of about five thousand feet on The Brothers, I can see the patchwork of logging below in the Hamma Hamma region. Planes are built of aluminum now, but the Olympics, on national forest land all around the park, continue to give up their forests; in the last fourteen years, almost half of the remaining old trees have been cut, leaving only 90,000 acres of virgin timber in the Olympic National Forest, which is now little more than a 600,000-acre tree farm for private industry subsidized by American taxpayers. For most visitors, this devastation is not always evident; by state law, the timber companies are supposed to leave a "visual corridor" of trees along the road. Behind this thin illusion are the big swaths of ripped-up ground, streaking mud and slash—one of many reasons why the Washington State Department of Natural Resources, or DNR, has long been nicknamed the Department of Nothing Remaining. During the recession of the early 1980s, when many of the logging towns were turned into welfare camps, the state and federal government continued to sell off the trees, practically giving them away in some sales concluded despite low demand. The state forests are sold to pay for new school construction, an archaic setup designed to ensure that teachers and parents root for clearcutting of ancient trees.

A take-no-prisoners style of logging is used on these six-hundred-year-old trees: all life, from ferns and huckleberry bushes on the ground, to eagles' nests on the tree crowns, is cut down, bulldozed into garbage heaps, stripped of commercial wood, and then burned. The great, deliberately set fires on state and national forest land are the main cause of air pollution in Seattle and Tacoma during the late summer, as the smoke drifts eastward into the Puget Sound basin and obscures views of the mountains. The giant trees of the peninsula are among the world's greatest storehouses of carbon. Once they are cut down, and the slash is burned, the fires release enormous amounts of carbon dioxide into the air, contributing in a small way to the greenhouse effect and shortening the planet's life span. A curious paradox is at work on the forests of the Olympic Peninsula: while the American government scolds Brazil for cutting and burning its tropical rain forest, the Forest Service is aiding and abetting the death of the American rain forest.

My legs move slowly in the deep, wet snow above the Hamma Hamma. The sky is starting to muddy. I'm not a technical climber; I know nothing of the fancy French rock-jock terms or moves, nor can I scale a granite wall. I can use an ice axe to keep from falling in a glacial crevasse, and I have a reasonable idea how to stay out of avalanche gullies. I can read a map. I understand when the sky is trying to tell me something, but like most climbers, amateur and hotdog, I don't always listen. Most of my life, I've stared out at The Brothers from Seattle—a two-breasted beauty that seems to sweep up from the very surface of Puget Sound. From the city, the tips turn pastel in sunset and then dark in silhouette, a very theatrical mountain, almost a custom fit of Winthrop's description of a peak that, viewed from a seat in civilization, stirs the soul. If ever there was a place where city and wild country could live side by side, this would be it, each needing the other, separated by the moat of Puget Sound. An irony of modern times is that the city dweller is often more appreciative, more protective, of the wild treasure than its rural neighbor. Thus, residents of the Columbia River Gorge fought the legislative protection of a National Scenic Area, and landowners around the Olympic National Park oppose further wilderness designation, just as many of their grandparents were against formation of the park. The larger question for the Northwest, where the cities are barely a hundred years old but contain three-fourths of the population, is whether the wild land can provide work for those who need it as their source of income without being ruined for those who need it as their source of sanity.

The sky continues to darken. I shift all thoughts to the summit. More than anything, at this instant, I want to stand atop this earthen cloud-grabber. Climbing is not something easily explained. The body gets to working, steaming, ploughing ahead with a single, all-consuming goal in mind. To the east, I can see the Puget Sound basin, wherein lies the Navy base of Bangor, home port for ten Trident submarines, each of which is longer than the Washington Monument is high and carries enough nuclear weapons to vaporize 240 cities. Farther across the water, Seattle can barely be made out. For the ice and rock ahead of me, I could be in the Himalayas, but instead I'm looking straight at a city with thousand-foot-high skyscrapers and ribbons of freeway clogged with traffic. Two hundred inches of precipitation can fall on this mountain, but just across the water Seattle gets less rain than New York, Boston, Philadelphia, Washington and Miami.

Now I come to a rock section too steep to hold the late snow of spring. I put my ice axe behind me, strapped to the pack, and start to clamber up the rock. This must be the last stretch of the mountain, and then I will touch the top and hurry down. But I'm having trouble. I'm slipping, and the way is not clear. Sweat stings my eyes. My fingertips are numb. My knee is shaking against the vertical rock. Only a few feet more, I think, just over the rise. Hold on, hold on . . . there—but what's this? I slip back, frightened. A massive white creature with a pair of big, wet eyes, two sharp horns and a full facial beard is staring back at me, not more than five feet away. A ghost. No. He's clinging . . . vertically. How? I don't know. He won't move. He's planted there, a two-hundred-pound, snow-white mountain goat. I fall back, startled. My mind was so intent on making this rise—which is not the summit at all—that I blanked everything else out. Now this—an arrogant goat. A warning, perhaps.

The clouds chase me down, spears of rain all around. I slip and slop, making a hasty exit from this high-country home of goats. I think nothing but dark thoughts, of being lost in a storm, buried somewhere, never to be found. Prodded by fear, my heart pounds harder on the way down than it did on the way up. The imagination runs wild. I stop and sit under the overhang of a boulder, shielded from the storm, and try to talk my way down. I have a compass. I know if I continue to descend, I will be in the forest, and then I can follow the runoff to the streams and down to the lake. The mountain goat—poor bastard—his days here are numbered. Once there were no goats on the Olympic Peninsula. Then, sixty years ago, a dozen of them were introduced as an experiment. Like every other form of life in the Olympics, they flourished, breeding madly, growing to absurd heights, some with pot bellies. Plenty of high-country meadows in the summer and rich valleys in the winter. No hunters. With the gray wolf extinct in these parts, and mountain cougars reduced to a handful, there are no natural predators. Now there are more mountain goats in the Olympics than anywhere else in the country. They tear up the fragile meadows, defoliate the shrubs, and drop large turds in the trickling fresh water of the alpine zone. The goats are cute. Very athletic. Their eyes are big, moist, brown, irresistible. But they are not indigenous, and are making life hard for plants that are, and so the Park Service has decided they must go. At a cost of $1,000 per goat, the rangers are airlifting them out and sending them to goat-deprived areas throughout the West.

The storm has picked up. Visibility about ten feet. Nothing to do but come out from under this rock overhang, wipe the cold rain from my face and slog down. Visiting a tree in a glass cage does have its advantages, but leaves nothing for the storyteller.

Chapter 3

TOE OF
THE EMPIRE

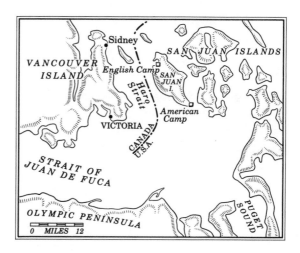

On the ferry to Vancouver Island, not more than a hundred yards from the international boundary, I look up, and there she is: Her Majesty Elizabeth II, Queen of England, ceremonially smiling under the weight of the Crown. She has a nice smile for a symbol, somewhat more human than a visage on a postage stamp. The Queen is framed in silver, a full-color photograph hanging prominently inside the bow of the ship, overseeing all the sensibly dressed white people. I'm crossing the Tweed Curtain, going from a land of E–Z terms and BBQ to a country full of fellows named Fisswidget, Craigenforth and Hangshaft. On the north coast of Washington, most of the settlements are small and ragged—some with get-to-the-point names like Whiskey Creek or Forks, others remnants from a Salish Indian past all but wiped out, places called Pysht, Sekiu, Sappho, Hoh, Yahoo, Klahowya, Sequim. Nothing regal. But away from the rain forest, across the swift-moving Strait of Juan de Fuca and up the Gulf Channel, are the mannerly burgs of Sidney and Ladysmith and Victoria, which was the last city in North America to give up the custom of driving on the left-hand side of the road.

At the moment, passengers are queued up for tea on the ferry, Her Majesty now smiling from another picture, this from the boat's dedication, complete with a tag line not seen on the American side of the Tweed Curtain: GOD SAVE THE QUEEN. Out the window, three bald eagles are circling for prey near the rock cliffs of an uninhabited island. A covey of harbor seals are crawling over one another on a basaltic perch next to the shore. Shiny red madrona trees stripped of their bark and polished by the wind lean out over the edge. Here and there, groves of Sitka spruce hold to shallow topsoil. The islands are dollops of evergreen that look as if they were plopped in the inland sea like raw dough on a cookie sheet. The rock shore is glacier-carved—lined, furrowed and cracked—a legacy of the last Ice Age, which retreated through here about twelve thousand years ago and carved out Puget Sound and most of the Strait of Juan de Fuca. Except for this strange hole of blue sky overhead, it looks like the rest of the Pacific Northwest.

In Victoria, which is neatly sewn into the southern tip of Vancouver Island, they grow cactus; palm trees are conspicuous in front of the several large estates. On the high bluff of the city's Beacon Hill Park, the old native cedars hold firm, but they are properly manicured, as evenly trimmed as a pensioner's mustache. On the vast grounds nearby, not a weed is in sight, not a single hawthorn hedge out of place, not a primrose or pansy in less than perfect health. The blossoms are everywhere, crowding ponds inhabited by royal swans (imported from the Queen's Preserve in Windsor Castle), bordering paths and playfields, all in flawless formation. The minute they start to droop or fade—gone, snipped away lest their sagging remains mar the effect. I wonder: don't flowers die around here? Archways drip wisterias. Small shrubs are cleanly topped. And near one of these ever-groomed gardens, two teams of eleven gentlemen in matching outfits and funny hats are playing . . . cricket. Yes, British baseball, with wickets and such. This is tournament play, the scores and details of which will be reported the next day in the Victoria *Times-Colonist*.

As manicured as a fresh-primped poodle, Victoria is the capital of the province of British Columbia, which spreads north in a mostly roadless expanse to the Yukon Territory and east to the plains beyond the Rocky Mountains in Alberta—an area about one-third larger than Texas. Much of the province briefly entered the American attention span during the presidential campaign of 1844, when "54–40 or Fight" was a slogan of James K. Polk, referring to the latitudinal point where Russian America, now the tip of southeast Alaska, snuggled into British Columbia, or New Caledonia, as it was known before Queen Victoria approved of the present name. Glaciers and wheat farms and forests—the barren, the bounty and the meat of the Canadian West—all are managed from under a pocket of blue sky next to a statue of an overweight Queen.

If the entire Northwest were ever to cleave from the continent and become a nation-state (a suggestion that has already prompted a name for the new country, Ecotopia), it would have not only geography but political sentiment in common. For just as Washington and Oregon were the only states in the West to vote Democratic in the 1988 presidential election, British Columbia went against the tide two weeks later and sent eleven additional members of the liberal New Democratic Party to Parliament. But those new Parliament members are among the harshest critics of the excesses of the American Northwest, which is considered a threat to their way of life. Many British Columbians who look south of the border ask: Why can't the Americans practice some self-restraint? In perhaps no other place in North America are the character quirks of two nations, one young and wild, the other old and reserved, so evident as here, on either side of the Tweed Curtain. Settling a land of benign extremes, the British reacted cautiously; the Americans never took a breath. The British chose to carve a small patch of perfection from the last unsettled edge of the New World; the Americans went to war against the land.

A visitor from New York City, who came to Victoria more than a century ago, made several observations which are as true now as they were then. He said, "The skies are ever clear, the air is always refreshingly cool, the people look quiet and respectable, and everything is intensely English." The New Yorker's only complaint was about Victoria's women, who "tend toward the ponderous." So, given the blessings of God and Queen, what have they done with it? Is Victoria a realization of the prophecy of Winthrop—the true city on a hill—the embodiment of a place he thought would emerge from a "climate where being is bliss"? Is this the civilization that would be ennobled by the elements? A land where the totem pole stands next to the statue of the Queen, and the twining of both cultures has produced an offspring of civility?

When Winthrop crossed the Strait of Juan de Fuca, there was no town of Vancouver (which is now the largest city in the Canadian West), just a Hudson's Bay Company fort at Langley on the Fraser River, which drains one-fourth of British Columbia. Victoria, by comparison, was a settled character who'd been sitting around the hearth long enough to be bronzed. The only major city on an island the size of Taiwan, Victoria has a metropolitan population of 250,000. Up until 1950, when emigration policies changed, opening the province to more Asian newcomers, more than eighty percent of Victoria's residents traced their ancestry to Great Britain. Now, only a third are English. Despite repeated admonitions from Canadian government officials, many Victorians still fly the Union Jack every day, fourteen thousand sea miles from the Mother Country.

While the rest of British Columbia—particularly the city of Vancouver, which is one-third Chinese, with healthy Greek, Indian, Jewish and German neighborhoods—has become a polyglot mix, Victoria clings to its English past, having transplanted many habits of the old island in the Atlantic to the new island in the Pacific. In Victoria, Empire Day is a showy holiday for members of the Imperial Order of the Daughters of the British Empire, which some less charitable Canadians call the Imperial Order of Dotty Englishwomen. The Royal Commonwealth Society and the Monarchists League also stage a variety of functions which inevitably conclude with tea-drinking and God-save-the-Queen-hailing. When Queen Elizabeth II last visited Victoria a few years back, the town spent thirty thousand dollars to dredge the harbor for Her Majesty's personal yacht, the *Britannia*. Few complained. On Empire Day this year, the Queen's representative to British Columbia, the Honourable Robert Gordon Rogers, visited the small town of Cumberland, and ten thousand people lined the streets in a rain storm to see him. He was astonished. Before the stroke of a pen changed him from Mister to Honourable, the former chairman of the board of Crown Zellerbach Company had been called timber baron, forest-stripper, strike-buster, and worse. But as soon as he became the twenty-fourth Lieutenant-Governor for the Province of British Columbia, overnight he was royalty. The Queen's Rep—he's played host to Di and Charles, chatted with Philip, and of course exchanged words with QE-2 herself.

The Tweed Curtain: a fuzzy black-and-white picture in the Royal Museum of British Columbia shows the Royal Engineers surveying the boundary of the United States and British Columbia. The line was drawn in 1846 at the 49th Parallel (Polk was now waging war with Mexico, and couldn't afford to fight the British over wilderness in the Northwest). Lower Vancouver Island, and a little tongue of land called Point Roberts fall below the line. The 282-mile-long island went to Great Britain. Point

Roberts, which is not much bigger than a stadium parking lot, went to the United States; it has essentially become a shopping mall with a border crossing. A dozen years after the border papers were signed, the Royal Engineers were sent out into the forest along the 49th Parallel to find and define this bloody line between Our Way of Life and the filthy Yanks in Washington Territory. In the picture, they are literally cutting and marking the border, a broad swath through the trees. And, while doing so, are dressed in pressed red serge uniforms and funny hats.

For introductory answers as to why this island in the North Pacific still clings to royal fussiness, I look up Molly Ingram, chairwoman of the Monarchists League. Four decades of life in Victoria have not softened the syllables as they march out of Mrs. Ingram's mouth in the accent of the Empire. A London native, she moved to India just before the war, and served the Empire in a variety of capacities, including espionage work. After the war, like many a British civil servant taking the slow route home to England, she stepped off the boat in Vancouver Island and never got back on. Now, she is the unofficial link between the monarchy and island residents who wish to stay in contact with royalty. A charming woman with a wonderful garden full of roses that blossom year-round, Mrs. Ingram has met the Queen a number of times. "She's so amusing, the Queen, and we get along quite well." And just what is the Monarchists League?

"Why, it's hundreds and hundreds of people here who think the monarchy is frightfully important," she says.

Every year, on April 21, the members of the Monarchists League hold a dinner in honor of the Queen's birthday. It's all very solemn and proper, and there's nothing funny about it. Aside from the dinner, they meet for cookies and tea and royalty-talk, and try to encourage more education in the Canadian school system about the role of the British monarchy.

"I think it's frightfully important to keep a sense of Empire, don't you?" says Mrs. Ingram. Her ancestors, she explains, did foreign duty in India beginning in 1816, and she continues the family tradition in the Province of British Columbia. "To me, the monarchy is all about continuity, which you don't have much of in the States."

When I ask her why the personality of Victoria is so different from that of the land just across the Strait of Juan de Fuca, Mrs. Ingram tries to maintain her politeness. "I'm very affectionate for the Americans, and I happen to like a great many of them," she says. "But our life up here is not like that of you people down there because . . . well, if you'll excuse my saying so, what you're all about is money, money, money. Yes? And that's not us. We live for something more."

Eighteen miles south of this toe of the Empire, on the American side of the strait, 150 men have just been given their pink slips from a timber mill at Port Angeles, a Resource Town that's been through one too many boom-and-bust cycles. Although the town's setting is breathtaking, in the foothills of the Olympics overlooking the water, nature and man struggle to get along, like a bad marriage sputtering through the hurt phase. Beat-up trucks with gun racks stop-and-go through the Lotto sales outlets. Ministers hold revivals in mobile homes. Billboards block views of the mountains and the strait with promotions for motor-home parks. Logs are stacked high around the port, the transit point for local timber ripped from the rain forest and shipped raw overseas. There is a sense that life is two steps out of reach and moving away fast.

Here in Victoria, the resource rat race is not as obvious. Although one in every two dollars generated on Vancouver Island comes from the forest-products industry, there are no sulfur-belching pulp mills, no clearcuts on the immediate horizon, no trailer-home parks on fresh-cleared stump-land, no drive-through booths for Jesus. Part of this picture is illusory: the interior of the island has been shaved to bare stubs; even sections of Strathcona Provincial Park have been clearcut. But in Victoria the land-scraping is out of view, not unlike the more abusive acts of British imperial rule at the height of the Empire.

This is not the England of Dickens, but the England of Hyde Park and Lord Byron. Double-decker buses cram streets named Royal Oak and Cadboro Bay. There's a pub and teahouse on every other corner. Clipped accents—real and contrived—thick ankles and sensible shoes are the rule, along with that peculiar British distaste for sweat. It takes me three days before I understand a joke. When a man's hat falls off, and he looks both ways and says "Excuse me" before picking it up—is that funny? In Victoria, it is.

Of course, there's a castle on the highest hill in town, a four-story haunt of sandstone and brick with thirty-nine rooms, eighteen fireplaces, a three-thousand-pound billiard table, and chairs with little notches in them (a place for the gentlemen to put their swords). "Those Victorian men were so imaginative then," says a blue-haired keeper of the Craigdarroch Castle, which looks like the Gothic home of Laurence Olivier and Joan Fontaine in the Hitchcock film *Rebecca*. On this side of the Tweed Curtain, the Resource Barons built great monuments to themselves after stripping the forests and digging up the earth. Craigdarroch is the stone dream of a Scotsman, Robert Dunsmuir. Having exploited the richest seam of coal ever found on Vancouver Island, he tried to build his Xanadu here, but died the year before it was completed in 1890. The British Empire was at its peak then, covering more than nine million square miles with a total population of 305 million people. However, the Empire had a trade deficit, importing thirty percent more than it exported. I culled this information from a hundred-year-old dish inside the castle, a commemorative plate from Queen Victoria's golden jubilee. "Don't touch, sir," the keeper scolds me, flashing a frown identical to the scowl worn by the Queen in the souvenir dish.

Walking away from the castle, I look out across the strait at the Olympic Mountains, still puzzled as to how this carpet of Anglo civility was laid over this land of glacial disorder. Some of the natives on this island were cannibals, others fierce warriors, but they are best known as artists, carvers of the totem pole and sculptors of animistic face masks. The Russians, the Spaniards, the French and the Yanks all nibbled at parts of Vancouver Island. It was the British, the apostles of rose gardens and high tea, who nicknamed this place "England of the Pacific," and sent boatloads of pipe-smoking, tweed-wearing, Queen-loving, tea-drinking gentlemen here to settle it. Unlike the American settlers, who brought bibles and guns to their new land, the British immigrants were urged to arrive with cricket bats, carriage harnesses and a library of the classics. In 1853, the same year Winthrop visited the Hudson's Bay Company outpost of Fort Victoria, the Honourable Charles Fitzwilliam, a member of the British Parliament, was also touring the colony on the Pacific. "The climate appeared to me particularly adapted for settlement by Englishmen," he wrote.

The monthly mean temperatures of Victoria are almost exactly those of London—both cities average 55 degrees Fahrenheit in May, 60 in June, 63 in July, 63 in August, and 39 in January. But climate alone does not make a cousin. Rudyard Kipling wrote after his visit more than a half-century ago:

> To realize Victoria, you must take all that the eye admires most in Bournemouth, Torquay, the Isle of Wight, the Happy Valley at

Hong Kong, the Doon, the Sorrento and Camps Bay; add remi-
niscences of a thousand islands and arrange the whole around
the Bay of Naples, with some Himalayas for backdrop.

Most early English visitors intended nothing more than a stopover on
the way home from Empire duty, expecting to find horizontal showers
and suicide-gray skies. Instead, they found the Blue Hole, a term used
by pilots cruising above the predominant cloud cover. The Olympic Mountains snag the Pacific clouds and wring them till they're dry, creating a
rain-scarce zone over the northeast tip of the Olympic Peninsula, the San
Juan Islands and the lower part of Vancouver Island. So, while it pours
150 inches or more on the Pacific shore, fifty miles away the American
town of Sequim gets less rain than Los Angeles. Victoria is at the north
end of the Blue Hole. As I look out now at the Olympics, the tips are
covered in dense clouds while sunlight saturates Victoria. This is Canada's Palm Springs; people from all over the Great White North come
here to "winter" in a town that is actually farther north than any of the
major cities of Eastern Canada.

In the last grip of sunlight, the world is as it would be if every square
inch of land had a benevolent keeper. Azaleas, dwarf junipers and the
yellow blooms of the marsh marigold crowd the view to the south. The
view the other way brings flowering Japanese crabapples near beds of
anemone and polyanthus. The land rolls and buckles, rippling color lines
in the fading light. Then, the sun drops behind the glass of Brentwood
Bay, fifteen miles north of the center of Victoria. A full moon is on the
edge of the tree line, sending light back into the lake below, an abandoned
quarry pit. From the center of the deep lake, water shoots up, a lavender-
colored spray followed by a pair of green bursts and now a rainbow finale.
The effect is of a giant blossom, a hydro-flower, unfolding then retreating
in the kind of fast-forward used in the old Disney nature films. Other
lights come on, spotlighting rockeries in full flower, archways of purple
roses. All around, a full 130 acres has been crafted into controlled beauty,
offset only by the odd sight of an old kiln stack poking above the trees.
It is not the muscled supergrowth of the rain forest, nor the wildflower
meadows of the high country. It is the stamp of the Empire in the land
of evergreen.

When the railroads were emptying thousands of newcomers into the
cities of the Northwest and the forests and mines were being scraped in

a frenzy, Robert Pim Butchart ran a turn-of-the-century limestone quarry here, from which he extracted material for cement. It made him a very wealthy man. When the quarry was all used up, Mrs. Robert Pim Butchart was repelled by the brutalized landscape left behind; it was ugly and offensive. She set out to remake it, planting poplars and rhododendrons, wallflowers and creeping ivy—anything that would grow and produce lasting beauty in the temperate climate of southern Vancouver Island. Thus began Butchart Gardens, a shrine as pulse-quickening to gardeners as Graceland is to Elvis Presley fans.

The Blue Poppy of Tibet, first planted in North America here from seeds given Mrs. Butchart by the Edinburgh Botanical Gardens, leaves an Impressionistic blur against the fountain of bronze dolphins cast in Florence. The poppies are a British colonial legacy, brought back to England by an army captain. I have never seen anything like them. Here, they coexist with a Japanese garden that is a hundred yards from the seashore, and an Italian garden surrounded by fifty-foot-high cypress trees. The mind rushes to overstatement. But this much seems obvious: not even the Tuileries of Paris can compare. Strolling on the grounds, I hear Hebrew, Russian, Chinese, French, Dutch, Japanese. They make the common sound of awe. In transforming this quarry pit to paradise, Mrs. Butchart has proven that the land of the Northwest does not have to be scraped bare to turn a profit.

The lesson seems lost on the rest of Vancouver Island. From the fjords of the east side to the ocean shore of the west, hill after hill has been completely stripped. On this week in midspring, the largest western red cedar in the world has just been discovered in the thin coastal sanctuary of Pacific Rim National Park. The joke around Victoria is that the tree is the only western red cedar left on the island. A marvel, this tree, twenty stories high, as big in diameter as a municipal water tower, sixty-two feet around, more than 2,100 years old. It was a seedling before Julius Caesar was born, an aging giant long before Columbus landed in the Bahamas. There are more of these monoliths hidden in the park, but few people know about them.

Going from the perfection of the Butchart Gardens to the fecundity of the island's remaining rain forest, I'm struck by this irony between the British view of natural beauty and the native perspective. In Victoria, they have taken virtually every plot of available land and whipped it into a proper, weedless, well-mannered thing of beauty—controlled at all times by the tastes of the master. Much of the rest of the island is a moonscape with stumps. Those groves of old trees still standing and the unmarred shores of rock and wildflower—the draws of a province which advertises itself to the rest of the world as Super, Natural—have received only belated attention from the government or the garden clubs. "Yes, that's the old-growth forest," you hear them say. "And where's the bloody horticultural identification tag?" The wild becomes beautiful only after it's shackled, put on a diet of chemical nutrients, and trained to perform on a seasonal schedule.

According to the native ideal common among most Coast Indian tribes, The Trees and The Rocks were thought to be as endowed with spirit and beauty as The People. When British civilization, then less than 1,800 years old (dating to the point of the early Roman invasions) landed on these shores in the form of fur-trading mariners, they met a people who had been building wood-framed homes, conducting religious ceremonies rich in theater and myth, creating artwork as startling as twentieth-century Cubism, and feeding themselves quite nicely, for nearly ten thousand years.

Before the arrival of Europeans, more than eighty thousand people lived in the land now called British Columbia, perhaps half of them on the coast of Vancouver Island in permanent villages enriched by a prosperous fishing industry. They dried and smoked enough fish to live comfortably through the winters, supplementing their diet with berries, seaweed cakes, roots. Cedar, the mighty Western Red with its waterproof, mildew-resistant qualities, was the source of all life, hollowed into forty-foot war canoes, shredded and twined into dresses, hats, baskets, mats and baby diapers. Their houses, most of which were much bigger than the typical home found on the island today, were built of planks cut from the big cedars. The tribes of the northern part of the island used more than 110 species of plants for food, tools, twine and art. They also traded in slaves and waged short, vicious wars with other native peoples, and killed the second of newborn twins.

"The vices of these savages are very few when compared to ours," wrote José Mariano Mozino, a Mexican-born botanist who visited the island more than two hundred years ago. "One does not see here greed for another man's wealth, because articles of prime necessity are very few and all are common. Hunger obliges no one to rob on the highways, or to resort to piracy." The natural bounty was so great that the natives actually fought some wars with food, trying to outdo one another with culinary gifts at their potlatches.

When Captain James Cook of the Royal Navy arrived in 1778, his men were sick with scurvy, having found little along the Northwest Coast to add to their diet of hardtack and pickled pork. The natives taught them how to brew spruce beer and catch salmon. What gave the Salish such a bad reputation was one particular feast with Cook's men, an imaginative meal that didn't go over well and may have doomed the tribes for centuries afterward. Cook's two British ships were looking for the Northwest Passage, that great geographic myth of four centuries, and they were in dire need of repair when they anchored in Nootka Sound on the western shore of the island in the spring of 1778. They tied up at a place Cook called Friendly Cove, known to the natives as *Yuquot*, meaning "Place-That-Is-Hit-by-Winds-from-All-Directions."

The sketch of Yuquot left behind by John Webber, Cook's official artist, shows several big houses perched up on the shore, half-clad natives tending their canoes, and the well-dressed emissaries of Her Majesty, Cook's men, greeting them with flag and handshake. A good enough start. Cook proceeded to repair the *Discovery* and the *Resolution* and to inquire about the local stock of animal pelts. From a book published in 1783, *A Journal of Captain Cook's Last Voyage*, by John Ledyard, one of Cook's officers, we pick up what happened next:

> These Americans are rather above the middle stature, copper-coloured and of an athlete's make. We saw no sign of religion or worship among them, and if they sacrifice it is to the God of Liberty. Like all uncivilized men they are hospitable, and the first boat that visited us in the Cove brought us what no doubt they thought the greatest possible regalia, and offered us to eat; this was a human arm roasted. I have heard it remarked that human flesh is the most delicious, and therefore tasted a bit, and so did many others.

Cook tried to dissuade the natives from this beastly custom, or so he said. There is some dispute over whether the roasted human arms were a joke, a warning to scare the big white ships away, or a legitimate snack of high nutrient value. In any event, the natives of Vancouver Island, now widely recognized as one of the most advanced of all aboriginal North American peoples, were tagged as cannibals. A few years later, an American trading-ship captain said of them: "A more hideous set of beings, in the form of men and women, I had never before seen."

Cook himself, of course, was hardly a paradigm of civility. With Cook was Captain William Bligh, and the two leaders made a spectacle of flogging their men, regularly and with great relish. Long before Bligh became famous for uprisings against him, his men nearly mutinied on the voyage to the Northwest Coast. His legacy here is a small tuft of land off the west shore of Vancouver Island—wind-flogged Bligh Island. Bligh's name will continue to be cursed into the next century: a reef in Alaska's Prince William Sound, also named for Cook's chief officer, snagged an Exxon tanker on March 24, 1989, causing the worst oil spill ever in North American waters.

For the Northwest, Cook's voyage was the most consequential of all the early European trips. He was not only the first British subject to set foot on what would become British Columbia—a minor accomplishment, considering where else he'd been—but also the first non-Indian to realize a substantial profit from a resource of the Pacific Northwest. While charting the west side of the island, after missing both the mouth of the Columbia and the entrance to Puget Sound, Cook purchased 1,500 beaver skins. He also picked up sea otter furs, which fetched $100 apiece in China, the equivalent of two years' pay for the average seaman. To the mandarins of Canton, the sea otter was a cloak of gold. Easily killed as they played while swimming on their backs, with a two-inch-thick hide, the otter wore the most valuable coat of fur in history. If you took all the hair on the average human's head and compressed it down to one square inch, you would have the thickness of the sea otter's pelt. In the trade marts of the Pacific Rim, one human slave was generally worth two sea otter pelts. When Robert Gray of Boston built a schooner in Nootka Sound in 1792, he sold it to the Spanish for seventy-five otter furs.

Cook, whose statue is second in prominence only to Queen Victoria's in the capital city's inner harbor, was killed by natives while wading offshore in Hawaii, where the British went for cheap labor and winter sun. When his ships returned to England in 1780, word of the valuable fur trade spread; the rush was on, and the end was near for the native culture. Captain John Meares arrived in May of 1788, loaded with fifty Chinese laborers who built a trading post at Friendly Cove. The next year the post was taken over by the Spanish, who claimed that most of Northwest America had been given them by the Pope three hundred years earlier. England and Spain nearly went to war over the seizure at Friendly Cove, which gives some idea of how much sea otters meant to the treasuries of both countries. The dispute was settled by treaty awarding the property to England, for a considerable sum. Captain George Vancouver was sent out to reclaim the land and resume the search for the Northwest Passage.

He didn't find the River of the West, but Vancouver discovered that this sylvan slice of property was an island, not the mainland coast. In the spirit of cooperation, he named it for himself and for the Spanish explorer Señor Don Juan Francisco de la Bodega y Quadra (although Don Juan's name was quickly dropped).

Between 1785 and 1825, about 450 European ships arrived on the wild shores of the island to trade; more than a quarter-million sea otter pelts were taken from the Northwest Coast to China. Many English sailors and many English merchants got very rich; the Coast Indians lost their way of life, corrupted and diseased by the trading tools of the Empire, especially Nicholson's London Dry Gin—"bottled and guaranteed by the Hudson's Bay Company." By 1885, two-thirds of British Columbia's native population had disappeared.

There were, of course, a few rebellions. Chief Manquinna of Nootka Sound attacked the *Boston* in 1803, killing all but two men, whom he took as slaves. The ill-fated *Tonquin*, piloted by the ill-tempered Captain Thorn of Boston, was burned in 1811 and all his men were murdered. The fierce Haidas of the Queen Charlotte Islands, with their huge war canoes which gave them a raiding range of six hundred miles, fought battles until the late 1880s and even skirmished into the twentieth century. Unlike the Yanks, the leaders of the Hudson's Bay Company— originally chartered by King Charles in 1660—never waged war against the native people. But then, after a while, they didn't have to: smallpox and alcohol did to the majority of traditional inhabitants what a few British naval officers never could.

When the Hudson's Bay Company scouts went looking for a northern foothold to hold off the Yankee wagon train invasion of the Oregon Country in the 1840s, they found only a handful of native women gathering camas bulbs on the rich plateau where Victoria now sits. The setting, at the southern tip of the island in a protected harbor under the Blue Hole, close to the mouth of the Fraser River, and close to the Pacific and Puget Sound, seemed a perfect place for the Western World's oldest monopoly to dig in. Even before a single log was cut for the fort, one of the company's Gentlemen Adventurers called the setting "An exact copy of English park scenery." When the island was declared the British Colony of Vancouver Island, the boys in the fur trade were rewarded with complete government control, for a nominal fee of seven shillings a year—the first time the Gentlemen had ever been given actual governing powers. They promptly raised the Union Jack and the flag of the Gentlemen's Company, an emblem with two elk holding a cross above the Latin motto *pro pelle cutem*. Roughly translated—"You give your skin to get a skin."

Victoria was to be no ordinary colony. No Irish castoffs, no hardscrabble exiles from other parts of the Empire, no Yankee religious fanatics, none of the indentured servants who toiled in the tobacco plantations of the British colonial South or the chained convicts sent to the penal colony of Australia. The company wanted only gentlemen to settle the toe of the Empire—generic gentlemen who could become Hudson's Bay Company Gentlemen. When the settlement was platted, one of the first things company factor James Douglas did was to set aside the stunning sweep of land on the bluff above the strait as Beacon Hill Park. In contrast to the founding of American towns, growth was controlled and orderly; speculation was discouraged. They set up four large farms as part of the Puget Sound Agricultural Cooperative; before long the Gentlemen were growing enough food to sell to the Russians up north and the Yanks in the south. Furs moved in and out of the post, although the sea otter, slow to breed and bearing only a single pup every two years, was fast disappearing.

By the time Winthrop arrived in 1853, the then ten-year-old fort consisted of seventy-nine dwellings, twelve stores, a library and 240 settlers. Winthrop didn't stay long; he was in a hurry to get back south and catch a caravan to the East. The Yankee traveler did not comment on what the Gentlemen had done with their settlement. The natural setting, however, drew a brief, favorable note from him: "The arm of the sea upon which Victoria is, looks beautiful in the sunny afternoon, with the smoke just obscuring the rocky, barren shores and veiling the white houses of the village." The weather, he said, was "like a New England October . . . warm and cloudless."

In Victoria today there is but one building left intact from the time of Winthrop's visit—Helmcken House. Cloaked in cedar shingles, it is surrounded by tall oaks and even taller totem poles—a blend of two arborist traditions, serene in its setting, an island of the past in the bustle of modern Victoria. I walk among the totems and oak trees, then sit on the porch of Helmcken House, seeking the distant scent of that Boston man from the last century. I find that we share an American distaste for royalty—the idea of glorifying someone whose most significant achievement is surviving the act of birth. Winthrop had a practical Yankee's loathing for the English, their formality and their trappings of class. What particularly annoyed him was all those English names on top of the high mountains of the Northwest: Baker, Rainier, St. Helens, Hood. Who were these people? Civil servants, British bureaucrats, hacks and bean-counters who might turn down the next voyage of discovery if not sufficiently flattered by the royal cartographer. The landmarks belong to their native names, Winthrop argued, not the "cockney misnomers" of "somebody and nobody" who had never seen the place.

The Gentlemen's idyll at Victoria lasted barely a generation; gold was discovered in the lower Fraser River valley a few years after Winthrop left. And though the Hudson's Bay Company at first tried to control who could go into the new mines, the dam quickly burst. More than thirty thousand prospectors, most of them non-tea-drinking, non-Queen-worshipping and non-tweed-wearing, came through the genteel island fort in 1858 on their way to the goldfields of the British Columbian mainland. Perhaps Victoria could have become a prettier version of London, but the railroad never crossed the Strait of Georgia. Instead, Vancouver was established as the road's western terminus, leaving Victoria cut off from the trends and action of the continent. By the start of the twentieth century, the city's influence had peaked. Though Victoria remained the capital, Vancouver soon passed it in population. There were a few last efforts to keep the British influence. The province was now, of course, a part of the Dominion of Canada, but by 1903 some government leaders were seeking more English immigrants to offset an influx of Russians. Two large horse-drawn exhibition vans toured depressed districts of rural England, looking for emigrants—this time, however, they didn't have to be gentlemen to qualify.

By 1917, Raymond Chandler found the toe of the Empire "dullish, as an English town would be on a Sunday, everything shut up, churchy atmosphere and so on."

Victoria will never give up England; by a quirk of history, the town's fate is now tied to maintaining the image of its past. With its huge Parliament Building lit up at night, the horse-drawn tallyhos, the double-decker buses, the city looks like a kind of English Disneyland. The ancient Empress Hotel buzzes with tourists. I see a man videotaping the hotel's rose garden, concentrating on one blossom. Inside the Empress, there is a long waiting list for the chance to pay twelve dollars and sip high tea, considered the quintessential Victorian experience.

The official, living link to all this British baggage is Robert Gordon Rogers, the Queen's representative. I went to spend some time with Mr. Rogers one day when the morning sun guided the blossoms in the Royal Rose Garden into a chorus of color. He lives in a granite castle called Government House, overlooking the strait. The grounds are exquisite, thirty-five acres of exotic flowers placed around ponds and old-growth evergreens. Mr. Rogers's personal secretary, a young man with Edwardian hair and flawless manners, had asked me several questions a few days earlier when I set up the interview.

"Eeee-gun?" He puzzled. "How do you spell that?"

"E-g-a-n."

"I see. The Irish spelling."

"Yes."

"Mmmmmm."

Government House is not open to the public except on New Year's Eve, when loyal subjects of the Queen are invited to the annual levee. Inside, the red-carpeted entrance hall is 150 feet long. The oak-paneled interior is filled with oil portraits of lesser royalty, while life-size paintings of Her Majesty the Queen and His Royal Highness the Duke of Edinburgh hang on each side of a granite fireplace. There is also a portrait of Mr. Rogers himself, wearing the gold breastplate, sword, and feathered hat of the Windsor garment. On this morning, servants in white uniforms and little headpieces that look like napkins tiptoe back and forth across the immense hall, carrying tea and coffee for Mr. and Mrs. Rogers, who live amidst the hush of elegance and the low hum of servant gossip.

I'm ushered into a private chamber, where I meet the Vice Regal. He seats me, and a servant brings coffee on a silver tray. Mr. Rogers looks a lot like Walter Cronkite: silver hair, slicked back, a neatly trimmed silver mustache, silver eyebrows used as conversational punctuation marks. He's sixty-eight years old, tall, trim, well manicured; he looks and smells the part. Mr. Rogers is having a typical day, welcoming visiting royalty, in this case the Crown Prince of Thailand and his accompanying swordsmen.

He tells me about his uniform, which is kept in a glass case when not worn on formal occasions such as the opening of Parliament. When fully dressed in the garment, Mr. Rogers is anchored in thirty pounds of formalwear. The gold-braided breastplate alone weighs more than ten pounds.

"It's quite a load," he says.

I ask him if all these trappings of royalty seem like a lot of blather for what is basically a ceremonial title. Not so, replies Mr. Rogers; in fact, he is the chief executive officer of the Province of British Columbia. Even though the Canada Act of 1982 gave Canadians full power to amend their own constitution, ultimate authority still, he says, rests with the monarchy. All bills passed by the B.C. legislature must be signed by him to become law. If he wanted to, he could veto any bill in the name of the Queen.

"However, if I chose to do so, it would set off a constitutional crisis," he says. No Vice Regal has done such a thing in recent memory.

Mainly, he flies the flag—his official flag, at that, a design of Union Jack melded with the B.C. symbol and topped by a St. Edward's Crown in proper colors—which is hoisted on the ferry whenever he crosses over to the mainland. And he drinks a lot of tea with a lot of visiting royalty. Upon appointment five years ago, his first guests were the Prince and Princess of Wales.

"Nice chap, Charles," Mr. Rogers said.

Well, what's he like?

"Puts his pants on one leg at a time, he does."

Mr. Rogers is very nice, very polite, within reason. What angers the Vice Regal is a woman in Victoria who does occasional parodies of the Queen for local television. She is not particularly vicious; her likeness to QE-2 is used in a gentle inducement to get viewers to buy certain products.

"It's an outrage!" says the Honourable Mr. Rogers. "An absolute outrage!"

I ask how Victoria would be different if the boundary had not been drawn at the 49th Parallel. He rolls his eyes. "We'd probably be like Los Angeles," he says, referring to a place that might as well be West Beirut. American cities, even Seattle, seem big and cold and hostile, overbuilt to accommodate the automobile and the egos of office developers. Victoria, he says with absolute assurance, is the British Eden, the prettiest spot in the Empire.

Late afternoon, back on the American side of the Tweed Curtain on the west shores of San Juan Island. I'm at the edge of a forgotten bay, empty of any visitors on this spring day save a wild turkey rooting through the woods on the hill. The Union Jack flies over an abandoned garrison on this far northwestern isle of America, a place of peace that nearly became a battleground. Here, on the eve of the American Civil War, a battalion of British Royal Marines and a motley crew of American soldiers nearly went at each other in a dispute over a dead pig.

Less than ten thousand people live on the 172 islands of the San Juan archipelago, which bask in the rain shadow in protected waters north of the entrance to Puget Sound. Most of the islands are uninhabited, green cones which rise from the sea, the tops of a mountain chain submerged when retreating glaciers melted away. For the most part, developers and bridge-builders and clearcutters have been kept away; the islands still look as if they were sketched from a Japanese woodcarving.

At low tide, much of the sea changes to land, and then more than seven hundred islands can be counted. People come here to hide, to find something they can't find on the mainland, to get religion through solitude. From June till September, nearly every day is perfect, with the 10,778-foot volcano of Mount Baker rising from the tumble of the Cascades to the west, blue herons and bald eagles crowding the skies, killer whales breaching offshore. The water is exceptionally clear, the result of a twice-daily shift-change in tide, when it sweeps north toward the Strait of Georgia, then back south toward the Strait of Juan de Fuca. In some places, the rip tides create white water like rapids on a foaming river. Being is bliss. But then the winters come and the tourists all go home and clouds hang on the horizon and unemployment doubles and the island dweller is left with whatever it is that led him to escape the rest of the world.

This seems an odd place for war. After the Treaty of Washington between America and Great Britain was signed in 1846, it remained unclear which country owned the San Juans. According to the treaty, Britain got everything above the 49th Parallel and all the land "to the middle of the channel which separates the continent from Vancouver's Island; and thence southerly through the middle of said channel, and of Fuca Straits, to the Pacific Ocean. . . ." The trouble was that several channels fit this description. No one much cared about the ambiguity, at first. The Hudson's Bay Company fort at Victoria sent a boatload of 1,300 sheep to San Juan Island, the largest in the chain, and they mingled with a handful of British and American farmers.

Then, on June 14, 1859, a pig owned by a British settler wandered into the potato patch of a particularly cantankerous American farmer named Lyman Cutler. Cutler shot the pig, and the two settlers had hot words, each calling the other a foreign trespasser, each declaring his country would back him in a jurisdictional dispute. Overreacting in the tradition of combat-hungry commanders, U.S. Army Captain William S. Harney sent a platoon of troops to the island to back up Cutler's right to shoot a British pig in his potato patch. The British responded by dispatching troops of their own. Before long there were more than a thousand armed soldiers facing each other, three ships from the British Royal Navy, and one howitzer-heavy American vessel on hand, with another due to arrive soon. Nine miles apart, each side set up camp and prepared for war.

But nothing happened. For the next thirteen years, the troops remained at their respective garrisons, in time getting to know each other quite well. The opposing forces held banquets and track meets together, shared whiskey and practical jokes, and in all those years never fired a shot. To kill time, the Royal Marines stationed at English Camp started a formal garden, a beautiful rectangular plot of land where only the finest of traditional English flowers would grow. Seeds came from all over the Empire, arriving on Royal Navy ships with fresh supplies and the implements of battle. The Pig War was eventually settled by the German Kaiser, acting as mediator, who gave the islands to America. The English went back to Victoria, or home.

What is left today at English Camp on the American side of the Tweed Curtain is the rectangular garden, the oddest legacy in one of the oddest troop deployments in the history of the Royal Marines. In the Pig War, the ground was turned to begin life, not to bury it. The roses are just starting to blossom on this spring day, the oak which shaded the soldiers is in full foliage. The air is sweet and salty clean—the air of a formal garden in a wild setting—evoking no sense of remorse or the whispers of the dead, a tribute to what happens when an empire leaves rose bushes and rhododendrons behind as its chief colonial legacy.

Chapter 4

THE LAST HIDEOUT

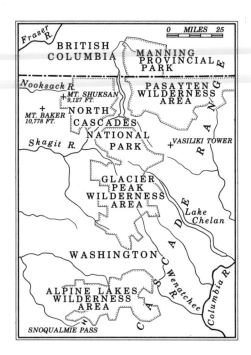

I 'm looking for Beckey. From peak to valley, from glacier to meadow, from fang to overhang, I hear nothing but talk of Beckey. His name echoes off the salmon-colored granite walls of the North Cascades and rustles through fields of waist-high wildflowers. Faces appear out of a fog, muttering Beckey, Beckey, goddamn Beckey. In the alpine villages on either side of the international border, the barkeeps and mini-mart merchants all know Beckey. They've seen him, oh yes. Just yesterday, or was it last week? Don't tell me about Beckey, son: I knew him before he was a statue. He never stays at sea level any longer than it takes to restock his supplies and slake the demands of his libido. In Marblemount and Mazama and Hope, tough little mountain towns pressed against the vertical edge of the Cascades, Fred Beckey is the rarest form of legend: one who's still alive.

Outside the walls of Beckey's kingdom, I look up at the sawblade skyline of the North Cascades. These mountains rise from the sea, holding the weight of every storm that blows east off the ocean, delivering an annual dump of 650 inches of snow on the summit barriers. Though uplifted by continental-plate collision and wracked by recent volcanism, the North Cascades owe their surface appearance to water, the master architect of the Northwest. A museum of ice, they are layered with all those low-pressure memories from the Pacific, more than seven hundred living glaciers in all. Think of glaciers, and what comes to mind are slow-moving frozen rivers viewed from the deck of an Alaskan cruise ship. But up here in the folds of the land between Snoqualmie Pass and the Fraser River, the glaciers are in constant and violent downward motion, actively reshaping the land. They crack, roar, scrape and tug, along the way polishing the vertical walls, depositing water in every available bowl, and feeding a forest of evergreens.

Nearly twice the size of Yellowstone National Park, the North Cascades lie within an hour's drive of four million people. Yet, while the rest of the range, stretching through Oregon and into California, is overrun with visitors, the year-round cannon fire of the north keeps people away from the high country here. Within sight of Seattle and Vancouver are flanks of the earth that have yet to feel a human footprint. Those peaks that have been touched, in all likelihood were first touched by Fred Beckey. Too harsh for prospectors, too high for the casually curious, the North Cascades—one of the last places in mainland America to be fully mapped and explored—have been the domain of the driven.

After crossing over from the lowland warmth of the San Juan Islands, I head east into the mountains, looking for Beckey. He's supposed to be here, somewhere. The only reason I know this is because Beckey usually migrates in the early summer from the High Sierra of California to the North Cascades of Washington and British Columbia. My first stop is at the Forest Service ranger station in the town of Glacier, deep inside the cedar tunnel of the Mount Baker Highway. Beckey? Sure, everybody knows Beckey, says the ranger. Behind him is a wall-sized map of the North Cascades, an area which William O. Douglas said contained "peaks too numerous to count." The high points on the map are called Terror, Fury, Despair, Forgotten, Forbidden, Formidable, Freezeout, Inspiration, Triumph, Challenger, Desolation, Isolation, Damnation, Illusion, Joker, Nodoubt, Redoubt, Three Fools. These are not the kind of names that come from dull-witted surveyors or Forest Service committees. These are climbers' names, many of them Beckey's, most of them recently coined.

Usually, you can tell a peak that's been named by Beckey because it has something to do with sex or alcohol. Aphrodite Tower, the Chianti, Burgundy and Pernod Spires—these are Beckey's peaks.

The forest ranger in Glacier has heard that Beckey is climbing the Nooksack Tower, just south of the Canadian border. Beckey's got to be getting up there in years, says the ranger. "I remember him from the forties." Fred Beckey is sixty-five years old, I tell him, same age as Chuck Yeager, the Beckey of the skies. For the last five decades, almost everything he's climbed has never been climbed before. "Yeah, he's something, that Beckey," says the ranger, "but he never checks in with us. If you see the little bastard," the ranger says, "tell him he's supposed to get a permit before he crosses Forest Service property into the North Cascade National Park." Right.

I slide down a wet clay bank above the swollen Nooksack River, cursing the Forest Service for not keeping up the trail system built under Franklin Roosevelt. The sky is in my hair as I begin this walk to the headwaters of the river, a typical Cascade Mountain stream born among glaciers and rushing quickly to tidewater. Stumbling up the low-elevation valley, I'm lashed by spindly alder branches that break out of the aging snowpack. Locked in late spring, the ground here is on mass melt today, new life popping out like kids crashing the school door at recess. After a few miles, the cloud ceiling lifts a hundred feet or so, and then something resembling frozen rain falls from it. The faint markings along the trees disappear, and I'm left with the chattering Nooksack. There is only one way to go, four miles up the river to the dead-end of the cirque wall, so I travel along rocks in the shallows of the milky river, my feet numb and thoroughly soaked. The river narrows, quiets, and then nearly disappears in the vast amphitheater of ice that is the Nooksack Cirque. It took me some time to notice, but the frozen rain has stopped, and the clouds are lifting. With the curtain up, the rippled ice flanks of the cirque enter from stage left, right and center.

Parts of this valley, fed by snow from the 10,778-foot volcano of Mount Baker and the 9,127-foot rockpile of Mount Shuksan, were trod by Theodore Winthrop when he passed by in 1853. When he paddled his dugout into Bellingham Bay and came ashore for a look, the Yankee got quite an eyeful. The local Lummi tribe told him about the volcano with fire in the belly and ice on top: *Koma Kulshan*, they called it, meaning "white, steep mountain." He was the first to commit the native name to print, but it didn't stick. "As to Baker, that name should be forgotten," Winthrop wrote in *The Canoe and the Saddle*. "Mountains should not be insulted by being named after undistinguished bipeds. . . ."

Winthrop ate a feast of boiled salmon with the Lummi, who never dreamed of trying to attain the volcano's summit, or that of any of the other big peaks in the range. The idea was absurd, as well as a form of spiritual trespass. The Lummi and the other tribes of Puget Sound would no more try to climb vertical ice towers than they would attempt to live underwater. It was always the outsiders, whether from England or from the Midwest, who wanted to go up among the eternal snows.

I see one tent, a red dome, inside this deep-shadowed hideaway. Looks new. I cup my hands around my mouth and call out, "Beckeeeeeeey."

The sound bounces from one snow wall to the other, and then falls away. It's late in a long day at a time of year when the light hangs around till nearly 10 P.M. I notice the fluted summit of the Nooksack Ridge, about seven thousand feet above me. I have to sit down in the snow to take it all in: the summit rim is an intense pink, lit by the fading sunlight from the west. It reminds me of a twilight hour in Manhattan when I watched the late color on the apex of the Chrysler Building. "It's like the spires of the North Cascades," I said at the time, my first visit to New York, and my friend looked at me funny. I dragged him into Grand Central Terminal, where I heard there was a full-color picture of Mount Shuksan, the centerpiece of these mountains. A Czech émigré named Dusan Jagersky had seen this picture when he first came to America in 1968, on the run from the Russian tanks that had rolled into Prague that year. Pointing to the mountain, Jagersky asked if he could purchase a ticket to such a place.

"I am not Beckey," says the man in the dome tent, which is obvious when he steps outside his shelter. He's from Germany, perhaps thirty years old, on a tour of America's national parks. He can't get over how much dead timber and snags are on the ground in North America: in Germany, the forest floors are clean of loose limbs and downfall. He's heard of Beckey.

"Everybody knows Beckey," he says. He shows me the little red book, Beckey's bible: *Cascade Alpine Guide*. There are three such volumes by Beckey, each one revered by the cult of climbers who've followed his every handhold. In the books, he gives a staggeringly detailed description of every climbing route on every mountain in the Cascade Range from the Columbia River to the Fraser River, more than 1,500 peaks in all. The language is insider jargon, coating high-risk alpine route-finding in a peculiar descriptive shorthand.

Beckey is also German, born near Düsseldorf, the son of a doctor. He was two years old when the family moved to Seattle in the early 1920s. Fred and his brother Helmy learned about the outdoors through the Boy Scouts, and on weekend trips to the Olympics the Beckey brothers usually went beyond the call of merit-badge duty. As teenagers they joined the Mountaineers, a formal climbing group whose members are given to long and somber discussions about their long and somber mass expeditions to the high points of the Cascades. By the age of sixteen, when Beckey started leading his own expeditions to peaks which the Mountaineers had declared unclimbable, it was clear that he would never be an organization man. He skied, played some football and ran cross-country, but directed most of his energy to the fulfillment of two passions: mountains and women. After graduating from the University of Washington (where he scaled the brick walls of the Gothic campus buildings in tennis shoes), he took a job as a delivery-truck driver, rather than pursue something more in line with his degree in business administration, because the job served both needs. It was part-time, which meant more time could be spent in the neighboring peaks near Snoqualmie Pass, forty-five miles east of Seattle. And along the truck route Beckey kept several girlfriends. During his days off, he pioneered new climbing routes; during the rest of the week, he pioneered an imaginative delivery route.

Early on, the Beckey brothers picked up with a climber from their neighborhood in West Seattle, an engineer named Lloyd Anderson. They drove to the mountains in a Model A, or hitchhiked. When the old mining and timber roads gave out, they slogged through thick brush or picked their way up streambeds and over goat paths toward the high ice. They sang dirty ditties to pass the time, and moved at an uphill, cross-country clip of better than five miles an hour. Where previous twentieth-century explorers, almost exclusively miners and government geologic surveyors, had called the North Cascades dark and chaotic and dangerous, Beckey came back with descriptions like "enchanting" and "stimulating." He compared climbing virgin rock to "erotic exercise." Even the savage storms that blew in from the Pacific were "morally uplifting," he used to say.

Until 1972, when the North Cascades Highway was opened, there wasn't a single east–west road that crossed the expanse of alpine country from Stevens Pass to the Fraser River. The Indians used trade routes, a few well-trodden trails over the mountains that brought the salmon-eaters of the west to the horse-riders of the east. Simon Fraser, a Northwest Company explorer who followed the river named after him from tidewater to headwaters during an adventure in 1805, said this part of the world was more rugged than any he'd seen in North America. "I have been for a long period in the Rocky Mountains, but never seen anything like this country," Fraser wrote. "It is so wild that I cannot find words." Alexander Ross, a trapper for the Pacific Fur Company, had claimed to be the first white man to find an overland route across the North Cascades: the Indian path from the east, up the Stehekin River and then westward over Cascade Pass and into the Skagit River. Whether he completed the route or not is still in doubt. But there is no record of any white crossing the mountains again for another forty years, until Washington Territorial Governor Isaac Stevens sent a railroad survey crew into the Cascades in 1853, the year Winthrop bumped into the surveyor near Naches Pass as the Yankee was making his own pioneering traverse of the range.

One other visitor of note came before Winthrop. In 1825, David Douglas, a young Scottish botanist, spent a year in the Cascades searching for specimens on behalf of the Royal Horticultural Society. Similar to a lunar explorer, Douglas discovered plants and trees that had never been found in the known universe. On the west slopes of the Cascades, he identified the tree that would be named for him, the Douglas fir, and measured its average diameter at seventeen feet in the lower valleys—the biggest tree found in North America at the time. When he sailed back to England, Douglas took with him seeds and samples from 150 previously unknown plant species.

Without exception, the early mountain visitors compared the North Cascades to the Swiss Alps. It was Winthrop who said the Old World comparison was not worthy of these New World peaks. While gazing up at the Cascade skyline from his canoe near the San Juan Islands, Winthrop argued that the new residents of the Pacific Northwest should forget Europe when discussing these mountains. He predicted that a regional style and outlook would evolve as the North Cascades were appreciated for their singular beauty. From the ice caps of the Northwestern summits would blow fresh inspiration for artists and climbers and everyday souls anchored in the mire of sea level.

In urging "recognition for the almost unknown glories of the Cascade Mountains," Winthrop wrote:

We are poorly off for such objects east of the Mississippi. There
are some roughish excrescences known as the Alleghanies. There
is a knobby group of brownish White Mountains. Best of all, high
in Down-East is the lonely Katahdin. Hillocks these—never
among them one single summit brilliant forever with snow, golden
in sunshine, silver when sunshine has gone; not one to bloom
rosy at dawn, and to be a vision of refreshment all the sultry
summer long; not one to be lustrous white over leagues of woodland, sombre or tender; not one to repeat the azure of heaven
among its shadowy dells. . . .

In the fifty years following his endorsement, most of the people who
wandered above timberline for a look were prospectors and surveyors.
Periodic goldstrikes fostered bursts of primitive road building in the valleys and construction of boomtowns which were often wiped out by avalanches. Unlike the Swiss, who built town-saving barricades where the
gullies drained into their villages, the Northwesterners never mastered
the avalanche. Early into this century, when the mother lodes were spent,
the North Cascades were mostly forgotten again. By then, the basin of
Puget Sound was filling up with people; only when pushed by urban
elbows did the city dwellers start to look up at the peaks in their midst
with anything approaching Winthrop's awe. Within easy distance from
the smokestacks of the new cities was a mountain range that could still
humble, or bring to the visitor a sense of discovery.

The first climbers were English, from Victoria. They compared Mount
Baker to the Jungfrau in the Bernese Oberland area of the Alps. Early
pictures show men in neckties, sometimes joined by women in ankle-
length dresses and floppy hats, slogging up steep glacial slopes. They
had little influence beyond their mostly upper-class circles. Bob Marshall,
the legendary Forest Service walker, hiked the Cascade Pass area in 1930
and recommended that the entire area be set aside as wilderness, an idea
that took form years later with piecemeal creation of the Glacier Peak,
Alpine Lakes and Pasayten wilderness areas and the North Cascades
National Park on the American side, and Manning Provincial Park and
Cathedral Park north of the border.

Beckey, singing his dirty songs, traveling in tennis shoes and carrying
a Boy Scout rucksack, made his first mark on the climbing world in 1939,
when he, Lloyd Anderson and Clint Kelley climbed Mount Despair in
the North Cascades. An ice pyramid of 7,292 feet, Despair had been
labeled unclimbable by a Mountaineers publication a few years earlier.

Whacking through the brush, Beckey's party found a way above timberline, then scrambled on rock and ice face to the summit, as if pulled by magnet. It was not so much the conquest of the peak that got Beckey excited as it was the conquest of his own fear. What triumph: to be unbound from the leash of mortality. He began to feel a certain invincibility.

From then on, he climbed virtually nothing but peaks that had never been ascended. All over the West, from the Teton Range in Wyoming to the Maroon Bells in Colorado to Yosemite in the High Sierras to the Cascade peaks of Mount Baker and Shuksan and Rainier, Beckey blazed a trail. By the end of the 1940s, he was the best-known climber in the West—and arguably in America—at least among the odd circle of European immigrants and loners who spent time in the mountains. But he'd also picked up a reputation as arrogant, dangerously careless, a youthful fireball who would soon burn out. Beckey was that rare athlete who knows he's the best and can't contain it. The climbing journals, feuding constantly with Beckey over his methods and routes, and the devil-may-care way in which he described his astonishing feats—on any given day, he could ruin an existing hero or make a longtime expert look silly—would give only passing mention to his first ascents, usually no more than a paragraph or two in the last pages of a mountaineering annual. In the late 1940s, he sought to have the Mountaineers publish his first climbing guidebook for the local peaks. When they turned him down, he went to the well-established, mostly upper-class American Alpine Club, and they agreed to print a few thousand copies for a flat fee—no royalties. Beckey made little money on the 1949 publication, and so he went back to driving a delivery truck. It would be years before he would return to writing about the mountains as a means of supporting himself.

Beckey's fame spread through word of mouth. There were stories about his wolf howl, a blood-chilling sound, which Beckey would use to scare tourists away from his favorite campsites. Whereas Mount Baker was first climbed by English gentlemen, Beckey went up and down like a vandal on the run; coming off the volcano in the 1950s, he found a logging truck at the trailhead, a violation, in his mind, of the wilderness. So he proceeded to disengage the truck's gear and roll it several miles down the valley. Climbing Devil's Tower in Wyoming, he was nearly arrested after urinating in front of gawking tourists in the parking lot below. Beckey had had no ill intent, he explained—it was just that he was stuck on the wall with no place to hide.

While many of his early climbing partners anchored themselves to desks at sea level, Beckey continued to take odd jobs, sleeping on friends' floors and cadging rides to and from the mountains. Lloyd Anderson, his partner on Mount Despair, founded Recreational Equipment Inc., an outdoor co-op set up as a way to get good European hardware at reasonable prices. After the war, with the surge in leisure-time activities and the surfeit of Army camping gear, the backyard operation took off. By the 1950s, Anderson's creation, known by the initials REI, had grown to be the largest consumer co-op in the nation. More than two million members have registered since Anderson's days with Beckey in the late 1930s, and there are now eighteen REI stores in ten states. REI is one of the largest sporting-goods retailers in the world. But the outdoors brought no riches to Beckey. The Man with No Permanent Address made few plans beyond the next outing.

He is supposed to be up there somewhere today, a sixty-five-year-old man who can't sit still. Beckey's apparent target, the Nooksack Tower, is a black hulk six times as high as the World Trade Center, coated in ice. Beckey was the first human to touch the summit, on July 5, 1946.

As the rose-tinted light bleeds out of the sky to the west, I leave the German and set up my own campsite below the walls of the tower. A moist wind invades the cirque, a harbinger of the next frontal system. Perhaps Beckey is bivouacked somewhere up high, and I'll catch him in the early morning. Then again, maybe he's gone. Now the light has disappeared, and the peaks are black and white, the shades of a killer whale just beneath the surface. At night, with a cannonade of avalanches all around, I have trouble sleeping. The sound comes first as a crack, and then *whooomppfff*. Mount Shuksan, joined to the Nooksack Tower by the shoulder ridge above me, means "roaring mountain" in the native tongue. Everything that any mountain could have—flower meadows, alpine firs, small lakes, glaciers, serrated rock walls, colors found only above timberline at a certain time of day, and a summit that defies easy ascent—is on Shuksan. But at night, all it does is roar. In the morning there is no Beckey, and the German is gone. I scan the tower, its peak bathed in the bronze of dawn, and see a speck of a man moving upward—the German—no doubt muttering directions from the Beckey book in his backpack.

———

At sea level, I look up Beckey's closest friend, a Lithuanian émigré named Alex Bertulis, who has an architecture practice in Seattle. I've put out the word that I'm looking for Beckey, and Bertulis has a message for me from the man himself: Beckey has gone to the Coast Range for the month. The Coast Range is a largely roadless spine of low-elevation wilderness rising from the fjords of British Columbia and stretching hundreds of miles north into the panhandle of Alaska. Most of the peaks are unnamed and unclimbed and heavily glaciated by year-round storms. The Coast Range, at his age? And then I remember a saying of Beckey's. Loveliness, he said, is paid for "in the currency of suffering."

Bertulis shrugs. Don't worry, he says. He'll be back.

"It's just something he has to do."

Bertulis has climbed with Beckey for three decades; he provides a couch for his sleeping bag whenever he's in Seattle. Beckey, he says, "goes through climbing partners like a gypsy goes through horses." Beckey may spend ten days on rock and ice, and within a few minutes of arriving back in Seattle he's on the phone, trying to find somebody to go with him back to the mountains. Usually his partners are half his age. While in town, he's constantly on edge until he's secured a mate for the next trip.

I ask Bertulis about the 1950s, when the Northwest was coming into its own as the climbing center of North America. The Army's Tenth Mountain Division, created as a ski unit to fight the Nazis in the Alps, was put together with climbers from Mount Rainier. After the war, many of them stayed together and started to pursue mountaineering as something more than a weekend hobby. Beckey was too young for the division; he enlisted near the end of the war and missed most of the action. By the late 1950s, an effort to put the first American atop Mount Everest was underway in the Northwest, led by Jim Whittaker, a West Seattle neighbor of Beckey's and an early manager of REI.

Like Beckey, Whittaker learned about the outdoors through the Boy Scouts, scrambling up the peaks of the Cascades and Olympics. Beckey, in the 1950s, had made three daring first ascents on comparatively unknown Alaskan peaks. He had done them all alpine style, a method of mountaineering later popularized by Reinhold Messner, the first man to climb each of the world's eight-thousand-meter peaks, fourteen in all. Rather than rely on an army of supplies and porters, the alpine idea is to travel light and fast without bottled oxygen or cumbersome support camps. Beckey, given his superhuman reputation, seemed a natural for the 1963 Everest trip. But he was not chosen. Four Americans made the high point of the planet. While Beckey was scrounging for gas money, Jim Whittaker became a national hero, joining John Glenn in the Kennedy circle of Camelot demigods, his picture on the covers of *Life* magazine and *National Geographic*. Whittaker went on to market a line of outdoor clothing under the label Because It's There.

"Fred was blackballed by the climbing community," says Bertulis. "There had been a tragedy while he was climbing in the Himalayas. Beckey's tentmate got edema and couldn't move. . . . In the same period, a man died climbing with Beckey in the Cascades. They were descending at night, and the man went the wrong way through the brush off Mount Baring and fell off a cliff. The climbing establishment never forgave Beckey. There was a stigma attached to him, perhaps it was envy. He had a reputation for being reckless, an undeserved reputation in my mind. But he was the most qualified mountaineer in America for that 1963 Everest trip."

Later, some members from the 1963 party conceded that Beckey was in a league of his own, a climber of extraordinary talent. But they said his personality—blunt, smart-ass, independent—was ill suited to a three-month expedition where teamwork and an even temperament were paramount concerns. Beckey himself had too much pride to ask for a spot, and he was never good at self-promotion, a virtual requirement for world-class athletes.

Beckey increased his pace in the 1960s, a time when rock-climbing developed as the new athletic frontier. More and more, younger climbers who'd heard about his spider qualities on rock and his ribald tales at night, sought him out. Among a circle of outdoor athletes, he obtained celebrity status, with one big difference: Beckey was always broke. But his sea-level charms could work wonders, often making up for what he lacked in money. Bertulis remembers numerous times when he and Beckey would descend into alpine towns, exhausted, and Beckey would want to go out. A few hours later he would return, arm in arm with the best-looking woman in the valley. He never married.

"Fred married the mountains," says Bertulis. "So, consequently, he looks at these peaks as his children. That's his life. That's all he's got. He's been very pure in that regard. He never compromised himself. Never endorsed Camel cigarettes or something like that. Never commercialized himself. As a result, he's always had to live hand to mouth."

Though Beckey has not slowed down, Bertulis has noticed one significant change in his friend. "For the first time in his life, he's thinking about his own mortality. He realizes his legs will not carry him forever."

In the Lost World Plateau, an attic of Beckey's past, I'm searching for clues to the young man. One look at Nixon's Nose, a protrusion of sloping granite high on Prusik Peak, tells me more about Beckey than anything he's written. To be intimate with that rock is to be divorced from the laws of physics. The dozens of lakes settled in the granite bowls above seven thousand feet here are known as the Enchantments; in mythological spirit, the landmarks were given such names as Excalibur Rock, Valhalla Cirque, Grail Tarn, Lake Viviane, Rune Tarn, Talisman, Valkyrie. Larch trees, a conifer which loses its needles after a show of gold, surround the lakes. The recipe that produced this beauty is unduplicated in the Cascades. I had to wait several weeks to get my permit from the Forest Service to enter this realm, now protected as the Alpine Lakes Wilderness area. In this waistband of mountain country, thirty miles north to south, are 692 lakes. In Beckey's heyday, he could run naked for a week in midsummer and bump into more goats than people. Now, the Enchantments have more company than they can accommodate and still live up to their name. As Winthrop urged in the last century, the captive of the city has discovered the freedom of the high country. And while the number of Cascade hikers has increased sixfold since 1960, nearly a third of the trail mileage has been lost to logging and neglect. Since the mid-1960s, the government has concentrated on road building for timber companies, largely ignoring the trail system built by Depression-era city workers.

Beckey first came to the Enchantments in 1948, intending to climb and name the unknown high points on the map above the apple orchards of the Wenatchee Valley. Like a sybarite stumbling into a convent, Beckey found himself surrounded by challenge. Traveling light as usual, he arranged for a crop-duster airplane to drop several weeks' worth of supplies to his camp. Flying low over the high rock, the plane crashed into boulders, but the pilot lived, and the supplies were salvaged.

I envy Beckey now, camped at Gnome Tarn under Prusik Peak. With the completion of the polar expeditions, discovery of the unknown corners of the planet became so much harder. Deep sea and outer space were considered the only places left, and to get Out There or Underwater required considerable technological help. Beckey, pushing the limits of a creature without hoofs or wings or sealed transport, found new land in his own backyard. When he reached the Lost World Plateau and set up camp in the Enchantments, he looked at a ridge where only eagles and hawks had perched, named it the Nightmare Needles, then climbed most of the serrated rock. He crawled up Nixon's Nose, up to the top of Prusik Peak, walked to the edge of Little Annapurna to see the sun set behind Mount Stuart, and scurried for handholds on The Temple.

Ira Spring, a photographer who has spent his life taking pictures of the Cascades, went into the Enchantments with Beckey in the 1940s and came out amazed at what he had seen.

"He exists on a different plane," says Spring. "Some of those climbs in there were just out of this world. Fred had taken lots of abuse because no one could believe he had done all these summits as fast as he said. I was impressed beyond description. But after that, I was the only one still impressed. He was written off as too controversial." Beckey refused to mend his ways with the Northwest climbing establishment. He would attend the rare slide show or annual meeting, but all the rock talk would eventually bore him.

Spring, holding rope to belay Beckey up the rock of the Enchantment Basin, heard nonstop prattle about women. "Girls, girls, girls, that's all he ever talked about. After a while I just shut up and listened to him. It made for interesting listening."

Now in his seventies, Ira Spring limits himself to hiking in place of the climbs of his youth. He can't understand why Beckey is not similarly bound by the handicaps of age. "Where does he get the energy? He looks like he couldn't walk across the street."

When it's time to leave the Enchantments, I scramble up to the edge of the Nightmare Needles as far as my ability will take me, a thousand feet or so below the Beckey threshold. I find a porch of salt-and-pepper granite and settle in for lunch. It's hot; the sun east of the Cascade Crest is not the same star that burns in the soggy west side. I slice a bagel open and layer it with cheese and salami. Leaning against the rock, the Wenatchee Valley to the east, I hear voices—two men and a woman, tied to each other in the upper reaches of the Nightmare Needles. They speak the same language I heard in the glacier bowl of the Nooksack Cirque: "Beckey says . . ."

Beckey lives. There is a voice to the legend. Back from the Coast Range, he says he's ready to meet me. I can barely hear him above an electric buzz on the phone line.

"What's that noise?" I ask him.

"I'm shaving," he says. "Don't like to waste any time in the morning."

He explains that he's chained to a desk in the Oregon Historical Society office, researching a book on the history of the Cascades. Can I meet him in Portland?

Crossing the Columbia into Oregon, where the Cascades are smoother, smaller and more rounded than the whitecapped ice fangs of the north, I have my doubts whether Beckey will actually show up; his reputation is that of a phantom, and an unpredictable one at that. We're supposed to meet at a diner on the shore of the Willamette River, Beckey's kind of place—"gets pretty wild after a while." I wait. No Beckey. After an hour, I'm ready to go, convinced I've been stood up. Then—Beckey.

He seems nervous and jittery, as Bertulis has described him whenever he's stuck at sea level, away from the familiar music of a storm and the living room under the sky. He walks in a stiff manner, back upright, about six feet tall. There is not an ounce of fat on him that I can see. Beckey's sandy hair is thinning on top, and his face is deeply lined, more from the sun than worry. He has a sort of hound-dog, wounded look to him until he smiles, and the accordion of high-altitude-baked skin slides back. His voice is hardly that of a sixty-five-year-old man; rather, it sounds like someone in his twenties. I think of all those young, glossy-faced ski bums and climbers I've met in the mountains, people who never have to go home on Monday morning. They're not supposed to age. Beckey's index finger on one hand is bent at a right angle, hanging like a useless appendage evolving its way out of the species. I ask him about the finger, and he looks at it as if for the first time.

"I don't know what the hell happened to that," he says. "Guess I'll have to get it looked at. That'll cost me."

Beckey gives the impression that he never planned anything in his entire life, except perhaps the next climb. Adventure drew him to the outdoors, the call of the unknown, he explains in short, precise sentences similar to the dry prose of his alpine guidebooks. He rarely talks about beauty in the mountains. His concerns are crustal fragments, thrust faults, gneiss. I wonder if the man has gone cold inside from all those years outside.

Talking about his youth, Beckey says he was always hyper. When he realized his limbs could carry him to sights unseen by other humans, he was hooked. It was all so easy, crawling up rock chimneys, dangling across faces with eight thousand feet of exposure, slogging through brush. What was hard was the sea-level stuff. Bringing a body back from a weekend trip, knowing the deceased had stepped one way and fallen to his death, while Beckey had stepped the other and come home un-scathed—how do you explain that? In the 1940s there had been an avalanche on Mount Waddington, in British Columbia, resulting in the death of a man from a Harvard team guided by Beckey. In the 1950s, a companion fell to his death while descending Mount Baring northeast of Seattle. And then there was the Himalayan accident, an episode still cloaked in mystery. Thinking about these lost companions, Beckey rubs his face. Like most mountaineers, he has a logical explanation for what happened; it's the only way to keep climbing.

Beckey says he wanted to be a cartographer, but most of the jobs for mapmakers in the 1940s were with the federal government in Washington, D.C., crawling up the walls of the bureaucracy instead of the flanks of the North Cascades. "I decided that was no man's land—too hot, too flat, full of ugly women." He didn't care that there was little glamour or career satisfaction in driving a delivery truck. "It was no-brain work. I liked that, because I spent all my mental time thinking about girls and mountains."

He talks about Liberty Bell, perhaps the best-known climber's peak in the North Cascades. Beckey named the true summit—it had been mis-placed on a neighboring rock tower—and was the first to climb it, in 1946. Today, alpinists come from all over the world to retrace Beckey's route up the pastel tower of Liberty Bell. It broke his heart to see the east–west highway carved through the mountains in 1972. He went back to Liberty Bell this summer, climbing familiar rock while tourists stared from a parking lot nearby, off the North Cascades Highway. He was like the aging Buffalo Bill performing the tricks of the Old West in a circus ring. Civilization, he feels, has crowded out the remaining wild country. A person has to go deep into Alaska, or the Yukon, to find a place to get lost. Off-road vehicles, which have been found by federal government studies to disfigure more land in the West than strip mining, are now allowed into many of Beckey's sacred places. "At least the miners knew what they were doing," Beckey scowls. "These idiots on dirt bikes and ORVs don't have any sense of the outdoors or how to treat the land!"

Oddly, Beckey calls himself a city person, and in that sense he is a Northwest archetype: someone who can tread water in the overcrowded urban pool knowing an ocean of freedom is only an hour away. But he feels cornered.

"The frontier is gone," says the last of the frontier explorers. "We've hit the Pacific Ocean and we're backed up. There isn't enough rock for everybody who wants to climb."

A few routes on a few high rocks in the deep shadows of the North Cascades have been omitted from his alpine guidebook trilogy, by design. Beckey wanted to leave some room, long after he's gone, for discovery. He says the books have brought him more stress than success. He lives on a few thousand dollars a year in royalties, and worries about the new litigious breed of urban outdoor enthusiasts. Recently, a woman went for a hike in the Cascades, following the directions of a popular trail guide. After she fell off the trail and suffered serious injuries, she sued the author and publisher, claiming they were to blame for her accident. The case was settled out of court. Beckey shivers at such stories. His publisher is always asking him to respond to some missive from a climber who is miffed because the Beckey route up a mountain took much longer than he had indicated in the guidebook.

Beckey seems little interested in recounting any of his expeditions, with one exception: the first trip to the bright-colored rock country near Liberty Bell, an area he compares to the Dolomites in northern Italy. At the time, Beckey was in love with a dark-haired, athletic woman of Greek background named Vasiliki. He met her while skiing at Stevens Pass and they hiked and played tennis and skied and partied together. She was one of the smartest women Beckey had ever met, fluent in several languages, but also outdoorsy and sure of herself.

Lovestruck, Beckey went into the uncharted mountains near Liberty Bell in 1952. The beauty of the area, baked in east-crest sun, only heightened his feelings. All around was fine-cut granite tinged in pink and orange. While bivouacked on a frosty evening, he witnessed the loveliest sunset he had ever seen in the mountains; in a lifetime of glorious alpine curtain calls, it was one of the few that ever stood out. He thought of Vasiliki, and then he remembered a quotation from St. Augustine: "There is a morning and an evening in all mortal things."

As the expedition continued, Beckey gave immortality to the woman he was stuck on. He named the sharp-edged, glacier-refined, pastel-colored rock of nearly eight thousand feet Vasiliki Tower, the only time he ever christened a peak for an individual woman. He named the surrounding summits for her favorite drinks—Chianti, Burgundy and Pernod spires—and two other high points, Aphrodite Tower and Bacchus Tower. Standing alone, any of those mountains would be far higher than any peak east of the Mississippi. In the North Cascades, they were ignored until Beckey bestowed his names on them. "Imaginative names," he wrote in a cryptic reference in his guidebook, "sometimes in abuse of such privilege, but adding character to the ridge."

Vasiliki was the one woman Beckey wanted to marry. "She would have made a terrific wife," says Beckey. "I wish I'd done something about it." She fell in love with somebody else, and prospered in a life where culture and money and civility mattered more than the spontaneous thrills of the climbing bum. Beckey went back to his old ways, seldom mentioning Vasiliki, flirting with death on new rock walls, meeting new women, but he left behind one strong hint of the man's soul. . . .

Near Vasiliki Tower, wildflowers grow from rock slits high above timberline. A hummingbird buzzes overhead, and I see goat prints on a patch of midsummer snow. I'm not wearing a wristwatch, so I can't set my expectations of the day against the clock. As it has for many late-century citizens of the Information Age, computer time has cut my attention span and reduced my patience. I absorb change in milliseconds. To come up here, looking for the better part of Beckey, I must slow to glacier time. Below, near the edge of a snow lake fast melting to turquoise, are heather fields aflame with color and little bell-cupped flowers. On the other side of the summit is a tarn, newly sprung from the Ice Age. My topographical map, based on a geological survey in the 1950s, shows several small glaciers in the northern basins of these peaks. They are no longer here, victims, perhaps, of the gradual warming of the earth.

Moving along a summit ridge, I chase Vasiliki Tower. It pokes in and out of view, guarded by the wine spires, never in full profile until I reach a rock summit. And then, there it is, in all its vertical glory, a magnificent hulk of rock and strength. I've had conflicting views of Beckey throughout the first months of summer—an egotist, an adventurer, a free spirit, a freeloader, an iconoclast, an athlete without equal, a man full of life, a man full of sadness, doomed to living out his years in high-altitude loneliness on legs that must grow weaker. But in his way, he has fulfilled Winthrop's prophecy, finding exalted life in the iced pinnacles. Yes, I know it now: feeling the breath of Vasiliki Tower at this range, I can think only one thought of Beckey: God, was he in love.

Chapter 5

WITH
PEOPLE

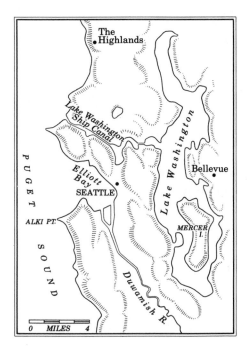

Here we have a city: black and beige and boxy up front, the towers of Chicago or Tokyo planted in soil that once held a glacier and fed a forest. Such bulk, piled on land so rumpled, pinched by an enormous lake on one side and an inland sea on the other. It's all very new, and all very tentative, for Seattle is a city that can't decide what to wear. The city has changed its look three times in the last thirty years, and half a dozen times in the last century. The hills that once rose steeply from the central waterfront—they've been cut in half. The Black River, a salmon stream that flowed from Lake Washington to the Duwamish and into Puget Sound—it's gone. And the tidelands which nurtured a bouillabaisse of sea life—buried. Still, the city is not finished; every wave of fresh tenants wants to remodel. So, the flat-topped hills of downtown, minus their natural summits, are sprouting new skyscrapers by the month, and the forested edge of the city is leveled for Weyerhaeuser's newest product: the instant neighborhood. When humorist Fran Lebowitz recently visited Seattle, she was asked what she thought of the city. "It's cute," she replied. "Why are they tearing it down?"

In the spirit of earlier inhabitants, I approach Seattle by kayak, entering Elliott Bay on a weekday morning; it's like landing at O'Hare Airport on a kite. Overwhelmed by ship traffic, I hug the shoreline, trailed by sea birds looking for French fries. The wake of a passing container ship, four city blocks in length, gives my small craft a muscular nudge. Rainier floats atop the southern skyline, a hooded cone above the industrial congestion of the Duwamish Valley. There is the Kingdome, a cement cavern without sufficient daylight to adequately support a baseball team, plopped on fill-dirt that used to be tidelands. Farther south is Boeing Field, where the Duwamish River was straightened and its old bed leveled to provide a runway for newly hatched jumbo jets. Towering over downtown is the Columbia Center. A thousand feet high and black as a charred forest, it's stuffed with enough lawyers to replace nearly half the attorneys in Japan.

Looking around, I see a few hints of traditional life in the temperate zone: a rock crab scrambling over exposed pilings, some loose kelp, a cormorant riding a northern breeze. At the entrance, Elliott Bay is nearly as deep as the Space Needle is high, a depth of six hundred feet that hides a half-blind octopus of three hundred pounds which paralyzes its prey with a toxic squirt. In these waters live squid twenty-four feet long, century-old clams with necks of pornographic dimensions, starfish bigger than an extra-large pizza—in all, more than two thousand kinds of invertebrates. All of that is below me, out of sight. What I see when I paddle into Elliott Bay is the dominance of one species.

I try to imagine George Vancouver, who was the first to pencil Puget Sound onto a map that showed no such thing. For one month in the spring of 1792, at the age of thirty-four, he had the feeling of God during Creation Week. Traveling up the Pacific Coast, the *Discovery* and the *Chatham* took a right turn at the Strait of Juan de Fuca and proceeded east toward an immense volcano anchored in the North Cascades, which Vancouver promptly relieved of its native name, Koma Kulshan, and replaced with that of his cartographer, Joseph Baker, the "undistinguished biped" cursed by Winthrop. Then south, to an inland sea and an even bigger volcano at its southern end, which he named Rainier. He passed through Admiralty Inlet, the weather clear, the water calm, the mountains polished on either side of him. All around, the land rose up in storm-sculpted detail, the islands carpeted by forests, streams leaping out of steep canyons. The air opened his sinuses and expanded his imagination. Vancouver, already ill with a mystery disease that would kill him before his fortieth birthday, was in the Northwest to map and chart a course for future commerce. A detail man, humorless, he would flog his men in front of other sailors to make his disciplinary point. But when he entered Puget Sound something happened, as if he'd tossed his old spirit overboard in a rush of spring euphoria. The first thing he did was give his men a holiday, their only day off since they'd passed Cape Horn at the toe of South America. From then on, his journals started to sing.

To Vancouver and other British explorers, wild land was evil land, bad until proven civilized. That attitude changed when he came upon the garden of Puget Sound. It was perfect as it was. Vancouver wrote: "As we had no reason to imagine this country had ever been indebted for any of its decorations to the hand of man, I could not possibly believe that any uncultivated country had ever been discovered exhibiting so rich a picture." Farther down the sound, he anchored off Bainbridge Island, just across the water from the future city of Seattle. Vancouver then penned what is perhaps his most famous passage:

> To describe the beauties of this region, will, on some future occasion, be a very grateful task to the pen of a skillful panegyrist. The serenity of the climate, the innumerable pleasing landscapes, and the abundant fertility that unassisted nature puts forth, require only to be enriched by the industry of man with villages, mansions, cottages, and other buildings, to render it the most lovely country that can be imagined.

In short order, the place would be full of villages and mansions and cottages, but their inhabitants felt compelled to assist nature. In Seattle, they nearly overwhelmed it.

On that spring evening in 1792, a six-year-old native boy by the name of Sealth is said to have looked out across the water at the *Discovery*, surely a vessel that could not have been assembled with any product of nature. The Olympics were topped by the gold trim of sunset, the Cascades dark blue in repose. Never again would such a view belong to one band of people. Sealth was the son of a native slave woman taken in one of the periodic raids which the Coast Indians engaged in to replenish the tribal stock of females. The city that was built around Elliott Bay was named for Sealth, changed to *Seattle* because the original pronunciation

(See-alth) made the speaker sound as if he had a lisp. But that came much later, more than a half-century after Vancouver passed by.

When Winthrop visited Puget Sound, Washington Territory had just been carved from the Oregon Country and contained fewer than four thousand whites. It was a wilderness twice as large as New England, stretching from the Columbia River to the Canadian border and east to Montana. Like Vancouver before him, he felt this land would need no customizing from humans to improve it; instead, things should work the other way, with the land reshaping its inhabitants—Winthrop's central prophecy. Already the cities of the East, some of them two hundred years old and falling into industrial mayhem, were not working. The nation was torn by slavery; seventy-seven years after the start of the American Revolution, a class system was still in place in many parts of a country where the theory of democracy and the practice of same were an ocean apart. Strange religious cults, centered around leaders who traded in ecstasy and redemption, sprang up in New England, New York and the new states of Ohio and Illinois and Indiana. Here in the Far West, in a maritime valley between two mountain ranges, was a fresh chance for a new nation to live up to its promise. Starting over is the oldest American impulse.

From my kayak today, I look one way at the forest of new skyscrapers and the other way at Bainbridge Island to a grassy opening in the trees where Sealth is buried. There is a white cross atop his stone grave; in his later years, he converted to Christianity, and the first historians of Seattle treated him well as a result. Had he remained true to his native religious beliefs, he would have burned every day he heard his name mentioned in relation to the ever-expanding city in his midst. Once a person died, his name was supposed to go with him, evoked by mortals only on the most solemn of occasions. Sealth had always been one to compromise; some would say he sold out, early and often. He was tall and tough, a warrior in his younger days who owned eight slaves at one point and eventually freed them after Abraham Lincoln did the same thing for blacks in the South. He lived to be a very old man, going from aboriginal king of Elliott Bay and the river that drained into it, to a withered curiosity on the muddy streets of what would become the largest city in the country named for a Native American.

Sealth was there when two dozen members of the Denny party landed off Alki Point in a November rain storm in 1851. The plan was to build a city on this narrow beach strip west of Elliott Bay. In the spring of that year, four wagons had left Cherry Grove, Illinois—a town which has long since left the map—and crossed the continent to Portland. They traveled the Oregon Trail at the same time that David Swinson Maynard, a clever, hard-drinking physician on the run from a bad marriage and a mountain of debt, was making his exodus from Cleveland. To this day, Seattle's divided character can be traced to the dual nature of its two founders. Maynard was a boozer and a visionary; Arthur Denny was a teetotaler and small-minded. Maynard quickly learned to speak the native language and set up alliances with several tribes; Denny despised the Indians and considered them useless except as snitches against their own people. It was Maynard who named Seattle, scribbling it into the territorial register after first scouting the location and conniving with Chief Sealth, who had been in exile while feuding with a rival native leader. Sealth planned to use the white party's arrival at his longtime fishing grounds as a means to his triumphant return.

When the twelve adults and twelve children of the Denny party landed at the wind-lacerated shore of what they called New York–Alki, the appearance of Sealth and his tribe shocked them. It was a collision of Midwestern, church-going, cow-eating, monogamous people with a Northwestern, polytheistic, salmon-eating, promiscuous band. The white women, their starched bonnets collapsing in the rain storm, broke into fits of tears. There was supposed to be a cabin waiting for them, built by one of the younger members of the party. There was; but it had no roof. From the very beginning, this place of brooding green was no Illinois, although the city founders would spend much of their time trying to make it so. The new reality set in quickly: Mary Denny, unable to nurse her screaming infant, came up with a formula of clam nectar.

Doc Maynard arrived in late winter and quickly concluded that the log cabin at the base of the windswept bluff would not do for his city. They could keep New York–Alki. He paddled his dugout around Alki Point and into Elliott Bay, protected from the winds and extraordinarily deep, and found the spot he had earlier scouted, where the Duwamish River drained into the bay. Several steep, forested hills rose above the tideflats. In accordance with the Oregon Donation Land Act, he claimed 320 acres for himself and 320 acres for the wife in Cleveland whom he had yet to divorce. Denny had also been exploring the Duwamish drainage; four months after settling into New York–Alki, he moved his party to the superior site on the bay. He platted one section of town in a neat grid patterned after Cherry Grove; on the same day, Maynard platted an adjacent section in a not-so-neat grid patterned after his native Cleveland. Thus was born the last great American city to rise during the frontier experience, 211 years after John Winthrop founded the Massachusetts Bay Colony and used the words "City on a Hill" to describe the New World promise.

Within a few years, Maynard's section of Seattle was wide open, a lumberjack's version of an eternal lost weekend. Denny's section was proper, picket-fenced. On Maynard's plat was the house of Madame Damnable, a two-story, Southern-style mansion and bordello that became one of the most popular destinations north of San Francisco, and the seat of local justice. On Denny's plat was built an Episcopal church. While the whorehouse thrived, the church folded for lack of attendance. Seattle still ranks at the bottom of all American cities in number and percentage of church-goers.

Most towns that were carved from the weeping forests of the Pacific Coast in the days before the Civil War were built in a spirit of speculation. Great chunks of land were free for the taking. Large sums of money were then made when that land was sold off, lot by lot, to immigrants who were convinced that their muddy plot would double in value within a few years. It was a kind of pyramid scheme, dependent on every new settler attracting three or four additional friends. As Winthrop wrote, "Whenever one has hit on a good site for a town, his next neighbor starts a rival one, so that there are often two settlements within a quarter mile in open warfare." While waiting for property values to rise, the towns had to do something to stay afloat and to make a name for themselves. In Seattle, they sold timber and sex—the only two reasons for a ship to tie up at the mud village in Elliott Bay. A few months after the Denny party arrived at Alki, they loaded a cargo of logs onto a brig bound for San Francisco, which the goldrush had transformed from a tent camp of a few hundred people to a rough city of 35,000. But every few months Baghdad by the Bay caught fire; in four years' time, San Francisco burned down five times.

The forests of northern California and Oregon were full of the straightest, tallest and thickest timber whites had ever seen, but the woods were impenetrable, and it was impossible to land a ship along most of the raging coastline. In Puget Sound, the lumber merchants from San Francisco found safe harbor, compliant pilgrims from the Midwest, and wood that could be purchased for a fraction of the price it would bring back in California. By 1853, the year Winthrop canoed past Elliott Bay, Seattle was home to the only steam sawmill on Puget Sound. Logs were cut from the hills above Madame Damnable's and skidded down a grease-planked road to Henry Yesler's mill. In San Francisco, after one of its town-consuming fires, those logs could bring as much as $300 per thousand board feet, which is not far from the price paid for raw logs today. As long as there were trees to cut, the people would prosper. Initially, the town looked no different than Port Gamble, the Pope & Talbot Company milltown on the other side of the Sound, or any other Northwestern timber village choking on sawdust and clay muck. Seattle was a filthy, foul-smelling lumber camp and vice pit that would, within a few generations, be called the most livable city in America.

By the time coal was being gouged out of the nearby Cascade foothills for export, Seattle was a full-blown resource colony, and a rowdy wart of a town at that. There were mob hangings, riots against the Chinese, saloon shootings, plagues of venereal disease. The Indian prostitutes who roamed the roughest parts of Maynard's plat were known as "sawdust women." A famous story has it that a hat remained in the middle of the muddy street for days on end because residents were afraid to pick it up and see who might be under it. Chief Sealth, appalled at how his emerald garden had been trashed so quickly, wrote a letter in 1854 to President Franklin Pierce. "The whites, too, shall pass, perhaps sooner than the other tribes," he wrote with the help of a translator. "Continue to contaminate your bed and you will one night suffocate in waste." To the white founders of the city, the new land was not a garden to be cultivated, but a wilderness to be crushed; it was not a paradise populated by an ancient race, but a vacant lot.

Sealth died in 1866, one year after the city which bore his name passed an ordinance to ban Indians from town. His youngest daughter, Angeline, continued to live in an eight-by-ten-foot shack on the edge of Seattle for another thirty years. She became a sad-faced curiosity, the frequent subject of sympathetic photo-essays. In the summer of 1889 the entire city went up in flames, and when the immense purple cloud lifted, all traces of the old town of driftwood shacks and wood-planked sidewalks were gone forever. Rebuilding in stone and steel, the new city musclemen went on a pell-mell push for greatness. The native land ethic and Sealth's warning to a president would return, but not for several decades.

There was a lot of work ahead in the reshaping of the natural setting. First, they took up pickaxe and shovel against the seven miles of earth separating Puget Sound from Lake Union, a canal project completed in 1916 with the help of an army of immigrant laborers, mostly Scandinavian. Then, on a belief that the city could not expand because of the steep hills, civic leaders began the most ambitious earth-moving project of any urban center in North America: the war against Seattle's hills. These bizarre regrades would take half a century, move more dirt than was displaced by the Panama Canal, and reduce the city's downtown elevation by 107 feet. Day and night, the glacial till of Denny Hill, Jackson Hill, First Hill and smaller city lumps were sluiced and gouged away—sixty-eight square blocks in all. "Some people seem to think that just because there were hills in Seattle originally, some of them ought to be left there," said R. H. Thompson, the chief city engineer, clearly disgusted by such an attitude. A few houses, their owners refusing to cooperate, were left teetering on the remnant towers of the old hills. At times, the city resembled a moist moonscape. The tidelands where Sealth's people used to dig for clams and set weirs for salmon were filled in, two thousand acres in all, first with sawdust, then with regrade dirt from the shrinking hills.

Murray Morgan, the Northwest historian, has said that the natural scenery of this city is better than if it had been planned. But from 1876 to 1930 more than 50 million tons of original Seattle was scraped away like gravel in a goldmine—a horror to the aesthete, a delight to the technocrat. Seattle was praised by the American Society of Engineers as a city "that had the courage to fill in its tideflats and regrade its hills." The great urban crew cut, they noted, "is the result of allowing full play to the imagination and creative energy of the engineers."

Winthrop would've been shocked at the initial appearance of the biggest city in the Northwest, an area he said was endowed with "the best, largest, and calmest conditions of nature." In this part of the world, poet would never be dwarfed by engineer, he predicted. Winthrop never mentioned Seattle in his book, in all likelihood because it appeared as nothing but a curl of smoke from a distant mill as he paddled past Elliott Bay, heading south for Nisqually. The prophet of 1853 found only the seven forested hills over which Seattle would eventually conquer and sprawl, but no city. He was high on Puget Sound, calling it by the native name, Whulge, and saying "Whulge is more interesting than any of the eastern waters of our country." Chesapeake Bay, Delaware Bay, Long Island Sound, "even the Maine archipelago cannot compare with it."

Stirred by the soft beauty of the Sound, Winthrop wrote:

> Again, I thought of the influence of this most impressive scenery upon its future pupils among men. The shape of the world has controlled or guided men's growth; the look of the world has hardly yet begun to have its effect upon spiritual progress. Multitudes of agents have always been at work to poison and dwarf poets and

artists in those inspiring regions of earth where nature means they shall grow as naturally as water-lilies by a lake, or palms above the thicks of tropic woods.

More than two million people live in metropolitan Seattle, a population larger than that of the entire states of Idaho and Montana put together. With all that open space just across the mountains, why cram onto a narrow band of land situated at a latitude farther north than half the homes of Canada? Tonight, stuck in traffic on a rain-slicked freeway at the edge of town, I grope for a type-A answer to this question. The new crowds of the city have forced the pace of thought and the pulse of routine. Gone from these streets is the favorite bumper sticker of the West: "If You Can Read This, You're Driving Too Close." Large, full-windowed houses with big yards and wonderful views are grafted to every available lot from south of Seattle to Everett, a forty-five-mile stretch. In between are three Boeing plants, each with its own police force, its own passports, and, at the 747 plant in Everett, a building so large clouds have been known to form inside. It's hard to see why jet factories have grown so naturally in this climate. An accident of timing, a world war, plenty of cheap property, and before you know it, the land of salmon and evergreen trees is the airplane capital of the world.

I turn off the freeway and head west toward the Highlands, which is where Bill Boeing settled after he sold his interest in the company. Overlooking Puget Sound and secluded by natural boundaries, the Highlands is to Seattle what Beverly Hills is to Los Angeles. It's much more understated and Northwestern, of course; this is a city where only lawyers, bankers and fresh-minted MBAs are consistent tie-wearers, and one in three residents belongs to the REI co-op. I pass the Tudor mansions and stone estates of old Seattle wealth, the descendants of timber barons who now live among some of the oldest and tallest trees left in the Puget Sound area, a long way from the ravaged stumpland of timber towns like Forks or Raymond. The homes are tasteful, devoid of ostentation, shadowed by the big firs. Each has its own stately view of the water, the islands, and the Olympics, an edge-of-the-world perch.

But, just as most of the big trees disappeared, these homes—this life— seem threatened, a feeling not limited to rich people in the Highlands. Stewart Holbrook, the writer of old tales about the young Northwest, described a feeling years ago that now is taken seriously by some. "Like many a native," he said, "I am privately of the opinion that this entire region should be set aside as one great park before it is wholly overrun by foreign immigrants like me."

A park it will not be. But a campaign essentially to freeze the region's biggest city, to do for Seattle what President Franklin Roosevelt did for the Olympic Peninsula, is gaining steam, even as it runs into the historic impulse of each wave of new residents to inflate and shape the city to their own liking. The idea of forcing newcomers to check their expansion plans at the city's door goes against the basic vision of the West—faster, bigger, better, the buzzwords of the American tomorrow. Seattle no longer wants to call itself New York–Alki, or even be compared to such a thing. After a century and a half of war, many in this city want to make peace with their surroundings while there is still enough of it left to bring them the good life prophesied by Winthrop. This sentiment has gone well beyond the sloganeering phase; taking the arcana of zoning laws into their own hands, Seattle citizens are set to vote on a measure that would cut construction of downtown skyscrapers by two-thirds. There is talk of banning cars from the central city, and keeping new houses from the last open spaces left in King County.

This movement began, in large part, with Emmett Watson, a newspaper columnist and author locally famous for founding Lesser Seattle, whose members commemorate month-long rain storms and civic failures with press releases to other cities. Watson is not a tree-hugger or backpacker; he chain-smokes unfiltered cigarettes, slurps black coffee 'round the clock, and walks with a half-step and hunched back. His constant companion is a runt poodle. Deaf in one ear, he briefly played semipro baseball for the Seattle Rainiers in 1942. When he was replaced on the roster, the coach was asked if the new player could hit. "I don't know," he answered. "But at least the son-of-a-bitch can hear."

Tonight, in honor of Watson's seventieth birthday, people from various backgrounds are crowded into the borrowed Highlands mansion to fete the founder of Lesser Seattle and talk up the promise of a restrained tomorrow. Off in one corner is Vasiliki Dwyer; she is with her husband, Federal Judge Bill Dwyer. I want to ask her about a certain mountain in the North Cascades, but I decide against bringing up Fred Beckey's legacy. I'm drawn to another face, that of a man who is nearly one hundred years old: Dave Beck, the old lion. Once he was considered, next to the President, the most powerful man in America. Now he has the countenance of an infant, free of hair and teeth and the dead weight of responsibility.

For much of this century, nothing on wheels moved in Seattle without

Beck's permission. Later on, little in America moved without his permission. As president of the International Brotherhood of Teamsters during the height of its power in the 1950s, Beck was the lord of labor. Born in 1894, a time when Chief Sealth's crease-faced daughter still prowled the streets looking for garbage to take back to her driftwood-framed shack, Beck is a living link between the mud village of New York–Alki and the overburdened megalopolis of today. His family came to Seattle in 1898, at the height of the Klondike goldrush, which enriched Seattle far more than it did the waves of argonauts who tramped through the snows of the Yukon. A brilliant publicity campaign convinced prospectors that they couldn't set foot in Alaska, 1,300 miles to the north, without first dropping most of their savings on merchants in Seattle. In two years' time, Seattle had more people than Los Angeles. In twenty years' time, it grew six times over. In the West, only San Francisco was bigger. Seattle had grown so quickly from primitive milltown to a showy urban upstart that a writer from *Harper's Weekly* remarked: "In the story of civilization, there is probably no record of more astonishing growth."

Like other immigrants, Beck's parents came to Seattle intending to board a ship for Alaska, but never got out of town. Beck himself was driving a laundry truck when Seattle was paralyzed by the only general strike ever to shut down an American city. Goldrush prosperity was followed by corruption so far-reaching that the police chief built and operated a five-hundred-room whorehouse with the full permission of the mayor. World War I heated up the timber, fishing and ship-building economy, all of which crashed following the Armistice. By 1919, the streets were swollen with newly unemployed shipyard workers, no-luck vets, three-fingered timbermen from the labor camps of the Industrial Workers of the World (the Wobblies), fruit pickers, foreigners fired up by the revolution then raging in Russia, and assorted hungry men from the sea and woods of the Northwest. There were several bloody riots between workers and company goons. Massacres made instant martyrs of Wobbly leaders. The city was ready to explode. A strike call, issued in sympathy for the shipyard workers, went out to the entire town, and on the morning of February 6, 1919, nothing moved in Seattle. In the labor paper, Anna Louise Strong, the onetime school board member and civic volunteer, wrote the words that would follow her to her grave in China, where she was an early supporter of Mao Zedong: "We are undertaking the most tremendous move ever made by labor in this country, a move which will lead—NO ONE KNOWS WHERE." The strike ran out of steam precisely because it had nowhere to go.

Dave Beck, the laundry-truck driver taking his self-improvement courses at night, learned a valuable lesson. He proceeded to organize every trade and profession with more than a handful of members, and he disciplined their leaders. In time, there was seldom any reason to call a strike; Beck had such control that most labor disputes were settled with a phone call. Business leaders came to like Beck, an Elks Club member, a teetotaler, a man whose word was law. His absolute power was predictable, which made for a smooth economy. Together, they promoted Seattle. Growth was oxygen, and the city inhaled it in great gulps.

Within a generation of the general strike, Seattle was no longer a scruffy labor town, but a citadel of the middle class. Union stevedores spent the weekends at their cabins on Puget Sound, or took off the first week in September to go salmon-fishing, same as their bosses. As president of the international, Beck became a wealthy man; union funds were used to pay inflated prices for property that he had purchased. The man who had once been so poor he shot rats for a bounty bought himself a mansion overlooking Puget Sound, complete with swimming pool. Despite repeated attempts by federal prosecutors and Senate racketeering inquiries to get him, Beck held on until 1962, when he was sent to prison for income tax fraud. He did three years' time at McNeil Island in Puget Sound, a prison term he said he found so restful that it added ten years to his life.

Now the growth crusades of Beck's prime have given way to a broad campaign to prevent too many people from moving here. The credo of many at this party is found in the words of Edward Abbey, who wrote that growth for the sake of growth is the philosophy of the cancer cell. Each person who comes up to Watson tonight has some story to tell about confusing a tourist or obstructing plans for the latest housing development at the edge of town. I hear much talk about the unbearable traffic, the frozen lines of cars on the Lake Washington bridges that connect Seattle to the generic neighborhoods spilling east to the mountains, and the forty thousand new people a year pouring into the Seattle metro area—a figure bandied about like the latest blood pressure reading of a terminally ill patient. An architect says too many of the new buildings look like Houston. Houston! And what about these Los Angeles drug gangs, the worst export of a town that has long been viewed as the Satan of cities? Unlike L.A., where residents don't look twice at the most popular yard sign in many neighborhoods—WARNING: THIS HOUSE PROTECTED BY ARMED RESPONSE—Seattle has not made the effortless shift to a siege mentality. Still, control seems to have shifted; more than ever, power is with forces from outside of the city, coming this way—a force of urban magnetism.

There is a certain smugness to all this talk; wouldn't Detroit or Cleveland or Buffalo or Denver like to have a little boom of its own? But beyond that, the growth angst has an edge because it goes to the very reason why people live in Seattle. Here in the corner attic of America, two hours' drive from a rain forest, a desert, a foreign country, an empty island, a hidden fjord, a raging river, a glacier, and a volcano is a place where the inhabitants sense they can do no better, nor do they want to.

The rain has always been the secret weapon. Winter days can be so dark and dank that a flashlight is helpful on a midday stroll. For nine months out of the year meteorologists issue one basic forecast: rain turning to showers. Turning to showers? How can they tell? The clouds are seldom forceful and usually tentative. The volume is nothing unusual—less rain falls here than in any city on the East Coast—it's the threat, the constant ambiguity in the sky, that drives people crazy. Now, however, with skin cancer and global warming, the sun is losing favor. On top of every other growth concern, even the Seattle drizzle has become fashionable, as good for the skin as a daily facial.

Watson gave the slow-things-down movement a name and a voice. As with many Seattle political trends, it started as a joke. While attending a luncheon of civic leaders who talked of further campaigns to expand the city—more industry, more people, more tourists—Watson squawked from the back of the room: "Who needs it?" Scorning formal organization and using his newspaper column as a bully pulpit, he commissioned anyone who shared his sympathies to become a "KBO agent." During an interview on the *Today* show, Bryant Gumbel winced when Watson answered his question about what the initials stood for: Keep the Bastards Out.

A writer with an ear for the talk of many lives, Watson has spent a lifetime chronicling the odd characters of the new city on Puget Sound. His father was a basement digger, and Emmett remembers tagging along as he cleared the sliding glacial till for new home foundations. Later, he moved to a farm east of Seattle near Snoqualmie Falls. The Depression broke his father, the bank took his farm, and he moved back to the city and went on welfare. He died shortly thereafter.

When Emmett came of age, the regrades and earth-moving projects were done, and the city was starting to show signs of fulfilling the Winthrop prophecy. A fine public university was built on a hill facing Mount Rainier—a promenade from the center of campus seems to spill into the mountain's north face, like the road to a glacial Oz—spread out over six hundred acres, accessible by water, and designed in Gothic style by a graduate of the Beaux-Arts school in Paris. Seattle attracted social tinkerers, lifestyle experimenters, political radicals. A Northwest style of architecture evolved, featuring windows big enough to allow the feel of winter storms, lots of unpainted wood, and clean trim lines in place of Victorian flourish. The subjects of native art—eagles and salmon and killer whales and wolves—and the muted colors of the sea and forest were evident in the work of many young artists. When Nellie Cornish arrived early in the twentieth century to found her school for the arts, she said the physical elements that surrounded the city would serve as the fount of a spirit and artistic style such as the country had never known. Eventually, Seattle became an important theater town. Ten professional stages provided Broadway and the West End with a steady source of original hits, although the directors of these theaters insisted they were creating original works for the people of the Northwest, not serving as a farm team for New York and London. When I asked Dan Sullivan, artistic director of the Seattle Repertory Theatre, why Seattle supports so much theatrical activity, he pointed to the drizzle outside his window. "The rain," he said. "It makes you go into dark places to tell stories."

Watson, who grew up listening to baseball games from distant ballparks, always thought he would move away to a real city. But he never left town. After baseball, he stumbled into the even cushier job of sportswriting, which led him to the better gossip tables in town and an expanded column format. He knew the bohemians and socialists, the Woody Guthrie crowd who sang until dawn at Lake Union houseboat parties; he followed Mark Tobey as he made a career painting the moods of the Pike Place Market; and when Ernest Hemingway passed his last day in Ketchum, Idaho, it was Watson who found out the death was a suicide and broke the news to the world. He helped the crusaders of the early 1960s as they campaigned to clean up Lake Washington, expand the region's park system and launch a world's fair that would leave the city with a landmark, the Space Needle, and a performing-arts complex.

Seattle was a place where a few citizens, not necessarily powerful but with access to a voice or a money source or a Senator, could change things. People moved here from the East or Midwest determined to do good, and in five years' time they were part of the power structure (and five years later some of them were part of the problem). Long before there was an Environmental Protection Agency or a Clean Water Act, a young bond lawyer shamed the city into paying for a massive cleanup of Lake Washington. Freeways which threatened parks or the quiet of settled neighborhoods were stopped in midair construction (they became known as the ramps to nowhere). A forested park was created on a lid covering Interstate 5, and an aging industrial plant was transformed into a public playground and kite-flying mound. Unlike Los Angeles, a city set in a Mediterranean paradise which long ago lost its resiliency, Seattle tried to practice some self-restraint.

But then things started to change. National magazines, beginning with *Harper's* in the mid-1970s, declared Seattle the most livable city in America. In the 1980s, Rand McNally rated the city the number-one vacation destination in the country, and *Savvy* magazine said it was the best place for women to live. *Sports Illustrated* pronounced Seattle a haven for the urban outdoorsman. The television news magazine 60 *Minutes* said Seattle was the best place in the country to have a heart attack because the emergency medical response was so good. Trade periodicals wrote that the average Seattle resident read more books, attended more movies and purchased more sunglasses (lost between solar appearances) than people in other cities. *Esquire* weighed in with a story on the Seattle lifestyle— "a major subculture of lawyers-turned-carpenters" and "some significant going home at four-thirty," and "on a famous ferry going into famous Seattle, dusk on a November night, the sky, the water, the mountains are all the same color: lead in a closet. Suicide weather. The only thing wrong with this picture is that you feel so happy."

All of this was acid in the face of Lesser Seattle. With each accolade came strangers who wanted a piece of Seattle and wanted it now, with some alteration. It was a curse, this Most Livable City tag, the revenge of Chief Sealth, coming at a time when the Northwest, like the rest of North America, was giving up its farms and becoming a continent of urbanites. Two-thirds of Oregonians now live within a hundred miles of Portland; seventy percent of Washington's population lives in the Puget Sound basin, and half of British Columbia's residents crowd the area around Vancouver. In Seattle, growth begat gridlock, drug wars and office buildings that broke through the ceiling of the cloud cover but greeted pedestrians like a basement wall. The Scandinavian business tradition which helped Nordstrom go from a single shoe store on Pike Street to the largest clothing retailer in the nation gave way to bigger money from the outside and bottom-line executives who couldn't give a damn about the water purity of Lake Washington or how some season-ticket holder felt about "his" Seahawks. To the old motivation of greed was added a new reason for the changing cityscape: ego. Martin Selig, a diminutive developer who owns a third of all the office space in the city, remade the skyline faster than a troop of volunteers had done just after the Great Fire of 1889. He reached the zoning code zenith with the seventy-six-story Columbia Center, the tallest building on the West Coast when completed in 1981. Paul Schell, who came to Seattle from Iowa, took a look at the Columbia Center and said, "If Martin Selig had been six-foot-five instead of five-foot-six, that building would be only half as big."

In the midst of Seattle's growing pains, Watson went to Switzerland to visit Mark Tobey during the painter's final years. Long after he left the country, Tobey continued to draw upon Seattle as the source of his inspiration: the sky could make four different faces in an hour; the wind jumped off the water and tumbled through the streets; anywhere you looked, from a hilltop neighborhood to a waterfront dock, at any time, the curtains might open and a mountain range would appear. If those peaks had been in hiding for a few weeks of winter, they looked new. Tobey was crushed by the march of the megalopolis toward the Cascades and the wave of generic skyscrapers downtown. Overnight, cities were shaking off their past and repackaging themselves in a single uniform. Seattle in the late twentieth century, once again ignoring the natural blueprint of its setting, was going the same way. "Landmarks with human dimensions are being torn down to be replaced by structures that appear never to have been touched by human hands," said Tobey.

Tobey's disgust became fighting words. The Downtown Seattle Association wanted to tear down the century-old Pike Place Market, heart and soul of the city and Tobey's favorite hangout, and replace it with a ritzy mall. They had their eyes on Doc Maynard's old plat, the century-old stone buildings of Pioneer Square, as bulldozer fodder. Both were saved by a vote of the citizens.

Land is finite and fragile; once it's capped by pavement or smothered with buildings, it will not answer to the laws of nature. The no-growth movement gained strength with people who said there was nothing wrong with big trees and steep hills and small buildings. They challenged the long-held assumption that the West was a blank slate that would only reach a semblance of civilization when it started to resemble the East, or Europe. Sure, more people brought more sophistication, but, for all the fine talk, it made for less room. The most audacious statement in the early days was made by Oregon Governor Tom McCall. "Come and visit us again and again," said McCall. "But for God's sake don't come here to live."

Watson's approach was along the same lines, with humor as the main weapon. The only National Basketball Association game ever to be called on account of rain (a leaky Seattle Coliseum roof) was touted as cause for a civic holiday. Presidential visits were rated by order of disaster: William Howard Taft was stung on the neck by a bee; Warren G. Harding caught a cold in the damp Puget Sound weather and died soon after his brief visit; Franklin Roosevelt was drenched when his open car was hit by a sudden squall; and candidate George Bush's motorcade at rush hour so backed up traffic that it helped to shift sentiment in favor of his Democratic opponent.

Still, all the Lesser Seattle talk only made those coveting a piece of the new city think the citizens were hiding some secret. And when they came and settled into their four-bedroom homes on a ridge bordering Mount Si near the site of the old Watson family pea farm, they joined Lesser Seattle. The city was caught in a paradox: As long as Seattle was seen as fresh and malleable, it would not be left alone. So, in the 1980s, the metropolitan area's population grew at twice the national average, and the central business core took on more office towers than downtown Los Angeles. Frustration mounted, pooled into those intersections wherever two or more waits to pass through a traffic light were frequent. In response, a group of citizens, most of them recent arrivals, put together an initiative to cut new skyscraper construction by two-thirds. And so the question of whether the premier city of the Pacific Northwest answers to the rhythms of the land or the demands of the marketplace has been reduced to a vote on how big and how fast new buildings can go up in the old haunt of Doc Maynard.

The obsessive need for growth is seen, in the Lesser Seattle view, as insecurity, a hangover from the resource-colony days. A city that has no confidence in its own ability to prosper is doomed to control by outsiders. While the vote nears, the debate is over who runs Seattle, what its true destiny may be. As when three owners of the same house try to decide how to remodel, there is no unifying vision. Some say Seattle should aspire to be the Paris of Puget Sound, accepting growth with grand European style and direction, a meeting of the ideal with the inevitable. This recalls New York–Alki, a city groping for greatness by trying to be like something else, instead of creating itself from the elements of its natural setting. Others want to seal the city entirely, drawing a line at the forested edge and putting up the Keep Out signs. The arguments rage for months, and then on a spring day when the Cascades hang in the grip of alpenglow till 9 P.M., a hundred years after the city burned to the ground, the verdict is in: by a nearly two-to-one margin, citizens of Seattle vote to curb future development drastically. What's important about Seattle, they say, is not glass and steel and money—those are the elements of Texas—but air and light and water.

At the Pike Place Market, where Emmett Watson lives and works and has decided to hang his birthday gift, a neon Lesser Seattle sign, I order a shot of espresso, buy a cigar from the woman at the Athenian Cafe who always calls me "Honey," and then walk out into the Marrakesh of the Northwest. The small-market concept has caught on in other cities of North America and in the suburbs as well. But Pike Place Market is little changed over the last century; Disney could never come up with this strip of commercial chaos on the bluff above Elliott Bay. The city that surrounds this market is all new. Yet Mark Tobey could sit here on his stool today and see truck farmers and crab-vendors and anarchists shouting to nobody; then as now, the market was the soul of the city.

Just below the market is the site of the old Longshoreman's Hall, where I used to go when I skipped college classes in search of a day's work. They'd call my number most times, and then I'd be sent to unload boxes from one of the big container ships tied up in Elliott Bay. The old guys would always talk about how their union could shut down the whole West Coast, and the young guys talked about getting laid and getting stoned. For one day's work, I'd make $75, about as much as I paid for my share of the monthly rent at our college house on Corliss Street. Then I'd walk up here to buy oysters and a piece of baklava and a bottle of good wine. After a plate of raw Quilcene oysters, I'd go home feeling as though I'd just had my blood changed, and not caring whether I ever made any money or finished school.

The Longshoreman's Hall is a condo now, peach-colored, I think. I meet Watson, and we talk about the recent vote and sports and a bunch of new writers he's discovered and how all the new construction has disemboweled the city. He shuffles and puffs on unfiltered cigarettes. We look out at the bay where I'd kayaked. Some of the towns on Puget Sound stink of sulfur and have poisoned their harbors by kowtowing to the mills. Seattle, having finally passed through its phase as a Resource Town, is healing, free at last of the forest-industry smokestacks. Perhaps, with the recent vote, it is also free of the need to pump itself up like an insecure body-builder. The last big sawmill within the sprawl of the city, a Weyerhaeuser plant near Snoqualmie Falls, has closed down. There is something in that news nugget for historians and prophet-checkers: built on the lumber trade, Seattle no longer has a sawmill, but has become a more active theater town than any other place outside of New York. Its two chief export products are now Boeing jet planes and Microsoft computer software.

Today is one of those days when Seattle can't hide: the sun makes everything appear fresh-painted and makes everybody walk as if fresh-charged. From the hillside market, we see the island where Vancouver parked his ship, the grave of Chief Sealth, the passageway of Winthrop. Cities are transient, reflecting the tastes of the time; but the spirit of a place is much harder to recast. Try as they did, humans have not been entirely able to shake Seattle from its inclination to be wild: blackberry brambles spring from cracks in the cement covering the sawed-off hills, and a few eagles still nest in the snags of Seward Park, a shank of old-growth trees ten minutes from the skyscrapers of downtown.

As we walk down the crowded market aisles, everyone says Hi to Watson. When livability replaced progress as the chief concern of many citizens here, he became one of the city's best-known celebrities. They give him slaps on the back and talk up the recent rain storms and the vote to cap the skyscrapers—that'll keep the bastards out, huh, Emmett? The Pope of Lesser Seattle puffs on his Pall Malls and moves on. He knows better than to encourage them.

Chapter 6

NATIVES

The dead are not powerless. Dead, I say?
There is no death. Only a change of worlds.

CHIEF SEALTH, January 22, 1855

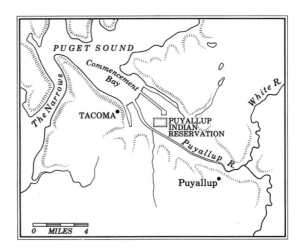

F
ull moon over Puget Sound, the last one of summer. Look at the sky, all full of doubt. The light is gone from the back side of Mount Rainier, leaving a coned cutout on the horizon. No wind tonight; the heat is stuck in the valley, where the smell of chemically cooked wood pulp lingers, the scent of a city that has long since taken over Indian Country. In place of wind, the hiss of human anger travels far. Somebody's drunk, screaming at the one he loves. A slammed door, an engine roar, screeching tires. Once again, the Puyallup Indian Nation is for sale, subject to approval by a tribal majority. In Seattle, the inhabitants voted on their future; here, they are voting on the past, perhaps the last resource they can call their own.

Frank Wright, Jr., a young leader of the Puyallups, rubs his bloodshot eyes. The stress of negotiating with the most powerful nation on earth and defending himself against charges of selling out his people has caused his marriage to break up. Wright wishes he could ask his father for advice, but the longtime tribal leader has cancer and can't speak from the intensive-care ward. In the hallways of the brick building which the Puyallups now call home, everybody stops young Frank Wright to ask about old Frank Wright.

"Dying," he answers.

"Any chance he'll pull through?"

"Nope."

The average Puyallup will not live to see his forty-fifth birthday. Among the young, one in five will commit suicide. Seven of every ten have no job. Nine of ten get by on less than six thousand dollars a year. They fight among themselves and watch too much TV and eat too much junk food and drink too much beer which their bodies can't tolerate. The elders try to keep the language alive, but the young ones want all-terrain vehicles from Japan and tickets to the Motley Crüe concert at the Tacoma Dome. Families crowd into skinny wood homes with exposed wires and no insulation in the walls. Too often, somebody goes to bed with a cigarette in hand, or leaves the door to the woodstove open, and then children wake up with their beds on fire. Their land is sick with pollution, and the river doesn't work any more. Devoid of spirit and strength, the Puyallup River brings no food to the tribe that used to feast along its banks. They have no weapons but the lawsuit. The Puyallup—loosely translated, the name means "People with More Than Enough."

And yet, as a tribe of indigenous Americans, they are still alive; that, to some members, is a miracle. Two decades ago, a court in Washington State pronounced them extinct, a nation no more. The vote today is a triumph of recognition, a climb back to the treaty table. In this century, there have been dozens of Indian land claims decided by judicial stroke of pen or Congressional vote. Usually, the land in question is barren or hidden, cold or depopulated. Never in recent times has a modern American metropolis been held up to such aboriginal scrutiny. As poor and powerless and alcoholic and tiny in numbers as the Puyallups may be— as a nation, they have about as many members as the average high school—tonight these 1,400 people, by virtue of their claim to the past, hold the destiny of a city in their hands.

At stake is the future of Tacoma, thirty miles south of Seattle, a gritty industrial port of 175,000 that sprouted on land which was given to the Puyallups for eternity. In this case, as with most of the 370 treaties signed between American aborigines and the government in Washington, D.C., eternity lasted only a few years. Passive people, never powerful, the Puyallups saw their landholdings shrink from more than two million acres to a thirty-five-acre cemetery. On the other side of the bargaining table is a representative of the United States of America, with 240 million members and a five-percent unemployment rate. The life expectancy of its citizens is seventy-two years.

The non-Indian property owners have houses and port facilities and skyscrapers and theaters and grocery stores and lumber mills and farms and malls—all told, property worth nearly a billion dollars—tied up on this land which the Indians won't let go of. They are not blackhats or thieves, these citizens of the U.S.A., just descendants. A legacy of land-grabbing has left them in this quandary. The non-Indians possess pieces of paper which say they own the property now, but the title companies won't clear the deed until they settle with the Puyallups, who have several pieces of paper, signed by several Presidents who've all been dead for more than a hundred years. In a suit filed in federal district court, the Puyallups assert ownership of the land on which sits some of the most valuable property in Tacoma. Rather than risk a losing verdict, the non-Indian property owners are negotiating out of court. Tonight, the final offer is on the table for a vote of the tribe. Two years ago, they rejected a smaller out-of-court offer. The whites say this is their final pitch. If the Puyallups give up all historical claims to the old riverbed, the port on Puget Sound, and the bluff on which sits downtown Tacoma, they will get cash payments of $20,000 per tribal member, a $22 million trust fund, nine hundred acres of land, job-training, and $10 million to try and bring salmon back to the ailing river—a package worth a total of $162 million.

One by one, the Puyallups drive under the freeway, up the hill, past the totem pole to the littered parking lot next to a sagging brick hospital building which is their tribal headquarters. Once, this was the site of a culture-busting government school, where young Puyallups got their ears boxed when they spoke the native language, and their feet were forced into tight shoes and they were told everything they knew was wrong. Then it became a state hospital for the young and disturbed. Finally, the Puyallups occupied it, saying the building was on their land. The state, after some resistance, gave in—a rare win for the tribe. Once, the Puyallups tried to take claim to the USS *Missouri*. They said the battleship on which Emperor Hirohito of Japan formally surrendered to the United States, long retired in Puget Sound, belonged to them under an obscure federal regulation which gave Indians first rights to surplus government property. To make their point, a young leader named Bob Satiacum paddled his dugout canoe out to the Mighty Mo and said he was going to tow the six hundred-foot-long ship back to the reservation. The newspapers ate it up. Bob Satiacum: now there was a leader with destiny written all over him. He could have been to the Puyallups what T. E. Lawrence was to Arabia. But he is not here tonight to stir the tribe, to dazzle the national press. He is in jail, in another country.

As the full moon rises, the Puyallups try to decide, on the eve of the last decade in the twentieth century, whether they want to give up land deeded to them by President James Buchanan in 1857. I never see a full family; men arrive with other men, women come with children, old people accompany old people. In the parking lot, the debate flows in shorthand. Nothing is more vicious than tribal politics, says Frank Wright, Jr. "Gary Hart getting caught with a bimbo? That's chickenshit compared to the rumors people throw around about us," he says. Back and forth the arguments go, in whispers and shouts: You can't sell land which is ours for eternity. It's just another Indian buyout. But we need this to stay alive. Yes, but if we vote to give up claims to the land, what assurance do we have that the United States Government will make good on their promise?

The Puyallup River, born among the blue glaciers of Mount Rainier, dies when it gets to Tacoma. In color and character, it resembles nothing in nature. Swimmers can no more frolic in the river's mouth at Commencement Bay than a goldfish can play in a bucket of battery acid. From the air, you can see how the Puyallup cuts a fine valley in its meander from Rainier to Puget Sound. At first, it winds and bends like any river, but then, approaching the city, it oddly straightens out and becomes an industrial sewer. Once the Puyallup was an unruly river, wild and free, its tidelands a maritime horn of plenty. They had a saying here, repeated up and down the coast of the Pacific Northwest: When the tide is out, the table is set. After World War II, the city of Tacoma handed the Puyallup River over to the Army Corps of Engineers, and they fixed it. They took the bends and gravel and spirit from the river, then gave it back to the city of Tacoma, dead but straight, a corpse from the Corps.

When Winthrop paddled down Puget Sound and into Commencement Bay in 1853, he saw a natural setting far more dramatic than the plot of ground on which Seattle was built. Few Yankees had ever seen anything like this: a 14,410-foot volcano, wedding-day white, rising from the valley floor of a river bordered by 250-foot fir trees. At certain times of the year, this river was so full of migrating salmon that they raised the water level. His introduction to Commencement Bay and the mouth of the Puyallup—at a time when the American East was trying on the first grubby boots of the Industrial Revolution but every inch of Puget Sound was still Indian Country—snapped Winthrop into a heightened state. He wrote:

> We had rounded a point, and opened Puyallop Bay, [sic] a breadth of sheltered calmness, when I, lifting sleepy eyelids for a dreamy stare about, was suddenly aware of a vast shadow in the water. What cloud, piled massive on the horizon, could cast an image so sharp in outline, so full of vigorous detail of surface? No cloud, but a cloud compeller. It was a giant mountain dome of snow, swelling and seeming to fill the aerial spheres as its image displaced the blue deeps of tranquil water.

He cursed the British name for the mountain. "Mount Regnier Christians have dubbed it, in stupid nomenclature perpetuating the name of somebody or nobody. More melodiously the siwashes call it Tacoma."

Rainier stuck. But Tacoma, the Salish name for the great volcano, was given to the town that would sprawl all over the bluffs and prairies and forests that rose from Puget Sound here, eventually including a neighborhood known as Winthrop Heights, named for the author of *The Canoe and the Saddle*. Boosters labeled Tacoma The City of Destiny; more than a hundred years after the birth of the nickname, there is still confusion and cynicism over what this destiny may be. Tacoma, unlike other Puget Sound ports, has yet to shed the mills in the center of town which foul the air and water for the quarter-million people living nearby.

There were no white settlers on Commencement Bay at the time of Winthrop's visit. But one year after he left, the Puyallups made their first pact with the Boston men. In 1854 they agreed, in the Treaty of Medicine Creek, to give up 2.2 million acres of land in return for thirty thousand dollars and a small reservation on the bluff. At the time, the Puyallups were a small, docile band of salmon-eaters, most of whom were somewhat overweight. For a society that did not farm or trade for food, this was almost unheard of—living off nothing but what swam up to their village or grew in the bushes nearby. They had no concept of property ownership—except for the inverse ownership of the potlatch, in which largess was given away to excess. Their language had no pronouns in the first person—no *I* or *we*. In the late summer, they caught enough fish in a few weeks' time to feed each family a thousand salmon a year.

They traveled up the lower slopes of Mount Rainier and filled their cedar baskets with huckleberries, blackberries, salal berries. For variety, they hunted elk, dug clams, caught crabs, boiled seaweed. The endowment from Puget Sound, where winter temperatures seldom drop below freezing, was unlimited. Without help of metal hammers, saws or nails, they built wood houses of cedar planks, some of them a hundred feet long and forty feet wide, with a stone hearth in the middle. Their universe was the river and its mouth at the sound. Each river valley was inhabited by a different nation whose members spoke a different Salish dialect.

In the elaborate potlatches, the chiefs of rival tribes tried to outdo each other in gift-giving. Trading goods, canoes, even slaves were offered as one tribe tried to show the other how well off they were. Though potlatches served as a sort of intertribal welfare system, they were repellent to the early Christian missionaries and government Indian agents, who outlawed them. Give away food? "An unsurmountable barrier to their material progress and civilization," said one American Indian agent of the potlatches. *Here*, the government men said, handing the maritime Puyallups hoes and plots of ground, *start farming*. Turning their backs to the sea brought instant starvation. And within a few years following the arrival of Europeans, there was no food to give away.

Of all the Indians in North America, possibly no tribes other than the Aztecs were more prosperous than the natives who lived near the Pacific Coast from northern California to southeast Alaska. In the Salish-speaking area, from midway up the Oregon coast to southern Vancouver Island, there were perhaps 100,000 people at the peak, living near the mouths of salmon rivers surrounded by thick forests—the densest population of aborigines on the continent. They were never big communities bound by geography or race, but rather a series of extended families whose members intermarried with other bands, or raided other tribes for their women. They had been living here—fat and happy—for more than ten thousand years. That much has been surmised from recent archaeological finds. The conventional scholarly wisdom is that the first people of North America crossed the ice corridor of the Siberian land bridge perhaps fifty thousand years ago and then spread out down the length of the continent, following herds of oversized creatures, chased one way or the other by ice sheets. A few clues have been left behind, bits of litter that tell a slice of a story, a hint of history. A 27,000-year-old stone tool was found in the Yukon. A rock spearpoint wedged inside the bone of a mastodon was unearthed on the Olympic Peninsula, dating back to 11,000 years ago; a Klamath Basin tool from southern Oregon dates to 13,000 years ago. Woolly mammoths, saber-toothed tigers, camels, American lions and other creatures of the late Pleistocene roamed this country just as the ice receded.

When North America was discovered for the third time—following the Siberian land-bridge travelers and the Norse seamen—the Northwest natives had already developed a fishing industry to rival that of New England today. They used seines, herring rakes, large nets and dozens of hooks attached to fishlines fashioned from kelp. In the streams a variety of weirs and traps were used to snare migrating salmon. Whales were hunted, speared by athletes in large canoes bobbing on the mean surf of the Pacific. They wore robes of water-repellent cedar bark trimmed in fur, conical cedar hats, and elkskin shoes. As woodsmen, they cut huge, even planks from trees, using nothing more than stone wedges. Some homes had gabled roofs. They had no agriculture, but they were among the few hunter-gatherer societies to develop a sophisticated culture of art, theater and mythology. They are best known for totem poles, but Coast Indian masks, figurines and dances are just as elaborate. When, after living thousands of years off the sea, they were forced in a single generation to become farmers, they gave up almost all cultural pursuits. The grim task of subsistence agriculture on rocky glacial till took up too much time to leave any for mask-making or totem-carving.

Captain James Cook did not expect to find any natives on the wind-lashed shores of the Northwest when he arrived in 1778. Although the temperature was mild, the rain was persistent, and the mountains that rose from the saltwater inlets appeared too inhospitable for human habitation. Of course, the land had long since been given away without regard for whether anybody might actually be living here. In 1493, one year after Columbus returned from the Caribbean, Pope Alexander VI divided between Spain and Portugal the New World outside of Europe. Spain acquired all of the Western Hemisphere except Brazil; Portugal got the rest, including most of Africa. The Pope ordered the two countries to convert as many of the natives as possible, by sword or fire, to Roman Catholicism. At first, there was some confusion about these people. What were they? Monkeys without tails, or wild children of God? The dilemma was solved by Pope Julius II, who issued an encyclical in 1512 declaring that the North American Indians were in fact descendants of Adam and Eve, and therefore had souls.

The missions of California were established before Cook set foot on

Vancouver Island. San Diego was the first, in 1769. In the next two decades, the Spaniards made it as far north as Neah Bay, on the Olympic Peninsula, but gave up that fort in less than three months. The rain proved stronger than the faith, and so Catholicism did not penetrate the forests of the Northwest for many years.

Following Cook's path came George Vancouver, whose assistant, Peter Puget, encountered the Nisquallies and Puyallups. The first recorded face-off between Puyallups and whites happened when Puget, after whom the inland sea is named, and some crewmen went ashore for water. The British found a band of naked men, their ears and noses perforated, guarding a salmon stream. Some of them had potbellies, much like the average American who now explores this territory in his living room on wheels, the ubiquitous Winnebago. Puget traded buttons for fresh clams, and he relayed his intent to stay away from the salmon waters. "Their appearance was absolutely terrific," Puget wrote. "Their paint only differed in the color and not the quantity used by our own fair countrywomen."

Spruce beer, given to Cook, Vancouver and other English explorers, kept the Europeans from dying of scurvy. In return, the King George men offered dairy products—cheese, in particular, which was considered odorous and vile—and alcohol, which the Indians could not tolerate. If the whites had left nothing but religion and other social diseases with the natives, the tribes might have held on to their land a bit longer. But the newcomers brought something stronger than any army: smallpox, against which the natives had no immunity. From the time of Cook's visit to the time of Winthrop's journey—little more than half a century—as much as ninety percent of the Northwest native population was wiped out. As young America grew and matured, a plague blew through the promised land of the Oregon Country, clearing away the original inhabitants as if they were scrub weed. No early white account of the Northwest is without a description of the bodies littered along the beaches, or in piles in the village center, or of babies sucking the dry breasts of their dying mothers.

In the year Winthrop found Columbia River natives "dying in crowds" and huddled in rancid huts at Port Townsend on the Olympic Peninsula, another Yankee traveler, Samuel Hancock, wrote that, "It was truly shocking to witness the ravages of the disease here at Neah Bay. . . . The beach, for a distance of eight miles, was literally strewn with the dead bodies of these people."

In the lower Columbia River region, where the Chinook tribe lived and

American society in the West began, 13,500 Indians were counted in 1811, six years after Lewis and Clark retreated. Thirty years later a census came up nearly empty of natives—this at a time when there were still less than a hundred whites living north of the Columbia. To some, especially the Protestant missionaries, the wave of death was the hand of God, wiping away one order to make room for the next. "The doom of extinction is over this wretched nation," wrote Methodist historian Gustavus Hine in 1850. "The hand of Providence is removing them to give place to a people more worthy of so beautiful and fertile a country."

The Jesuits were a bit more sympathetic, viewing the decline in typically logical, realistic terms. "The poor Indians of Oregon will finally disappear, victims of vice and malady, under the rapacious influences of modern civilization," wrote Father Pierre Jean de Smet, who was considered a friend of the natives. These "blackrobes," as they were called, conducted a bitter rivalry with Presbyterian missionaries over how to treat the tribes of the Northwest. The Catholics had been introduced through the Hudson's Bay Company, who built their fur-trading network without trying to take Indian land. Many of the Gentlemen traders married Indians and shared their cultural views while clinging to a hybrid Catholicism. The Protestant missionaries, on the other hand, were Americans fired by Manifest Destiny and fundamentalist irrationality. By divine design, they felt, it was their duty to convert the Indians and then clear their land for settlers. They demanded that the native people cover their bodies, then they told them to abandon hunting and fishing and take up farming. Once the Indians were domesticated, the missionaries thought, they would be easily Christianized.

As the short history of the Northwest was written, the missionaries were given a free ride, pegged into the blank holes that promoter-historians reserved for martyrs. In Washington one such missionary, Marcus Whitman, is celebrated as a kindly saint and hero. Thousands of people flock to his mission site near Walla Walla to read about the good doctor. Close by, just over the Idaho border at a state park near Lewiston, an Indian snitch and traitor, Chief Timothy of the Nez Perce, is held up as a model native because he became a Christian and farmer. The truth is a bit muddier.

For centuries, the Nez Perce and their ancestors had been living continuously in the desert high country where the Snake River roars out of Hells Canyon and joins the Columbia. Of all the natives whom Lewis and Clark came in contact with, they were most impressed by the Nez Perce. They were a huge tribe, six thousand members living in forty-one bands at the time of white contact, superb horse-riders, powerful in build, wealthy, with a structured society. In a place where extreme landforms meet—the second-deepest canyon in the Western Hemisphere, bordered by desert on one side and mountain meadows on the other—these people lived the best of both Northwest Indian worlds. They built homes with underground basements, sheltered by sod-covered roofs and driftwood, that were cool in the 105-degree days of August and warm in the subzero temperatures of January. In the summer, they crossed the Continental Divide and hunted bison. In the fall, they fished for the goliath salmon which swam six hundred miles up the Columbia to spawning grounds in the desert. Camas bulbs, dug from the ground in late spring, provided spice and other nutrients to season meals of fish and meat. They formed bread into flatcakes, twisted reeds into snowshoes, made huge fishing dipnets from pine poles and twine. But, as strong and established as the Nez Perce were, they had one other quality which perhaps led to their doom. "Their hearts," Lewis and Clark noted in their official journal, "were good."

Try as they might, at first the whites could not break the Nez Perce. In 1812, French-Canadian fur trappers set up a trading post near the village of Alpowai. But the Nez Perce considered fur-trading to be the work of weaklings; so, while tribes on the coast, from the Puyallups to the Nootkas, were knocking each other out to find pelts for the Europeans, the Nez Perce wanted no part of it. They were plenty wealthy, and didn't need to chase beaver for a few bullets and beads. Next came the Presbyterians, Henry Spaulding and Marcus Whitman. In the late 1830s, they managed to convert one local Indian, christened Chief Timothy, set him up with a wood-frame house and garden, and dressed him in the clothes of the white man. He was held up to the Nez Perce as a role model; they called him stooge and traitor.

Dr. Whitman established a mission near the present-day town of Walla Walla, just southwest of Alpowai, and tried to get all the Indian children to attend his stern sessions on death and the devil. He spent much of his time chasing them out of his garden; at one point, he spiked selected melons with ipecac to sicken the children. By the late 1840s, wagon trains were disgorging newcomers into the Oregon Country at a rate of six thousand people a year, and smallpox was killing a nearly equal number of Indians. Whitman, seeing the tribes as headed for extinction, tried to get the Nez Perce, the Cayuses and the Walla Wallas to give up fishing and hunting and move into grounds near his mission and become Christian gardeners. The Nez Perce, except for Timothy and a few others, stayed away and held to their freedom. But the Cayuses gave in. In 1847, several Cayuse children enrolled at Whitman's school came down with measles, which spread among the already ravaged tribe. The disease killed half the tribal population in one year.

Dr. Whitman proclaimed himself their savior, medical and spiritual. But as they came into the mission, they continued to die in droves. The tribes, by then, knew all about the power of white men to spread disease. Downstream, at Fort Astoria, one fur trader used to toy with a small black jar wherein resided the dread smallpox virus. Or so he said. He lorded this jar over the Chinooks whenever he wanted to control them. Feeling that the missionaries had plotted to spread the disease among them, the Cayuses at Walla Walla went on a rampage. On the night of November 29, 1847, two warriors went into the mission and split Dr. Whitman's head with a tomahawk, killing him on the spot. Then, joined by other Cayuses, they murdered Whitman's wife and ten other mission hands, and took about fifty men, women and children hostage. They were eventually released, unharmed. But for the next fifty years, the whites used the Whitman massacre as an excuse to pummel, hang, starve and cheat the Nez Perce, the Cayuses, the Walla Wallas and other tribes of the inland Columbia River region.

The year Winthrop directed his gaze up the Puyallup River valley at Mount Rainier, a child was born nearby, the son of a Hudson's Bay Company trader and his Puyallup bride. Jimmy Cross would live his first months as the child of a free nation of Puyallups, and every year after that, would fight to retain what he'd lost in infancy. Washington became a territory in 1853, when Jimmy Cross was born. The land was carved from the Oregon Territory at the Columbia and stretched east beyond the Idaho panhandle to the present western boundary of Montana. In 1850, a census count came up with less than five hundred whites living north of the Columbia, or about the same as the number of Puyallups around Commencement Bay. To encourage settlement of an area still controlled by Hudson's Bay Company traders and commerce-smart tribal leaders, the United States Congress in 1850 passed the Oregon Donation Land Act, a singular act of thievery given the full legal blessing of the young democracy. Under this act, any white American could claim 320 acres and his wife another 320, regardless of whether that property was part of Indian country or not. In just a few years, all the choice land in the Puget Sound basin and in the Willamette Valley was taken by homesteaders and the surrogates of real estate speculators. Coupled with the smallpox epidemic, this set the stage for an initial round of treaty-making that would cede the most heavily populated Indian country in America— more than 200,000 square miles—to the government in Washington, D.C.

Isaac Stevens, arrogant and blustery, Napoleonic in height and self-confidence, was the first territorial governor of Washington. Stevens, called "a tiny, bandy-legged tyrant" by his personal secretary, was an officer with the Army Corps of Engineers, age thirty-four, when he was sent west to govern the new territory. A reputed alcoholic, he had the temper of a Brazilian soccer fan. He was sent to the Northwest with a twofold mission: to extinguish all aboriginal title to the land, and to survey the mountains for a railroad pass.

On Christmas morning, 1854, seven hundred Indians from lower Puget Sound gathered in the rain and chill at the Nisqually Delta to sign a treaty with Stevens. "The Great Father feels for his children," Stevens told the shivering natives. "And now he wants me to make a bargain with you in which you will sell your lands, and in return be provided with all these things. . . ."

His speech was translated into Chinook Jargon, the trade language used up and down the Northwest Coast, a blend of French, English and Salish with a three-hundred-word vocabulary. Winthrop was fluent in this shorthand language, and his book was the first to print a glossary of Chinook Jargon. Many of the treaty nuances were lost on the tribes, but they understood one thing, and to them that was the most important: they would retain fishing rights. In the Medicine Creek Treaty signed that day on the delta, the Puyallups and nearby Nisquallies gave up 2,240,000 acres in return for $32,500 to be paid over a twenty-year period and three reservations of 1,280 acres each. Article 3 of that treaty stated: "The right of taking fish at all usual and accustomed grounds and stations is further secured to said Indians in common with all citizens of the territory."

In the next few months, Stevens made four other treaties, until all six thousand Indians in Puget Sound had given up their homeland. The next year, two-year-old Jimmy Cross was ordered off the land near the Puyallup River and sent to the new 1,280-acre reservation on a bluff above the river. In that first winter of the treaty, 1855, the Puyallups saw that the tiny plot of ground assigned them would never do. The Nisquallies, accustomed to roaming the banks of the swift river that drained Rainier's longest glacier and plying south Puget Sound in their dugouts, were equally angry. A few of their members, as instructed, took up farming;

but glacial till produced dust compared to the gold of elk, salmon and berry country. A Nisqually leader, Chief Leschi, who claimed a thumb-print had been forged next to his name on the Medicine Creek Treaty, called for war. Only a handful of the natives joined him, but there were enough of them to put a scare into Stevens, who had called the Coast Indians "a docile and harmless race." In 1856, Leschi's guerrilla band attacked the fledgling settlement of Seattle, but were driven back by cannon fire from the Army ship *Decatur*, anchored in Elliott Bay. Minor skirmishes followed for much of the next year, a shot here and there, a settler killed, a native ambushed, a farm set on fire.

Plans were underway to unite all the Indians north of the Columbia in one big war when Leschi was captured in late 1856, after he was betrayed by his nephew. Stevens charged him with murder. Leschi's white supporters argued that the Nisqually leader had done nothing more than engage in normal acts of war. The first all-white jury to hear his case was deadlocked, and a mistrial was declared. Leschi was tried again in the spring of 1857; this time he was found guilty and sentenced to death. After he was hanged from a tree not far from the land where he grew up, his executioner, Charles Grainger, said, "I felt I was hanging an innocent man."

Leschi's revolt, however minor in military terms, resulted in more land for the Puget Sound tribes. The Puyallups, including young Jimmy Cross, were given an expanded 23,000-acre reservation; most of them moved down from the bluff to their traditional land near the river and the bay, the very land that would be up for vote in the next century. Jimmy Cross learned to fish as his ancestors had, setting up weirs in the small streams which fed the Puyallup. In the spring, some early chinook would come home; later in the summer, they were followed by coho and fall chinook. Some years, the coho kept coming back right up until Christmas. When Jimmy Cross got older, he used to tell stories about why he was never hungry as a boy: all he had to do was reach down and pull up a salmon. For so many years, it was that simple.

Buoyed by his triumph in the initial round of treaty-making, Stevens sent a delegation east of the mountains to make pacts with the horse-riding, better-organized tribes of the upper Columbia River region. Five thousand Indians from the Nez Perce, Cayuse, Umatilla, Walla Walla and Yakima nations showed up for the Council of Walla Walla in 1855. Stevens wanted to clear the great river and its major tributaries of its traditional inhabitants to make way for miners, loggers and farmers. The Nez Perce, who had resisted the missionaries and were spared most of the recriminations that followed the Whitman massacre, held out for a large chunk of land, more than ten thousand square miles stretching from the salmon-rich desert streams that fed the Snake River to the elk country of the Wallowa Valley in northeast Oregon. Largely unsettled by whites, the Nez Perce land was conceded to the tribe. The other nations were to be sent to reservations on either side of the Columbia. Eventually, leaders representing the pro-treaty faction signed for all the tribes. In turn, each tribal leader was promised $500 a year over a twenty-year period. And that was it—in less than a year's time, Stevens had convinced seventeen thousand Northwest Indians to give up 64 million acres. The treaties cost the federal treasury $1.2 million, or less than 2 cents an acre. But the ink was hardly dry when the tribes realized they'd been taken. Although Stevens had promised a two-year cushion before the Indian nations would be moved to the new reservations, he opened up their ancestral lands to settlers twelve days after the Treaty of Walla Walla was signed.

Kamiakin, chief of the Yakimas, forged a loose alliance of several inland tribes and declared war on the United States. But his grand plan to unite the coastal tribes and the inland tribes in one big campaign never bore fruit. The war was vicious on both sides: a sympathetic Indian agent was killed when he ventured into a Yakima tribal camp seeking justice for them; a chief of the Walla Wallas, Peo-peo-mox-mox, was captured at a peace parley and then murdered while in custody. The white troops paraded his scalp and ears before settlers. Small battles were fought throughout the year, but by winter the war had temporarily died down. During the hiatus, the government built two forts, one near the Yakima River, the other at Walla Walla near the Whitman mission.

In 1858, with the Coeur d'Alenes and Spokanes now aligned with Kamiakin, the fighting picked up again. In one battle, 1,000 natives routed 164 federal troops from Fort Walla Walla. Emboldened by the victory, the tribes took on a larger cavalry force near the Spokane River, but were badly beaten. They were pursued to their villages, their families killed, homes burned, leaders hanged.

Governor Stevens was called to the Civil War; on September 9, 1862, a Confederate bullet shattered his brain.

The Nez Perce, content with their ten-thousand-square-mile reservation on the Snake River and in the Wallowa Valley, had avoided the bloodshed of the Yakima Wars. As long as the whites left them with the land they had been formally awarded by treaty, they were fine; if they could live through the still-fatal vestiges of the smallpox epidemic, the

Nez Perce expected to maintain themselves as one of the strongest Indian nations in the West. With the land they'd been allowed to keep, they might even prosper.

Soon, however, gold was discovered in the Wallowas, and precious-metal lust brought in a horde of well-armed trespassers. Pressured by miners, government officials called another treaty council and reduced the reservation by ninety percent, down to a thousand square miles, all of it in the high desert of western Idaho. One band of Nez Perce, led by Old Chief Joseph, refused to move, and returned across the Snake River to the longtime home in the green Wallowas. He lived there for ten years, until more trespassers claimed title to his land.

By the 1870s, there was a growing sympathy in the East for the remaining tribes of Indians in the West that had not been moved to the designated Indian Territory of Oklahoma. President Grant bent with the wind in 1873 and allowed the Joseph band of the Nez Perce to stay in their Wallowa Valley home. The tribe had received good press in Washington ever since they had fed the nearly starving Lewis and Clark expedition. But Grant's order infuriated the white homesteaders, who placed him under great pressure; he promptly bent the other way and reversed his order. In May of 1877, General Oliver Howard ordered the Wallowa band, now led by young Chief Joseph, out of the fertile valley and across the Snake to the desert reservation. He gave them thirty days to close out their homes and leave. Enraged, a group of Nez Perce teenagers attacked several white settlers. More troops were called in for a big push against Joseph's band, but the Nez Perce slipped away.

Leading 700 tribal members, 550 of whom were women, children and old men, Joseph crossed Hells Canyon and retreated up the eastern banks of the Snake, heading for high ground and reinforcements. Two battles were fought in Idaho, both stunning defeats for General Howard and his six hundred men, who were slow-moving—a big, blue-coated target—and unfamiliar with the territory. The Nez Perce, having sent their families farther east, broke up into small commando units and picked off Howard's troops at random. They were first-rate marksmen, as are most hunters of today who chase the big game in the severe terrain above the Snake. While Howard's bluecoats licked their wounds and called for help, the handful of Nez Perce warriors broke through the Bitterroot Range and headed toward Montana, hoping to gain an alliance with the powerful Crows. Traveling hundreds of miles on foot and horseback, they traversed harsh mountain country and entered Yellowstone, which had recently been set aside as the world's first national park. Tourists camped at Old Faithful in the late summer of 1877 were stunned to see a fast-moving band of Indians pass through the park in the middle of a war. On the way to Yellowstone the Nez Perce had eluded one ambush but, after regrouping with their families, got trapped in another; eighty-nine people were killed, all but twelve of them women.

In Montana, the Crow refused to help them, so the Nez Perce headed for Canada, planning to hook up with Sitting Bull, the great chief of the Sioux who had been granted political asylum north of the border. A long wilderness trek through some of the meanest country in the Rocky Mountain West lay ahead. Many of the horses were lame, and the Nez Perce families began to starve. By late September, winter was closing in on the tribe just as hundreds of newly arrived troops were fast approaching them. Snow fell, hungry children woke up chilled by hypothermia, infected bullet wounds turned gangrenous. Joseph tried to keep hope alive, pressing toward Canada. Finally, on the bitterly cold morning of September 30, 1877, fresh infantry troops spotted the Nez Perce camp at Bear Paw, within a few days' march of Canada. With howitzers and rapid-fire guns, the Americans pummeled the retreating refugees. On the second day of the siege, it rained; on the third day, it snowed. Howard and his regiment caught up with the new troops and prepared to finish off Chief Joseph and his bedraggled band, who had eluded capture for 1,700 miles and gained the attention of the world. Reluctantly, Joseph surveyed his frostbitten, starving, dying people, the remnants of one of the strongest and most prosperous nations to live in the Americas, and gave up.

In his speech, recorded on the scene, Joseph said:

> The little children are freezing to death. My people, some of them, have run away to the hills, and have no blankets, no food. No one knows where they are—perhaps freezing to death. I want to have time to look for my children and see how many I can find. Maybe I shall find them among the dead. Hear me, my chiefs, I am tired. My heart is sick and sad. From where the sun now stands, I will fight no more forever.

The last treaty ever made between the American government and an Indian nation was with the Nez Perce, in which their Wallowa land was given to the whites and they were scattered to the Indian Territory of Oklahoma and other places without salmon or elk. Years later, the federal government named a dam on the Columbia River after Chief Joseph; it was built without fish ladders, effectively killing off the last of the wild salmon runs that had been on the upper Columbia as long as the Nez Perce could remember.

With the Indian Wars over, government policy-makers tried to assimilate natives into the American melting pot by teaching them farming and property ownership. If the tribes had only been left with their reservations, they might have fared better as the twentieth century approached. Instead, things got even worse, especially for the Puyallups. President Lincoln had signed a bill in 1864 chartering the Northern Pacific Railroad for the purpose of laying track from Lake Superior to Puget Sound. Construction started in 1870, and approached the Cascades three years later. Every lumber town and three-shack burg around the Sound competed to be the railroad terminus. Tacoma, just beginning to take shape on the bluff near the Puyallup tribal village, got the railroad. But there was one big problem: the twenty-three-thousand-acre Puyallup reservation bordering Commencement Bay. This reservation had been granted to the Puyallups for eternity; by the terms of the treaty, it could never be sold. But that didn't stop President Grant from signing an executive order, later judged to be illegal, which allowed the railroad to run right through the reservation. The Puyallups, of course, were never compensated for this passage. And as speculators caught the railroad fever, Puyallup land, once considered wetland trash, took on the gloss of a rough diamond. Joined by other real estate promoters in search of a loophole, the Tacoma speculators lobbied Congress for passage of the Allotment Act of 1887. Under this act, each male Indian head of household was given a chunk of reservation land, between 40 and 160 acres, which he could then sell as an individual.

This proved to be almost as devastating as smallpox or the wars. Impoverished, sometimes plied with liquor, most Indians quickly sold their allotments. In Oregon, the Siletz tribe went from owning 1.1 million acres in 1856 to less than three thousand in the mid-1890s. Nationwide, Indian landholdings shrank from 140 million acres to 48 million in less than fifty years. By selling their reservation lands piecemeal, the tribes lost their strongest hope for prosperity: a unified control of resources. Today, two-thirds of all Indian-reservation property is not owned by the tribes, a legacy of the Allotment Act.

Jimmy Cross took his allotment, a piece of valley land that flooded in the spring and brought salmon in the fall, and held on to it. He grew corn and carrots and berries, but mainly stayed alive with fish, which he caught and smoked and sold and ate year-round. By the time his grandson, Silas Cross, took over the family allotment in the mid-twentieth century, most of the fish had stopped coming back up the Puyallup. The tidelands at Commencement Bay, which were never sold in allotments, had been filled in; railroad and port facilities rose on the new ground. The river, also promised for eternity, was straightened, and the Puyallups were told they had no treaty rights to the new river or the old, dried-up bed. What siltation and industrial sludge didn't do to the salmon run, the state did by allowing overfishing, all the while denying the Puyallups their seasonal access to fish, saying they would have to fish for salmon like everybody else. The Puyallups pointed to their treaty of 1854, approved by Congress and signed by the President, which guaranteed them the right "to taking fish at all usual and accustomed grounds." The non-Indian fishermen were taking eighty-five percent of the catch. When a handful of Puyallups—Silas Cross, Bob Satiacum and Frank Wright, Sr., among them—tried to fish the new river outside the formal state fishing season, they were arrested, labeled poachers. Thus began the Fish War. The Puyallups would sneak out at night under cover of darkness and try to get a few salmon; the state game wardens were there waiting with manacles and TV cameras. Rocks were thrown, boats were sabotaged, occasional shots were fired. Marlon Brando came to the river in 1964, and was arrested with Satiacum.

After losing the Fish War in the river, the tribe took to the courts. And while Frank Wright, Sr., and Silas Cross continued the fight in the legal trenches, Bob Satiacum went another way, setting up a network of smoke shops that sold tax-free cigarettes, booze and the kind of fireworks a kid couldn't get at the local Safeway booth. A convincing speaker, Satiacum soon became the most powerful Puyallup in modern times. Tracing his ancestry to a leader who signed the Medicine Creek Treaty with Governor Stevens, Satiacum declared himself chief, a title which was soon elevated, at a national Indian conference, to Chief of Chiefs. At his height, he owned four smoke shops, liquor stores, casinos, a pizza house, a wholesale tobacco company, a cabinet shop and a gift shop, and he sold his own Chief brand of liquor. In a few years' time, he went from being a welfare recipient and onetime semipro baseball player to the overweight lord of the Puyallups, with a business empire worth $80 million. He owned a Mercedes, a Cadillac and twelve fishing boats, and lived in a million-dollar house with an Olympic-size swimming pool. As the salmon runs continued to shrink—providing sustenance for a mere handful of Puy-allups—the Chief's empire became the main economic engine of the tribe, employing nearly a third of its members. He expanded east of the Cascades, opening smoke shops on the land where Chief Joseph was buried, and announced plans to unite all the American tribes in a tax-free business juggernaut. He bought up other allotments within the old reservation boundaries, saying his goal was to return all the treaty land to the tribe.

But instead of being hailed as a model capitalist, Satiacum was shunned by non-Indian business leaders and by many within his own tribe, who distrusted him, comparing the Chief to a mafia don. By the late 1970s, Satiacum's activities had drawn the attention of the federal government; ever since the Medicine Creek Treaty, the ears of government agents had never been far from the tracks into Indian Country. FBI agents turned an ex-con and Satiacum employee into an informer and wired him. He was sent into Satiacum's den with instructions that if he could nail the Chief, drug charges against him would be dropped. The feds believed Satiacum was behind several arson fires and attempted shootings of tribal business rivals. The two months their informer spent with Satiacum formed the basis of a sixty-seven-count racketeering indictment filed against him in 1980. Then the IRS hit him with $24.7 million in liens against all his property, and the Supreme Court ruled that states could collect taxes on cigarettes sold on reservation land.

Satiacum, the Chief of Chiefs from the lowly, nearly extinct Puyallups, was finished. A jury found him guilty on two counts of racketeering, one of arson, and forty-four of bootlegging cigarettes. By 1982, he was facing a sentence of 225 years in jail, and the movement for self-sufficiency among the Puyallups was dead. On a cold night in December 1982, while out on bail and awaiting sentencing, he said goodbye to his wife and seven children and fled north. He lived for a year on the lam in Canada, until he was arrested by the Royal Canadian Mounted Police in Saskatch-ewan. Dirt-poor, tired and sick, he was thrown in jail. He requested political asylum. After more than three years in British Columbia's cus-tody, he was granted political refugee status—the first American citizen ever given such designation in Canada. Unlike Joseph of the Nez Perce, the Chief finally found a home in the land of the Hudson's Bay Com-pany.

While the Chief was on the skids, the lawsuit pursued by his two former cohorts in the Fish War took a dramatic turn. After a three-year trial, Federal Judge George Boldt declared that all the Indians in Puget Sound who had signed the original 1854 treaties with Stevens were entitled to half the salmon caught in Washington waters. For the first time in their lives, Silas Cross and Bob Satiacum could take fish from the "usual and accustomed grounds" of their ancestors.

My friend Benjamin, who is five years old and loves the woods much as I did as a forty-five-pounder, is going through his Indian phase. In the week the Puyallups were trying to decide what to do with the offer for their land in Tacoma, I went for a walk with Benjamin. He wore his feathered headdress, buckskin pants and moccasins, and carried a bow and arrow. I told him that when I was ten years old I'd wanted to be an Indian and even made plans with a friend to float down the river in our canoe and never come back to the city. We'd just live off the land, hunting deer and fishing and sleeping outside every night and never going back to school. Man, what a life. Benjamin asked me if I'd ever seen a real Indian, and I said yes, lots of times. His face lit up as his mind filled with the images he'd been seeing in all his Indian books. Are they good horse-riders? Did you ever see them spear a whale? Is it true they can split a tree with just a bunch of stone wedges? Could you take me to see an Indian? I started to tell Benjamin that the Indians I knew worked in smoke shops and 7-11s and cinder-block government offices, but he wouldn't let me finish. He started crying, then kicked me in the leg.

"No! No! No! I want to see a real Indian!"

Driving home from Benjamin's house, I realized that my perception of the American natives was not all that different from a five-year-old's. Earlier this summer I had gone looking for the Chief Joseph band of the Nez Perce, but all I'd found was a broken little town in a reservation north of the Grand Coulee Dam. At nine in the morning, I stopped to ask two men for directions to the grave of Chief Joseph, which is the question outsiders almost always ask when they arrive in the arid pine forests of the Colville Reservation in central Washington State. One of the men was clearly drunk; his buddy was on the way. He told me I could drive down to the main junction, where they had a little plaque atop a rockpile in the lot of an abandoned gas station. The inscription said Chief Joseph was buried on this reservation and that he was a military genius who evaded capture for 1,700 miles. But, what about the actual gravesite, I asked. "You can't see that," said the second man. Why not? He looked at me coldly, then walked away. Driving through the reservation I saw the worst poverty in the Northwest; homes without electricity or front doors, rusted cars lying in dried streambeds, emaciated animals prowling through backyard garbage.

When I went to the Warm Springs Reservation in Oregon looking for the horse-riders and fishermen of the inland Columbia River, I found a suicide epidemic. Within a two-month period, seven young tribal members had killed themselves. "It's so hard to stay alive," said a Paiute boy of eighteen; two of his brothers had hanged themselves. For most of my life, American Indians have existed only as icons, naturalist heroes of the past; I'm like Benjamin.

The people who took over the Northwest did not treat the Indians any better or worse than other Americans had treated other tribes. Winthrop cast a cold eye on the "fishy siwashes," as he called them. He was disgusted by their inability to contain themselves after drinking alcohol. But in writing that civilization in the Northwest would be different from any other, more attuned to the land and its influences, Winthrop might as well have been talking about the Indians. They were different from others on this continent, and they still are. The Salish-speaking people along the misted coastline, so wealthy in pre-European times, have now used the lawsuit so effectively they have become role models for the rest of the 1.6 million American Indians. Their efforts have led to a renaissance among some tribes. If old trees are saved because the Nisquallies threaten lawsuits against loggers who damage the salmon watershed, we have them to thank. If Puget Sound is kept free of toxic dumping for the same reason, the tribes are a big part of the reason why.

The aboriginal people of the Pacific Northwest never saw anything like the riches that came to the fallen nations of Japan and Germany after World War II. After all the Indian wars and deceptive treaties, the legalized land-grabbing, the allotment schemes and the assaults of state courts, the tiny nations that lived at river mouths draining the Cascade Mountains were left with nothing but the lawsuit.

And so it was that the non-Indian property owners of Tacoma came to offer $162 million for the land that was supposed to belong to the Puyallups for eternity. If the tribe approves the package, it will be one of the largest Indian land claims in history—second, in this century, to the Alaskan native settlement in 1971. The full moon is well over Commencement Bay, flooding the water in silvery light. All the votes are in. Silas Cross, who runs a small smoke shop and has a satellite dish in his backyard and still farms part of the original allotment given his grandfather, says, "They're asking us to give up something you can never give up. It's just another Indian buyout." But Frank Wright, Jr., doesn't see it that way; after nearly 150 years of passive restraint, the Puyallups can now control their destiny, he says. His father, the tireless Fish War leader, cannot lend his voice; he's too sick to talk. And Bob Satiacum is back in jail, facing charges in Vancouver of having sex with a minor.

If the offer is approved, the Puyallups will get cash, their own deep-water port on Puget Sound—offering them the opportunity to become the first Native American tribe to control a Pacific port—nine hundred acres of tideland, some forest land, a permanent trust fund, and $10 million to rebuild the fishery in the Puyallup River. The river? Why would the Puyallups want anything to do with a limp channel bordered by industrial parasites and sewage-treatment plants? You can't breathe life back into a body that's gone cold. Frank Wright, Jr., looks out from the old brick building, beyond the freeway and the smokestacks, and sees a river that one day will bring salmon back to his people. He has no idea what the Puyallup River used to be like, but his father, his body now atrophied from cancer treatment, has told him stories. Plenty of stories.

The vote is 319 to 162 in favor of accepting the offer and dropping the historical claim to the land. A few days later, Frank Wright, Sr., dies of cancer at the age of fifty-nine. By modern standards for the Puyallups, he was an old man.

Chapter 7

FRIENDS
OF THE HIDE

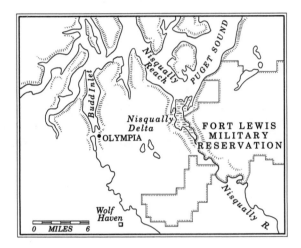

At the Nisqually Delta, where Puget Sound picks up the runoff from one of Mount Rainier's longest glaciers and then doglegs north, creatures of the air and water have hunkered down for their last stand. It's an odd place for a sanctuary, this intersection of man and aqua-beast, of freeway and marsh, of fresh water and salt. At the time of Winthrop's visit, the mouth of the Nisqually served as regional head-quarters for the otter- and beaver-hide trade; it was a swap mart for hard-edged men carrying furs to be worn by soft-edged urbanites in distant cities. The fashion designer stood atop the predator chain then.

I come to the Nisqually Delta, not by canoe as did Winthrop, but on an interstate that carries eight lanes of traffic through eighty miles of megalopolis. As the road drops to cross the delta, leaving behind acres of inflatable exurbs and Chuck E.

Cheese pizza palaces, the land turns shaggy and damp, a sudden reappearance of the original form. What used to be the fortress of man, surrounded by wild, has become the fortress of beast, surrounded by city. I find a handful of Nisqually Indians holding to a slice of land along the river, and soldiers playing golf on a bluff once guarded by the Hudson's Bay Company. The mosaic of salt water and river rush—one of the last true wetlands left on the West Coast—now is a federal wildlife refuge, the animal equivalant of the Indian reservation. Hunters pick off returning loons as they near the Nisqually, but once the birds make it through the firing line to land on the fingers of the river, they find a smorgasbord of food, and federal government protection. The refuge designation came just in time: the Weyerhaeuser Company, owner of 1.7 million acres of timberland in Washington, wanted to build a log-export facility in the Nisqually Delta to help speed the shipment of fresh-cut trees to Japan. When the company backed off during the timber recession of the mid-1980s, conservationists stepped in and saved the delta. However, it may turn out to be wildlife under glass; the county surrounding the delta is the fastest-growing community in the country outside of Florida, and Weyerhaeuser, which calls itself the tree-growing company, plans to build a new city of fourteen thousand people on its acreage bordering the refuge.

A sponge for winter rains, and feasting grounds for species that thrive in the blend of mud and grass, the wetlands in this wet land have always been looked upon as ill-defined and malformed. Not suitable for human habitation, they were judged to be worthless. One by one, the estuaries of the West Coast have been filled in, paved over, planked up. Puget Sound, with more than two thousand miles of inland shoreline, has only a few small places left where river and soil and tide converge to support the bounty of delta life. The Snohomish, outside Everett, has lost three-fourths of its marsh; the Duwamish marsh has disappeared altogether, its tideland filled in with 12 million cubic yards to accommodate Seattle's early-century expansion. Commencement Bay, where the Puyallup has lost all but a few acres of its wetland cushion, is a toxic nightmare, home of the three-eyed fish and a pulp mill which has been the source of one of the most lasting nicknames in the Northwest—the Aroma of Tacoma. For the last century, oxygen-starved marine life in Commencement Bay has been fed a diet of heavy metals, PCBs and algae.

The Nisqually, for the time being, looks as it did when Winthrop saw it: wide and wet, a stew of shorebirds and marine mammals, more than 240 animal species, with tall grass growing around scattered firs, thick cottonwoods along the river, and in early summer, waves of pink blossoms from the thorny blackberry bushes. I could set up camp here, as the Nisquallies have for centuries, as Winthrop did overnight, and never need to walk more than a few miles to find every food source necessary to lead a long life. But I don't need the delta for food.

Walking a trail planked over the mud and eelgrass on a warm summer morning, a day when much of the country is praying for water and trembling about the prospect of global warming, I pass through a window to the air-conditioned wild; with each step, traffic noise gradually recedes and the full-throated sounds of marsh creatures gain. Inside this thousand-acre garrison eagles nest atop box springs of heavy twigs, mallards feast, needle-legged blue herons and big-headed belted kingfishers dive for prey, and assorted others of webbed toe and water-resistant coat hide out for a few weeks. But where are the sea otters? Winthrop found stacks of their furs inside the palisade of Fort Nisqually here. Where are the packs of wolves that howled outside the gates and disrupted his sleep? Where are the whales he dodged while paddling down the length of Puget Sound? Where are the geoducks he called "large, queer clams," century-old bivalves with necks half as long as a jumprope?

To find a sea otter in the Northwest in the last years of the twentieth century, you go to the Seattle Aquarium, where a trained mammal does tricks for tourists. Otherwise, the animal that brought white men to this corner of the world has largely disappeared—officially extinct off the Washington, Oregon and British Columbian coasts for nearly half a century. A few transplants introduced under the protection of federal laws have since been placed in Northwestern waters, but their fate is uncertain. A recent spill from a barge carrying heavy bunker oil killed several of them; with their fur soiled, sea otters lose their coat of warmth and die a painful death from hypothermia. Otter Crest, on the Oregon coast, has no such creatures swimming near its beach. Nootka Sound, where Captain Cook first noted the easy-kill, big-money mammal, has no descendants from that era playing in its waters.

Sea otters have never caused great fear or awe. They backstroke through cold channels looking for new places to make water slides. They plunge to great depths, seeing how long they can hold their breath. They sing to their young, which gave rise to the myth of the mermaid; horny sailors, hearing the distant song of a sea otter mother to her pup, imagined a large-breasted amphibian calling them to shore. Few things are funnier to one otter than sneaking up on another otter and biting the mate's tiny ear. They never migrate, food is easy, the water's always fine.

To be a comedian in nature is to have a short life. While the pursuit of spice and the cultivation of tobacco may have led to early colonization of the eastern part of North America, it was this mammal, among the most docile in all of nature, that was responsible for bringing the hordes of Boston and King George men to the Pacific Northwest. Once otter pelts replaced the nonexistent Northwest Passage as the only justification for sailing eight months around Cape Horn and up the Pacific Coast, it took less than half a century to kill most of them. By the 1820s, up to 500,000 otters had been caught and stripped of their thick, luxuriant hide. Thus began a pattern: as long as this land brought wealth to those who stepped ashore, it was prized. Winthrop, and others who said the lasting value of the Northwest was not extractive, were lonely voices until the time came when there was very little left to take.

Peter Pans at heart, sea otters shy away from early attachment; when at last they do breed, the females seldom produce more than a single pup. A standard ploy during the early nineteenth century was to snatch the baby, thus luring the mother out, who was then clubbed. The orphan, more often than not, died without the mother's milk or drowned without the benefit of maternal swimming lessons, accelerating the decline of the species. But through it all the otters kept on their backs, balancing clams on their noses, playing pinch with Dungeness crabs. A large sea otter pelt, in perfect condition, could fetch as much as two thousand dollars in London during the early nineteenth century. Such money— one pelt could bring the equivalent of five years of wages and a stake in the bank—was earned from the simple task of slamming the skull of a smiling eighty-pound mammal. By the early 1820s the Hudson's Bay Company was calling for conservation measures. Their network of trading posts, so English and orderly, so profitable and legally monopolistic, was in danger of losing its chief source of income. But by then it was too late.

Asked to assess the value of all land north of the Columbia River before the United States and England settled their boundary dispute, an American government expert wrote that "The country north and west of the Columbia, extending north to the 49th degree of latitude and west to the sea, is extremely worthless." A marsh, thick with marine life, had no value. A mountain range with glaciers and streams and spires enough to fill an area twice the size of the Swiss Alps, was dispensable. A dozen rivers, each carrying enough salmon in a single run to feed every native and every Boston man in the new country at a single sitting, was a trifle.

The great problem with the area north of the Columbia was, as the American wrote, "There are hardly any furs." Having depleted the Northwest of the first resource to be exploited here, the Boston men were already pronouncing it worthless.

Young Teddy Winthrop and three Clallam Indians arrived at the Nisqually Delta on a hot day in late August of 1853. Seattle, fifty miles to the north, was a mudflat with a handful of timber beasts and a waterfront whorehouse. Olympia, one inlet west of the delta, housed a few rotting territorial-government structures. But the Hudson's Bay Company post at Nisqually, situated on land that had recently become American territory, exuded an air of permanence and authority. When Winthrop pulled up his canoe at the river's mouth and hiked inland to Fort Nisqually, the company was already turning to agriculture, growing strawberries, gooseberries, carrots, potatoes and other vegetables in such quantities that they kept the other forts supplied with food and sold the surplus to the Russians in Alaska. Winthrop, gazing up at the twilight-pink flank of Rainier behind the ten-foot-high walls of the fort, found the setting enchanting. He wanted to get closer to this "giant mountain dome of snow swelling and seeming to fill the aerial spheres." The Nisqually Glacier, one of the longest tongues of ice on the mountain and the river's headwaters, gleamed in late sunlight. A climate barometer, the glacier has shrunk by more than a mile since then.

The fort was full of the commerce of dead-animal dealings.

Winthrop wrote: "Rusty Indians, in all degrees of froziness [sic] of person and costume, were trading at the shop for the three b's of Indian desire—blankets, beads, and 'baccy—representatives of need, vanity and luxury." He noted a great quantity of "otter, beaver and skunk skins and similar treasures." Winthrop again enjoyed the civil company, imported wines and fine china of the Gentlemen running the company post. He obtained two horses for the trip across the mountains, another guide, this a Klickitat Indian from east of the Cascades, more hardtack and pork, some roots. The shopping spree cost him thirty dollars. Bedding down inside the fort at night, he heard the howl of timber wolves. Lucky man. The true call of the wild has not been heard in this part of the world for some time. The poison campaign which killed upwards of two million wolves in less than fifty years was already underway in the mid-nineteenth century. Even the Gentlemen of the Hudson's Bay post at the Nisqually Delta, who showed some conservationist leanings despite the nature of their business, took up one of the favorite weapons of the frontier—strychnine—against the wolves that attacked their livestock.

To find a wolf in the Northwest in the last years of the twentieth century, you must go above the Nisqually Delta to the bluff and travel south for about thirty miles until you reach a somewhat spooky warren of orange-eyed carnivores—Wolf Haven, it's called. The Gray Wolf Valley on the Olympic Peninsula has no such creatures. Bounty hunters killed off the last wolves in the state fifty years ago in that valley, which is one big reason why helicopters are chasing goats in the Olympics this summer, trying to thin a herd that no longer has a predator.

At Wolf Haven, everybody has a beard. People who stay together long enough are supposed to start looking alike; a similar trend is evident at Wolf Haven, where peacocks perch from the misted branches of spruce trees, and the evening air is filled with the jabbering of humans trying to communicate with three dozen wolves. Two volunteers proudly show me their bite marks. One of them says, "There is no better feeling in the world than French-kissing a wolf."

On summer nights when the sky is clear and the great black Out There is full of mystery, cars drive along the old Hudson's Bay Company fur-trading trail, turn off into the woods and pull up at Wolf Haven. Here, the people take pictures and then gather around a big bonfire and howl. A whole gaggle of captive wolves howls back. And then the Wolf Haven leaders try to get everybody to howl together. A "howl-in," they call it. It's all part of the job of trying to remake the image of one of the most maligned creatures in history.

I walk among the wolves with their benefactor, a chain-smoking thirty-six-year-old man named Stephen Kuntz. He has a beard, a bit of a beer gut, a baseball hat with a wolf emblem on the front. His van carries a personalized license plate—WOLF 1. He stops to chat with Windsong, a female buffalo wolf who spends a lot of time on the rubber-chicken circuit, appearing before Rotary Clubs, at county fairs, in an occasional spot on the *Today* show. Nearby is a timber wolf named Rogue, retrieved from the garbage dumps of Portland, now learning to howl for the first time. The star of this sixty-acre spread is a white arctic wolf named Lucan. This ghost-colored carnivore was once an habitué of a rich man's private zoo; upon his death, the owner left Lucan with Wolf Haven.

Steve Kuntz has spent the last thirteen years of his life living with wolves; on the whole, they make better companions than humans, he says. His chief assistant, an earnest, bearded biologist named Jack Laufer, goes even further: "For me it's easier to talk with these wolves than it is to talk with people," he says. "They're a lot more open and honest with their feelings."

They share their feelings with you?

"When they howl, it's vocalization, it conveys plenty. I can't think of anything important that I can say which they can't say." Laufer speaks a few lines in English to Lucan, who says nothing. "What's more," he says, "wolves are a lot more compassionate than most humans. The pack—the community—is the most important thing to them. The pack always works together. They are monogamous. They breed for life. And they're faithful. You won't see a sadder thing than a wolf who's lost a mate."

The two Wolf Haven leaders go through the numbers: wolves used to inhabit all of North America above the 30th Parallel, but now they've disappeared in every state but four; wolves were not only poisoned and gunned for bounty, they were set on fire; during the height of the cattlemen's poison campaign, a thousand wolves a day were killed; Oregon does not have a single wild wolf; Idaho has six, and Washington has zero. I correct them: Last summer, while exploring a meadow near the moraine of the Carbon Glacier on Mount Rainier's north side, I looked across the flower fields and saw a gray timber wolf, *Canis lupus*. His tongue out, tail down, the wolf strode across the meadow, moving at a fast clip. I snapped a picture, backpedaled, then headed for higher ground. Like everyone, I grew up with the myth of the man-eating wolf, the lecher with bad breath, a devil in disguise.

The image problem, I think, has to do with the wolf's appetite. There is no getting around their love of fresh, raw meat; after a kill, usually carried out by a pack closing in on a lame animal, a single wolf can eat up to a fourth of its body weight. They sometimes kill more than they can eat. The sight of eight wolves bringing down a deer—nipping at the thighs, then going for the jugular—is blood-spurting violence of the type seldom discussed at Audubon Society meetings. The Indians, for the most part, were not afraid of wolves and attributed spiritual qualities to them. Lewis and Clark ate wolves during the lean days of their cross-country expedition. It wasn't until the wagon trains came west with livestock in the 1840s and '50s—presenting an easy meal for the wolf packs—that *Canis lupus* became the homesteader's worst enemy. In some counties of the West, it was against the law *not* to put poison on the fence post.

Yet, as Kuntz and other neo-wolf lovers point out, there is not a single documented case of a healthy wolf ever attacking a human.

"Of course, I've been bit a couple times—feels like somebody smacked you on the hand with a hammer—but that was from playing around," says Kuntz.

Wolves still are hunted in British Columbia, often from helicopters by sportsmen who've paid up to $15,000 in a lottery. The provincial government says the aerial hunts are necessary because too many moose, caribou and mountain sheep are being killed by the wolf packs of British Columbia, whose numbers may be as high as five thousand. Some biologists accuse the government of hiding their true intentions; they say the game managers who approve the wolf kill want to build up the herds of trophy animals in British Columbia, where hunting is big business. During Expo '86, the wolf kills were stopped; 20 million people visited Vancouver with nary a peep heard about the helicopter hunting. In the years since, however, the kills have resumed.

Much of the change in attitude has come about because of people like Steve Kuntz, who calls his captive wolves "ambassadors for their lost brothers in the wild." A native of Trenton, New Jersey, he was the kind of kid who put a frog in his pocket and then kept it in his room until his mom forced him to get rid of it. He once had a snapping turtle for a pet, but preferred big dogs like German shepherds. On his own at age thirteen, he never finished high school, moved all over the Northeast, and then to the Southwest, where he lived for a while in a hippie commune. Working a construction job in Colorado, he saw an ad in the paper offering a stray wolf pup for sale. He took the pup home, named it Blackfoot, and became quite attached. It was a buffalo wolf, one of the descendants of the great packs that used to attack bison on the plains east of the Rocky Mountains. Kuntz treated Blackfoot like a dog, keeping it on a leash, taking it for walks. But something was wrong.

In Washington with his wife, Linda, and Blackfoot, Kuntz looked up a man, Ed Andrews, who kept several wolves on his property. Andrews was having a hard time holding on to the property and the wolves at the same time, so he turned his pack over to Kuntz. Reluctant at first, Kuntz and his wife soon took on the manners and attitude of orphanage owners—bring us your stray wolves, your zoo rejects, your urban misfits. The early years of Wolf Haven were lean, but then they started the howl-ins. In an age of theme parks, the idea of sitting around a bonfire under spruce trees with a bunch of wolves and howling at the moon has terrific appeal. Tourists come by the carloads, entering the grounds as curious, usually neutral visitors and leaving as true believers, heads full of the new gospel of the wolf. The wolves inside the mesh-wired compound are their own best pitchmen. They play tag. They kiss each other. They bite each other's ears.

Before coming to Wolf Haven, I read a book by Barry Lopez, *Of Wolves and Men*. Devoid of sentiment, Lopez makes a good case for the wolf, decrying the national tragedy of our annihilation of this animal in the wild, stripping away the myths. But he brings up something that comes to mind now as I walk among Lucan and Rogue and Windsong, the half-moon overhead dipping in and out of the stretch clouds. "I do not wish to encourage people to raise wolves," Lopez wrote. "Wolves don't belong living with people." I want to ask Kuntz about this. He's howling away with the arctic wolf, a beautiful creature with its thick, pure-white coat; the animal seems like a spirit at play, jumping and yelping with Kuntz. I decide to let them howl, uninterrupted; such is the best language at Wolf Haven.

Coastal Indian legend has it that the killer whale is a wolf that was stranded at sea. Like wolves, *Orcinus orca* are the top of the predator chain, are very smart, and travel in packs. Their sense of family would put a Mormon patriarch to shame; the offspring spend their entire life within their mother's pod, a traveling unit of up to twenty whales. One pod of killer whales in Puget Sound includes an eighty-three-year-old grandmother; slow-moving and revered, she is the keeper of family secrets and tips on how best to ambush a harbor seal. Orcas don't howl, but they communicate in dialects unique to each region. They use sonar to hunt and are capable of distinguishing one small species of fish from another at a distance of three hundred yards. After a few days' absence, returning whales greet their pod mates with a showy ceremony. There is no documented case of an orca killing a human. But until a few years ago, they were considered black-and-white villains.

To find an orca in the Northwest in the last few years of the twentieth century, you must get in a boat and go to the deep, clean waters around the San Juan Islands, a place of great hope for those who believe humans can get along with other creatures without clubbing or caging them. Whaletown on Vancouver Island has no such mammals off its coast; it's a shell of a shore town, condemned to die by previous avarice. Blubber Bay, similarly named by the nineteenth-century men from Nantucket and New Bedford, is devoid of the animal oil that used to light the world's lamps in the days before electricity. The blue whale, largest creature ever to inhabit the earth, has disappeared completely from Washington coastal waters and Puget Sound. For thousands of years, the Makah Indians chased various whales, looking for thirty-foot-high spouts in raging surf off the northwestern tip of Washington. They threw harpoons attached to sealskin floats at the flanks of the big creatures. Finally, exhausted after days of chase, the whales would be towed to the beach. The Makahs have not hunted any type of whale since 1913. The efficient whaling factory ships of the 1920s eliminated the blue whale from Northwestern waters. And you won't find a killer whale at the aquarium in Seattle, which was one of the first places in the country to put this twenty-five-foot mammal on display, inside a small cement tank. Prodded by a change in public attitude, the state of Washington has since outlawed the capture and containment of orcas, the only animal with a brain physiology comparable to that of humans.

The current in Haro Strait is so swift during the twice-a-day tidal shift that it produces whitecaps which look like Colorado River rapids. Three pods of killer whales live year-round in Puget Sound, and once every few days most of them pass by Haro Strait, shared by the United States and Canada. From a whale's point of view, it's a great fish-funneling spot; in late summer, sockeye salmon come in from the ocean up the Strait of Juan de Fuca and pass this point on their way to spawning grounds in the Fraser River. The whales find the schools and open their mouths, straining out lesser edibles.

Whale-watching requires the patience of a gardener in winter. I'm in a small boat, trying to hold the binoculars with one hand and the guard rail with the other as I scan the water around the northern San Juan Islands. The day is bright, as they almost always are during the warm months in this archipelago. People who come to the San Juans, no matter their background or degree of sensitivity to the earth, invariably fall in love with the natural world; in turn, the natural world repays such affection. Man is but one resident, in places a fairly insignificant one, in the habitat of the San Juans. The islands are fir-covered mountains with all but the summits buried by sea. Just offshore, the water is a thousand feet deep in parts; year-round, it stays at a temperature of forty-six degrees Fahrenheit. As species continue to die out in most other places of the world, the San Juans belong to creatures on the comeback—killer whales, harbor seals, bald eagles. Eighty-four islands in the San Juan chain are wildlife refuges; of those, humans are allowed to visit only three.

We stop for a while to watch harbor seals. About six feet long, they sprawl atop rocks close to water, soaking in sun. As we approach, their personality quirks reveal themselves. Their heads are like those of fashion models—sleek and clean, with slicked-back hair. They have front-end flippers, and no external ears. For years, the harbor seal was considered an enemy; the state of Washington paid a five-dollar bounty for any seal snout brought into a game office. Hunters would motor to within a few yards of their targets, then shoot the seals from the boat. Between 1946 and 1960, about seventeen thousand harbor seals were killed this way. Now, they are protected by federal law. However, they do have a predator.

We move on, out toward Canadian water, passing Spieden Island—a grassy, open isle with large madrona trees latched onto bits of hardened soil in the rock outcrops. In the 1970s, a group of investors purchased the island and imported to it a variety of exotic animals. They intended to have a sort of safari theme park here, a place where hunters with no sense of sport and deep pockets could sit on stools and shoot transplanted exotic animals who had little room to roam and no room to hide. When residents of other San Juan Islands found out about this, they orchestrated a publicity campaign that, at its peak, brought the crew from 60 *Minutes* to tiny, uninhabited Spieden Island. Under pressure, the investors shelved the idea of a safari hunters' island and sold the property.

In Haro Strait, not far from Lime Kiln Point, somebody spots a pod of orcas; few things set the human heart to racing as hard as the sight of black dorsal fins on the horizon. When they break the surface, jumping ten feet or more, the killers show the grace of ballerinas. Hearing them breathe, you find it hard not to feel a sense of mammal kinship. Through their blowholes they spout a blast as grand as a geyser gush—the sight and sound of large lungs exhaling warm air. Cleanly black-and-white, the orca would be ruined by colorization.

One larger whale, apparently the bull, leaps high and crashes down, displacing enough water to flood a subdivision. They move fast. I want to get closer, but we can't; it is against the law to come within a hundred yards of killer whales or to harass them in any way. From Lime Kiln Point, the nation's only whale-watching park, the orcas can often be seen thirty to forty yards offshore. In the chill waters of Haro Strait, chasing fish, playing with each other, they seem like regal creatures. Later in the day, I hear a story from one of the naturalists at the Whale Museum in Friday Harbor on San Juan Island. A few harbor seals were sunbathing on rocks near a steep edge on one of the small islands when they were approached by a pod of orcas. One whale snatched a two-hundred-pound harbor seal, then the rest of the pack moved in, tearing the seal apart.

The killer whale has had many friends in this part of the world for at least two decades. Most schoolchildren can describe the orca's intelligence, its strong family ties, its sense of humor, its dorsal-fin size. Every killer whale in the waters of Washington and British Columbia has been identified and named; their pictures are published in a book, not unlike a high school yearbook. When Winthrop toured Puget Sound by canoe—passing the spot on San Juan Island where orcas play 'most every day—the killer whale was the most feared creature of the deep. Efficient carnivores, a pack of thirty orcas may attack a gray whale, for example, and tear the larger creature apart, shredding the tail flukes, then stripping away the blubbery flanks. Another type of orca attack includes the coup de grâce: forcing open the other whale's mouth and ripping out its tongue. In such a case, the victim dies from shock and blood loss. The orca also eats dolphins, sea lions and occasional shorebirds.

As recently as the early 1960s the United States government issued bulletins stating that the orca would attack and kill any human in the water. A *National Geographic* book published about the same time repeated the myth. This perception helps explain the worldwide publicity a man named Ted Griffin received when he purchased a killer whale in 1965 for $5,000 from a group of Vancouver Island fishermen. While press helicopters buzzed overhead and newspaper reporters sent daily dispatches from the sea, Griffin took eighteen headline-filled days to tow his caged orca five hundred miles south to Seattle. He named the whale Namu, put it inside a small tank, and charged admission from the curious who came to see him swim with a creature that was supposed to rip him apart. Soon, Griffin was a celebrity, invited by Pentagon brass to formulate a plan to put the orca to military use. In 1968, the Defense Department purchased two killer whales from Griffin, believing they could be trained as a sort of watchdog on the high seas. Meanwhile, United Artists had paid Griffin $25,000 for the rights to film *Namu, The Killer Whale.* When the picture was shot off San Juan Island in 1966, a fake whale manufactured in Hollywood was used in place of Namu, who had died in his cement pen in Seattle. The cause of death was listed as drowning brought on by sickness from polluted water.

Griffin proceeded to catch a total of thirty orcas, selling most of them to places like Sea World in Southern California and Florida. By the early 1970s, the killer whale had become the world's leading aquarium attraction. Nearly forty orcas, more than a third of the Puget Sound population, were captured by aquarium hunters in a ten-year period up to 1976. So, even after the landmark whale treaties of 1966 protected blue and hump-back whales from further predation by man, the orca hunts accelerated. Killer whales were netted, sedated, taken from their families and put into tiny tanks for amusement purposes. In the open sea, moving at a top speed of thirty knots, they cruise up to a hundred miles a day. In the cement tanks, their range is usually just several lengths longer than their body size.

Few Puget Sound orcas, conditioned to a stress-free life of roaming in forty-six-degree water with their families and friends of the pod, have lived very long in captivity. At Sea World, they have been taught to breach on command for their food and generally treated like circus dwarfs in the last century. One transplanted orca in Los Angeles was trained to wear sunglasses for a car dealer's ad. Like the sea otter and the wolf, the orca is known to have a well-developed sense of humor in the wild, playing tag with friends, doing cartwheels and back flips. But at aquariums such as Sea World, their humor appears stiff and forced—Pavlovian routines of hoop-jumping and fin-standing in order to get their dinner. Some have rebelled and turned surly or refused to eat; a few captives have died of anorexia, baffling trainers who can't understand why such an intelligent mammal would starve itself to death. Most of the captured orcas have died well before their natural life expectancy of seventy to eighty years.

In the early 1970s, a onetime Vancouver Aquarium whale expert named Dr. Paul Spong led a worldwide campaign to keep the orcas free. While Spong fit the generational stereotype—during summer months, he lived in a treehouse off Blackfish Sound and played his flute to the whales as a way of communicating with them—his early research was gaining a foothold of credibility in the scientific community. Initially, Dr. Spong was laughed at when he talked about similarities between whale and human brains and claimed that orcas had a sophisticated way of com-municating with one another. By comparing the evolution of human brain size with that of orcas, Spong concluded that the cerebral cortex—that part of the brain which houses language, abstract thought and logic—is strikingly similar in the two mammals; no other warm-blooded creatures have brains of such sizes compared to their body weight. In 1976, while Spong was speaking at an orca symposium at Evergreen State College in Olympia—a school whose official mascot is the geoduck, the "large queer clam" which so fascinated Winthrop—eight killer whales were captured nearby in Budd Inlet, just a few miles from the Nisqually Delta. The seizure, by hunters from Sea World of Japan, made front-page news for days on the West Coast. A few of the whales were released from their holding nets by midnight saboteurs. The others were ordered released by Governor Dan Evans.

Soon after the Budd Inlet capture, the state banned all types of commercial whale-hunting in Puget Sound. This upset columnist George Will, who wrote a piece in *Newsweek* criticizing Washington Secretary of State Ralph Munro. A fourth-generation Northwesterner, Munro wondered why children of Washington State should have to travel to San Diego and pay ten dollars to see a creature whose home waters used to be in their backyard. Munro said people in the Northwest "are tired of these Southern California amusement parks taking our wildlife down there to die." His statements set George Will off. "If Sea World is denied a permit for ten orcas," Will wrote, "I hope 230 million Americans go to Puget Sound, unfold lawn chairs on Munro's lawn, ask for iced tea and watercress sandwiches and watch the whales. It will be good for their souls and it will serve him right."

The orcas were never captured. Ted Griffin retired from the business of riding killer whales around by the dorsal fin in small cement pools. He was forced out, he admitted, by a tidal shift in public opinion—the wolf of the sea had become a teddy bear. But just as the orca was given its freedom, a group of bottlenosed dolphins were drafted into indentured service at the Trident nuclear submarine base at Bangor, on Hood Canal. These swift-moving mammals, part of the same family as killer whales, are being taken from their home waters in the Gulf of Mexico and trained to guard nuclear submarines in Puget Sound. Having marshaled some of the best scientific brains to build an underwater nuclear arsenal that can destroy the planet, man now attempts to put the smartest creature of the sea at work as a co-conspirator.

At high tide, the horizon at Bowerman Basin is covered with the pastel undersides of a million sandpipers. They come here from South America, heading north; or they fly down from the arctic, heading back to Colombia. In small part, the basin reminds me of the Ngorongoro Crater in Tanzania, the great watering hole of nature where pink flamingos blot the sky and sleepy lions and moody water buffaloes roam the crater floor. In the ten-thousand-mile length of the Pacific flyway, there is no better truckstop than here, a mudflat just outside the broken Pacific logging town of Hoquiam on Grays Harbor. The town lost almost a third of its population during the last timber recession; now log prices and demand are high, but Grays Harbor County still has an unemployment rate three times the national average. The winds blow steadily in from the Pacific; logs and jobs sail steadily out to Asian countries that no longer have forests.

For migrating birds, the old wetland haunts of the West Coast are mostly gone. Hungry and desperate, they finally land in the mudflats of Bowerman Basin. Unlike the Nisqually Delta to the north, the basin has tidal goo uniquely suited for sandpipers. Frantically digging into the mud with their pencil-thin beaks, the birds gorge themselves on marine life, carb-loading for the two-thousand-mile flight ahead, the final leg north. Their stomachs on autofeed, they slurp and peck, and chomp and slurp on a patch of tidal mud. Then, something happens, something changes, and they hit the sky—a sheet as big as a stadium flag.

I arrive at Bowerman Basin on a day when many in New England have yet to see their summer songbirds. For some reason, they didn't show up. Shutters in New England opened to spring mornings, bulbs came forth in the usual color, but there were no songbirds in the land of Winthrop. They must be late, delayed by a seasonal quirk. But then spring dragged on, and still no sound of the early morning worm-chasers. For most people, it's a mystery. Others blame the loss of wetlands and estuary stopovers. We are losing plant and animal species in North America at a rate a hundred times greater than before the arrival of Europeans. Most of us don't notice until the morning begins with no other sound but the dreary radio news of traffic tie-ups, or the backyard is overrun with a certain type of insect, or the sun burns hotter than ever.

In the Bowerman Basin area, civic leaders think they should continue filling in the marsh; already, a third of the basin has been covered up by the Army Corps of Engineers, acting on some vague plan by local business leaders. They have no specific economic outline; just a gut sense that mudflats can't mean much of anything to a broken community. The mayor of Hoquiam, a timber town so depressed its leading citizens are paying $100 a night to hear motivational speakers from Seattle tell them how to feel good about themselves, says he eats shorebirds for lunch, a line that gets a big laugh at Rotary. His remark is a response to a proposal to save the last bit of mud in the Bowerman Basin. With four thousand acres of Grays Harbor marshland already filled in, conservationists want to save the remaining thousand or so acres for the sandpipers. The basin hosts the largest concentration of these birds in the West. Hoquiam civic leaders are against the idea of a wildlife refuge; they think filling in the mudflats is a better idea: solid ground in Bowerman Basin will make it even easier to export the logs which are yanked out of the fast-disappearing rain forest to the north. But nobody knows for sure; the word in the Hoquiam business community, freshly rejuvenated by the Seattle motivators who tell them they can do anything as long they feel good about themselves, is that mud and birds don't add up to a whole lot.

When I ask for directions to the basin, the Chamber of Commerce folks shrug. Apparently, I'm not alone. Dozens of people have dropped by the visitors' center this morning—up from Portland, down from Seattle—inquiring about these goddamn sandpipers and the stinking mud. A woman gives me a brochure which tells all about the world's first tree farm up north, and I tell her I don't want to see a bunch of uniformsized, corporate Douglas firs, thank you. I want to see the sandpipers. Well, then go out past the mill and the loading dock facility until you get to the airstrip, you can park there. But you're on your own.

At Bowerman Basin, about twenty people with cameras are positioned at different spots, sitting in the grass onshore or wading through the mud. I feel like a visitor to Capistrano before the hordes descended on the little mission town to watch the returning swallows. The birds don't seem to mind the human presence; beaks down, they slurp and chomp. I find a weather-beaten log and settle in. I start to read something I brought along; ten minutes later, when I look up, my log is surrounded by a swarm of birds. I watch them for perhaps twenty minutes, and then they swarm away to another location in the mud. Hitting the sky, thousands in one mass fly in unison at a high speed. As natural thrills go, this one gets the adrenalin pumping. In the distance, logs are stacked to the low end of the cloud cover, putrid smoke belches from a mill, and the people in the broken town wonder what to do to save their community, and I wonder: in all the West Coast, is there no room left for a bird that only wants a thousand acres of mud?

In New York a month later, I meet a man who lives on the forty-second floor of a building in the Lincoln Center area, two blocks from Central Park. He strikes me as a sort of graying genius, in his mid-sixties with a wrinkle-free face and thick glasses, the kind of man who can talk for an hour without taking a breath because his head has been buried in a computer screen for so long. He works at his terminal in sweat pants, massaging questions through his IBM. When he talks about his home, he says he's an environmentalist, angry at skyscrapers which block the sun from Central Park, incensed at New York's garbage being dumped at sea. As we talk, he proudly points to the view across the Hudson River to New Jersey. It's the kind of view I used to think I wanted, in the heart of the world's greatest ambition refuge, the streets pulsing with the kind of activity one needs to lead a full life.

I ask the New York environmentalist about estuaries: are there any fish or migrating birds across the way where the Hudson River empties into the Atlantic? I tell him about the Bowerman Basin; the very week I'm in New York, Congress votes to set aside part of the mudflats in Grays Harbor for the sandpipers. He takes off his glasses and gives me a quiz-zical look, blinking. What do you mean? I ask if the Hudson and Atlantic convergence fosters any marine life. He shakes his head and says you wouldn't want to eat anything that came out of the water below, then points to the bank that rises up from the water, New Jersey, and the narrow band of mud at the foot of the cliff.

"The estuary, you mean? Is that where it is?"

"I guess," he says. "I'm not sure what you call it—I'm not familiar with the terms—but isn't it pretty?" I tell him not to apologize; some words leave the language when they no longer have any use.

Chapter 8

UNDER THE VOLCANO

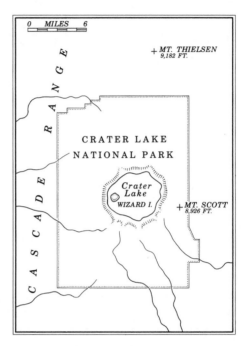

The hot breath from the belly of Mount Rainier is stale and sulfurous, the distinct odor of a restless land. Fourteen thousand feet above the lowlands of Puget Sound, one hour into a new dawn, the August sun has yet to soften the ice over which we walk. The summit is near, so says the nose, picking up the scent of the volcano's crater vents. Now the glacial surface turns to sun cups, knee-deep bowls melted during the heat of the day and then frozen in position as soon as the mountain goes back in shadow. They look like petrified waves. We are cold, three of us tied into one rope, and silent— a unit of chill inching upward through the sun cups. No more of the crude jokes and high-fives which helped jump-start us out of camp at midnight. My brother Danny has lips of blue and fingers that won't wrap around his ice axe. My friend Grim, son of a Norwegian who escaped the Nazis on cross-country skis, is stoic as usual, but his eyes have taken on a glaze that doesn't fit his usual summit face. We want only to stand atop the broken crater rim of Tacoma, as Winthrop called it, he being the first to commit to print the native name for the highest point in the Northwest. To get here, we drove to the parking lot at Paradise Inn, crossed the deep-wrinkled Nisqually Glacier, put in camp under a thirty-story icewall at the 9,800-foot level, and then woke this morning for the final push through Fuhrer's Finger, a narrow stretch of deceptive glacier and a funnel for fast-charging boulders, named for two Swiss brothers who should have known better than to come up this way. When the temperature reaches a certain point, the ice that bonds broken rock to the mountain loses its grip, sending a constant shelling of stone down this steep couloir.

None of us likes the route; it is too hazardous for fun, too long for weekend challenge. The exhilaration of last night, when we stared down at the pink-tinged sea of clouds from a seat carved in the glacier, wrapped in an evening as still as cathedral air, is gone; we are left scraping the barrel of our motivation for putting one strained leg ahead of the other. Grim and I are as different as the national characters of the two countries from which our ancestors came. But we share a love of the high country, a friendship developed over years of testing avalanche gullies and passing a flask in the alpenglow. In the Northwest, where one can flee the social divisions of sea level in a few hours' time, friendships that flourish above timberline are not unusual.

We have the standard tools, feet of spiked crampons and a rope that tethers us to each other's pace. They bring some sense of security. In town, my pile of climbing equipment looks formidable. At this elevation, it seems laughable. What's to keep a fortress of ice which has clung to this mountain for several millennia from suddenly crumbling, as it did in the summer of 1981 when a party of eleven was killed while crossing the Ingraham Glacier, the most common route up the mountain? Gravity tugged, the bond broke, and in ten seconds they were all gone, swept away by van-sized chunks into the Pleistocene depths of the glacier. It was the worst disaster in American mountaineering history, an act of God, the investigators concluded. Coming up through the bowling alley of Fuhrer's Finger this morning, I'm reasonably certain no such divine mood swing is in store for us. Of course, the very thought of danger is part of the attraction.

The only storms that truly matter in this part of the world are those that shower up and out of the volcanoes. As the cities grow, and comforts increase, we place more distance between us and the molten rock that smolders under blue ice. We understand what's going on (or at least we think we do), and we've got terms that help to explain it all. But subterranean pressure—plate digging under plate and forcing hot crushed rock upward—hasn't gone away just because we no longer attribute such violence to a temperamental deity.

On the summit Danny finds a steam vent and plops on top of it. The land lives. Just below the summit, the glaciers are hundreds of feet deep, a choppy sea of frozen séracs and snow-covered cracks. But on top there are patches of bare land on a ridge kept warm by the mountain's inner turbulence. A small lake hides under the middle of the crater ice cap, long mythologized as the haunt of summit demons. Here, where the air has a third less oxygen than at sea level, we are too tired to explore further. Grim and I fall on our backs, the ultraviolet stare hot on our faces, stars still visible in the bruise of an early sky. At this height the mechanics of the shift-change from night to day are more transparent, the atmosphere cluttered with backstage maneuverings. I fall asleep. When I awake, my brother's pants are wet, soaked from the steam vent, but he is much warmer. We laugh, silly with exhaustion. The volcano is friendly now, a source of wonder and curious extremes—all this ice on the outside, all this fire inside, and no place higher for a thousand miles in any direction.

Without snow on top or verdant trimming of fir below, without its ice-cream-cone shape in the sky, Rainier would still inspire. We are drawn to the quirks of the planet, those deformities of landscape which mock convention. Even more, we are drawn to power. In one day of discontent, this mountain could bury the city of Tacoma, level Seattle, smother the most productive fruit orchards in the world and fill much of Puget Sound to such a height it would become a lifeless prairie. The impulse to reassure says that geologic time moves too slowly for such disasters to affect us; that wasteland of St. Helens to the south of me this morning says otherwise. It is hard to hold a grudge against any of the sixteen major volcanoes of the Pacific Northwest, a string of elevated portholes to the inner earth stretching from Mount Garibaldi in British Columbia to Lassen Peak in northern California. No matter how much hill-leveling, tideland-filling or river-rechanneling takes place, the volcanoes will remain lord of the landscape.

The old forests which cloak these cones and the wild streams which scramble from their glacial tops are mere façade, the mask of the outer earth; we look at them and see beauty, the perfect picture of the Northwest. Beers are sold and vacations are made from this scenery. What we don't see is the hellfire below, yet we want some intimacy with it, sensing in the ticking of the earth's heart something greater than the pulse of our own lives. Volcanoes brought life to much of the planet and hold the potential to cause massive death. To live within close range of such power prompts humility and fear even while it inspires. The naturalist John Muir, touring these volcanoes a hundred years ago, said Mount Hood was "a glorious manifestation of divine power." Rainier, he said, "was so fine and so beautiful it might well fire the dullest observer to desperate enthusiasm."

There has been much firing to desperate enthusiasm in the last century. An Army pilot, flying through the cloud halos which blow off Rainier's summit like smoke rings from a cigar, swore he ran into a swarm of flying saucers in 1948. His account, widely publicized but never completely put to rest in the tidy bed of government conclusion, produced the first use of the term Unidentified Flying Object—UFO. Since that time, friends of the extraterrestrial have gathered annually on a summer evening in a meadow at the base of Rainier and linked hands, calling forth the saucers from Out There. Inevitably, they are satisfied. Farther down the mountain, near the damp taverns where out-of-work loggers shoot pool and curse the spotted owl, the New Age movement has set up base. First, Ramtha, the thirty-thousand-year-old spirit who resides inside a young woman with a gift for mass marketing, moved into a million-dollar home in the Nisqually valley. Then Shirley MacLaine bought a house nearby. They both believe the volcano attracts an unusual amount of psychic energy.

I feel today as Winthrop did when he walked the Cascade Crest east of here in August of 1853. Though he would live only another seven years, to his thirty-third birthday—my age on the day I stand atop this peak—the alpenglow of the volcano brought him a hint of eternal life. In that, he was surely ahead of his nature-savaging countrymen when he wrote:

> And, studying the light and the majesty of Tacoma, there passed from it and entered into my being, to dwell there evermore by the side of many such, a thought and an image of solemn beauty, which I could thenceforth evoke whenever in the world I must have peace or die. For such emotion years of pilgrimage were

worthily spent. If mortal can gain the thoughts of immortality, is not his earthly destiny achieved?

Another generation would pass from the time of Winthrop's visit to the first successful climb of Rainier. In 1853, he considered the summit unclimbable, a view shared by many. "No foot of man had ever trampled those pure snows. It was a virginal mountain, distant from the possibility of human approach and human inquisitiveness as a marble goddess is from human loves." But his prophecy on that day came in the form of a command: "Up to Tacoma, or into some such solitude of nature, imaginative men must go, as Moses went to Sinai, that the divine afflatus may stir within them."

Today, we are but three of six thousand climbers who attempt to walk this crater rim every year, of which about half succeed. I look to the west and see the Puget Sound basin, wherein reside those millions who stare back at us in first light. Beyond are the Olympic Mountains, and farther, the Pacific, shrouded by the blue wall. To the north, Mount Baker and Glacier Peak tower above the spine of the Cascades, two white cones among the jagged edges. To the south, I see Hood and Helens and Adams and Jefferson and even a wisp of Mount Shasta, which last blew ash from its northern California base in 1786. All the majors in the Ring of Fire are visible this morning. I move closer to the north edge of Rainier, where the mountain was cleaved and sliced, losing perhaps a thousand feet of the top some 5,800 years ago. The north wall drops down a straight vertical mile. Weakened by hot volcanic fumes, the upper part of this side of the mountain was shaken loose and then slid away, eventually carrying a half-cubic-mile of mud 45 miles down the valley toward the tidelands where Seattle originated, covering 125 square miles. If a similar event happened today, a half-million people would flee for higher ground. To the natives who lived near the shoreline, the mud storm of long ago fortified the mountain's position as forbidden high ground, a place for angry gods.

Any doubts that the land is alive and in command of all that lives atop its surface are removed by the view to the south. Still smoking and stuffed with debris, Mount St. Helens, the youngest of all Cascade volcanoes, looks like an ashtray after an all-night party. Denuded, it nonetheless pulses with new life as the dome inside the crater rebuilds. Surveying this lineup when Helens still had its Mount Fuji top, Winthrop wrote:

> The dearest charmer of all is St. Helens, queen of the Cascades, queen of Northern America, a fair and graceful volcanic cone. Exquisite mantling snows sweep along her shoulder toward the bristling pines. Sometimes she showers her realms with a boon of light ashes, to notify them that her peace is repose, not stupor, and sometimes she lifts a beacon of tremulous flame by night from her summit.

His view, typically romanticized, erred only in the gender assignment: Helens was not named for a woman, but rather for the British diplomat Lord Alleyne Fitzherbert, Baron St. Helens. Fitzherbert himself never saw the mountain. Baron St. Helens spent most of his years in the Court of Madrid. During his lifetime, and that of Winthrop, Helens erupted on a regular basis, providing an ash-and-fire show powerful enough to keep most settlers out of the valleys immediately below. Different tribes had different names for the peak, but they conveyed the same point. One native name was *Louwala-Clough*, meaning "smoking mountain." Another was *Tah-one-lat-clah*, "fire mountain."

Among the other volcanoes in the Ring of Fire, Mount Baker had minor eruptions in 1843, '54, '58, '59, '70 and then blew an unusual amount of steam and some ash in 1975, causing many a sleepless night in the cities of Vancouver and Bellingham. Glacier Peak, at 10,541 feet just slightly smaller than Baker, exploded with a great burst twelve thousand years ago, sending ash and debris as far as Saskatchewan. Hot springs at the base of Glacier Peak are a token of the heat that courses beneath all that ice. Mount Adams in Washington, and Jefferson, the Three Sisters, Thielsen and McLoughlin in Oregon have been relatively quiet in the eyeblink of geologic time since the arrival of whites. Mount Hood steams intermittently, giving off a sulfur stench to compete with any open sore in the Cascades. But only Mount St. Helens and Lassen Peak, which erupted off and on between 1914 and 1917, have thrown fire to the sky in front of a modern audience. Mount Mazama in Oregon, which lost enough of its top 6,800 years ago to cover much of the West and eventually become a caldera filled with the deepest lake in America, left a volcanic legacy that doesn't need interpretation to demonstrate its power.

Were it not for volcanoes, it's doubtful there would be water and atmosphere. They helped to produce a habitable planet. In the early years of the earth's life, volcanic vents released massive amounts of steam from the interior. Condensed, the steam formed oceans. Over millions of years, ocean algae took carbon dioxide from the primitive atmosphere, and, through the labor of photosynthesis, released oxygen into the air, creating a breathable blend of gases. On a much smaller scale, this primal act of creation continues today. Like all Cascade volcanoes, St. Helens is a product of the collision of ocean plates and continent, which forces magma and steam up through the summit openings. Seventy-five million years ago, the Cascade Range was still underwater; fossils of that period have been found in rock now high enough to hold a glacier. So many shells cover one place north of Mount Baker, for example, that it's called Chowder Ridge. As the rest of the land settled down, the volcanic hot points continued to blow, venting magma from below and building new formations above. The fifty thousand square miles of the Columbia Plateau—the vast near-desert in central Washington and Oregon—was created by more than ten million years of intensive volcanic activity. The present peaks of the Cascades are anywhere from a million to twenty-five thousand years old. In that time, they were carved and given their craggy alpine look—the U-shaped valleys and numerous lakes and tarns—by Ice Age glaciers which draped most of the northern edge of present-day America in blue. Puget Sound was buried in an ice sheet four thousand feet thick. The basin's unveiling is relatively recent; the ice left a mere twelve thousand years ago. St. Helens is about forty thousand years old, an infant compared to Rainier's million-year age. The cone blown off in the 1980 blast was built up by eruptions since the time of Christ.

The land here is a long way from completed. While Winthrop felt a sense of immortality in the presence of these mountains, the volcanoes also remind us of the planet's irascibility. Temperate and lush, fertile and flush with bounty from the sea and the alluvial valleys, the land here could all become uninhabitable overnight. I realized this on May 18, 1980—a day that has been seared into the collective psyche here. Suddenly, we realized that the sky could turn dark at noon, and cars could not start because of ash-clogging, and rivers could be buried and forests leveled and lakes displaced, all by something over which we had no control. On May 18, 1980, I felt transitory, a passenger on a short ride in time.

At 8:32 on a clear Sunday morning an earthquake registering 5.1 on the Richter scale shook residents of southwest Washington out of bed. The north side of Mount St. Helens, which had been bulging outward at a rate of six feet a day, exploded with a force said to equal several hundred times the power of the atomic bomb that destroyed Hiroshima. Such comparisons are meaningless, on the whole. Reid Blackburn, a photographer with a shaggy beard and quick wit, was shooting pictures for *National Geographic* nine miles north of the crater. He took a few snaps, then ran to his car. He was found a few days later, buried and petrified in ash up to his neck. The heat from the blast, more than 680 degrees Fahrenheit, had killed him instantly. Farther down the mountain, David Crockett, Jr., tried to find his way through darkness and choking ash. Speaking into a recorder, the television photographer said, "Oh, dear God . . . my God! This is hell, hell on earth. Right at this moment I honest to God believe I am dead." Crockett lived. But fifty-nine people were killed that Sunday morning. The valleys around the mountain are sparsely inhabited; an annual rainfall of about a hundred inches keeps most people away. Logging crews, which during the week were working well within the blast zone, had the day off.

Within a few minutes, the mountain went through three transformations. First, more than half a cubic mile of rock, snow and ice—the entire surface of the mountain's north face—avalanched at speeds of two hundred miles an hour. Spirit Lake, surrounded by an ancient forest and lodges to house the summer hordes, was raised by two hundred feet; in other spots, the debris piled eight hundred feet. The Toutle River, which flows from this lake that the Cowlitz Indians believed to be a home for the dead, was blocked by a mile-wide dam of debris. Blue went to gray, green went to black, all life was smothered.

A lateral blast followed the avalanche. This explosion carried pulverized pieces of rock, organic material and hot gases at speeds of up to four hundred miles an hour. Imagine a hurricane, blowing at twice the speed of the highest winds ever recorded, with a temperature just under 700 degrees Fahrenheit, and you have some idea of the blast that carried the north side of St. Helens with it. All trees, including firs which had clung to the ground for three centuries, all shrubs, meadows and grass, all deer (more than 5,000), elk (1,500), mountain goats (15), black bears (200), birds and small game (several million), snakes, fish, bees and anything that might later have contributed to new life were wiped out within 150 square miles.

A third phase carried ash to a height of ninety thousand feet, the dark upper ceiling of the stratosphere. The ash darkened the orchard country of eastern Washington, clouded parts of Montana nine hundred miles east, and eventually circled the globe. All told, 540 million tons of ash rained down on more than twenty-two thousand square miles. An estimated 4.7 billion board feet of timber was blown down—an amount equal to the entire annual harvest on all nineteen national forests in the Northwest. Such are the numbers from one small act in the ongoing formation of the earth.

A few days after the eruption, a helicopter full of reporters started up the Toutle valley on a survey of the carnage. As they flew over the deforested lower slopes, gasps were heard and jaws opened.

"I can't believe it," said one reporter. "Everything is gone."

"Like the surface of the moon," said another, pointing to gray-covered stumps and creekbeds shaved to bristle. "There's nothing left standing."

Their frenzy was interrupted by a reporter from the Seattle *Post-Intelligencer*, the only local writer on board.

"This area wasn't destroyed by the volcano," he said. "We're not over the blast zone yet."

"Oh?"

"That's a Weyerhaeuser clearcut below."

Nearly a decade later, I stare down at the lava dome inside the crater of St. Helens. The dome has grown to a height of nine hundred feet, oozing up from the floor, gradually refilling a two-thousand-foot-deep crater. Blue-tinted plumes rise from cracks and fissures; the texture looks like fresh-cooked oatmeal steaming in a bowl. Sometime within the next two hundred years, the volcano will have regained much of its form; these mountains grow fast, especially the young ones. The previous top took just under four hundred years to build. Standing so close to this oozing mass of hot land, I feel as if I am present at the maternity ward of nature: raw earth at birth. A festive mood predominates on top, unlike anything I've ever seen on a mountain summit. Two dozen or more people, an assortment of characters, some in costume and drinking wine, have made the long hike up the south side of the snow slope to the new 8,365-foot summit ridge above the crater. We crossed a young forest, walked over light pumice slopes and kick-stepped up the final three thousand feet to reach this sharp-edged apex. Some of the other volcanoes are out in full glory this morning: Rainier just to the north, Adams on the east side, Hood and Jefferson to the south.

Spirit Lake now has a touch of color, but it looks as if it belongs in Nevada—devoid of green, surrounded by lifeless banks of brown and stuffed full of rotting timber. To the south, where the volcano did little damage, is a patchwork of large clearcuts on Forest Service land, as devastated in parts as the mountain valleys cleared by the lateral blast of 1980. Despite all the apparent wounds, the mountain has a relaxed atmosphere to it, much in the way of Spirit Lake before the eruption. Every day, several hundred people wait in the dark of 2 A.M. in hopes of receiving the handful of permits issued to climb St. Helens. They are warned about getting too close to the crater rim, warned about the explosive potential, warned about staying out of the crater, warned about disturbing the National Volcanic Monument. Helens seems too healthy again for such talk. Like many newcomers to the Northwest, the mountain has remade itself—the volcano as metaphor.

Though the inside may seem like a newborn, the rest of the mountain is growing like a toddler. Three months after the eruption, asters, fireweed, lupine and avalanche lilies sprouted. A few elk were spotted nibbling on alder saplings. Weyerhaeuser foresters brag about trees they planted in the summer following the blast which are now twenty feet high. The ash, which is sterile and has the chemical composition of glass, doesn't help the trees; they were planted in the topsoil that's buried beneath the volcanic cover. Inside the blast zone, John Fraenzl, a Forest Service ranger, is showing off the new trees he's planted. This tree-growing-in-a-wasteland business can get competitive. On the other side of the mountain, Weyerhaeuser is raising a tree farm, not a forest—a "plantation," as it's called in industry parlance—which will be cut in thirty to fifty years. Their trees, greenhouse-bred for maximum growth, are to the rest of nature what silicone-filled breasts are to a beauty contest. They stand out, but there is something . . . odd . . . about them. No snags. No variety. No slow succession through the different life stages of a forest. No sense of what came before.

"Time is nothing to nature," says Fraenzl, standing at the head of the slowly recovering Clearwater valley, east of the crater. "We want to see trees out here right now. We're in a hurry. Nature could care less. A natural forest will come back here, but not for a long time."

Two days before the May 18 eruption, Fraenzl worked in a section of woods so thick and overgrown it looked like the Olympic Rain Forest. On Monday when he returned to work, he flew over the gray, desolate land that he used to know as well as his own backyard, and he could not find a single landmark. That summer, his boss asked him if he wanted to be transferred, perhaps to some national forest with trees in it. The work ahead would be tough; never before had anyone tried to reforest an area that had been so thoroughly bereft of life. In places, the ash was three feet deep. Fraenzl decided to stay. He did a literature search, looking for hints on how to proceed, a model from anywhere else in the world—

nothing. For a forester, working on a surface that resembled the moon, the job was like that of a war zone medic.

Two years after the eruption, he started planting trees in earnest: a patch of lodgepole pine here, a quilt of Douglas fir there, a few noble and silver firs higher up, even some cottonwoods. On weekends, he would return with his seven-year-old boy, to plant more trees as volunteers. Standing among the skinny saplings with his son, he thought about the future—fifty years down the road—when the boy would come to look at the forest he helped to plant with his father. It took three hundred years to grow the old forest, John Fraenzl told his son, and just a few minutes to wipe it out.

By the mid-1980s, Fraenzl noticed that the firs were growing up to three feet a year. Soon, he would need to start thinning them. To his astonishment, a few trout started showing up in Clearwater Creek. Now, even in the worst part of the blast zone, no more than five miles from the crater, some trees are ten feet tall. The scraggly hardwoods, particularly alders and willows, grow without help in the draws where moisture gathers. Fireweed and lupine, the vanguard of a forest that will take hundreds of years to return to climax phase, seem to need nothing more than air and water to proliferate. We walk over a flat stretch where the pumice is so deep nothing will ever grow, and pass a small lake which survived because it was covered by a protective floor of ice. We go up the hill, and then drop down a little bit.

"I want to show you something," says Fraenzl, leading me to his secret.

"There—look at that." A few acres of lodgepole pine, green and thick, among noble fir, Douglas fir and hemlocks. Not a plantation, but a slice of forest. Like most scientists, foresters are not given to emotion or descriptions tinged with romance when discussing their subjects. Under this volcano, lost in his thatch of green, Fraenzl now hoots like Tom Sawyer on a rope swing over the river.

When young Winthrop headed up the Willamette Valley, the deepest lake in America had yet to be discovered by white men. The Klamath and Modoc Indians knew about it, but for a long time the secret never leaked outside tribal circles. The great mysteries of the world, natural and spiritual, were kept in the caldera of cobalt blue buried inside the Oregon Cascades; it was a place so sacred the natives were forbidden to speak of it to others. Only a few Indians were allowed to even gaze upon it. By the 1820s, the Hudson's Bay Company had a fur-trading post on the Umpqua River to the west. They conducted a vigorous business with the Indians, married their women, raised families, and crisscrossed the mountains within sight of the Big Secret. Still, no native told them about the blue waters inside the old volcano. The natives grew up with legends, born in eyewitness accounts, about the fiery fight between gods that led to the decapitation of a twelve-thousand-foot mountain. To have told others of the living conclusion of those legends would have been to risk further disruptions of the land. Throughout the 1840s, wagon trains pushed over the Continental Divide on the Oregon Trail and emptied twenty thousand people into the new country of the Willamette. Before long, they spilled into the south, to the Rogue and Umpqua river valleys and into the Siskiyous. At the same time, goldminers from the spent lodes of the Sierra pushed north, finding precious metals in the Rogue, which drains the west slope of Mazama. Still, the natives kept the secret of Crater Lake.

Then, on June 12, 1853, just a few days after Winthrop left the Umpqua valley and returned north, three prospectors looking for a lost goldmine came up to the seven-thousand-foot rim of the hollowed volcano and fell to their knees. A thousand feet below the rim was the bluest lake any white man had ever seen, filling a crater six miles across, with a cinder cone growing inside it, and off to one side, a basaltic rock that looked like a ship. The entire mountain had been sheared off at its midsection. No water flowed into the lake, and nothing poured out. With all the imagination expectable of someone who spent his life scraping at the rocky edge of the planet looking for gold specks, John Wesley Hillman named his discovery Deep Blue Lake. And then he led his prospectors back down the slopes of Mazama and continued looking for that lost goldmine, which he never found. There is no record of any whites returning to the lake for ten years. Then, found again, it was called Crater Lake.

The lake has a proselytizing effect on most people who stare down the pumice and ash slopes to its surface. By 1902, less than fifty years after the prospectors' accidental discovery, Crater Lake became the nation's seventh national park—a Teddy Roosevelt legacy—a few years after another volcano, Rainier, was added to the park system. Justifiably suspicious, Roosevelt felt that the forests and rock around Rainier and Crater would be scraped bare if they weren't locked up. He was right.

I come to the rim of Crater Lake, arriving at the spot where the prospectors fell to their knees, on a day when a small, one-man submarine with two mechanical front arms is being lowered by helicopter down to the lake. I walk over to a park rangerette in a Smokey Bear uniform and ask about the sub. She tells a story about the struggle for the inner power of Crater Lake, a fight over geothermal vents. The land is alive here in a caldera that lost five thousand feet of its summit in an eruption forty times greater than that of Mount St. Helens. A power company from south of the border—those hated Californians, the scourge of Oregon—has leased seventy-six thousand acres in national forest property just east and south of the park. They are drilling a series of holes four miles from Crater Lake to find the best place to construct a hydrothermal power plant. Once built, the plant is supposed to pipe steam out of the ground and use it to power turbines for producing electricity. The power, of course, would not go to Oregonians—who still have such abundant supplies of hydropower they sell it to California—but would be sent to users in the San Francisco area.

The company was encouraged to drill near Crater Lake by James Watt, the early 1980s Secretary of the Interior and trustee of all the national parks. Watt once told a Senate committee that man was ordered by God to take over the earth and conquer all living things, a view that used to be shared by many of the new residents of the American West.

The scientists guiding the submarine are trying to find hydrothermal vents on the floor of America's deepest lake, in Oregon's only national park, hoping to use the evidence to stop the power plant. Perhaps, they theorize, these vents influence the color and water level of the lake. In some places where geothermal vents were tapped into for power purposes, hot springs and geysers have been reduced to warm carbonated spit. The rangerette explains it this way: "Ever try taking a shower when all the other water faucets in your house are turned on? You can't get much water, because you don't have any pressure. We're afraid if you start tapping into these vents just outside the park, you'll reduce the pressure underneath the lake."

The rangerette also wonders what it would look like to have an industrial plant on the border of a national park that has consistently been judged to have the cleanest air in the country. People drive up here to the seven-thousand-foot rim of the broken volcano, far removed from any population center, just to breathe. Random comments from the Crater Lake Lodge guest book: From a Texan—"Fantastic! I've died and gone to heaven." From a New Yorker—"What do you do to the air up here?" From a German—"Eighth wonder of the world."

In the evening, I walk along the rim away from the crowds. Like most of America's national parks, Crater Lake is designed to funnel thousands of drivers into one main visitors center where they can buy a Crater Lake Twinkie and take a picture and then be on their way. A few hundred feet away from the traffic jams, the natural wonder comes into better focus. As Rachel Carson said, you don't need to be able to identify a pine tree to love nature; at Crater Lake, you don't need to be a geologist. Windprints track across the wide surface of the lake; stiff-limbed, anorexic trees grow in pumice slopes; the mystery of the rock island called the Phantom Ship enchants.

Meditations in blue: because there is almost no marine life in Crater Lake—all the water comes from rainfall and snowmelt—the color is a product of the interplay of sun and water. As sunlight passes through the lake, it is absorbed color by color. The reds fade first, followed by orange, yellow and green. Blue, the strongest hue in the color spectrum, is the last to be absorbed. From a depth of three hundred feet, the limit of light's ability to penetrate water on the planet, the blue gets reflected back.

Crater Lake is a product of destruction, essentially Mount Rainier without the upper mile of its cone. In the year 4860 B.C.—carbon-14 dating of charcoaled wood has established the exact date—the volcano erupted with a force that hurled eighteen cubic miles of pumice and ash all over the West. St. Helens sent forth little more than half a cubic mile. Parts of this mountain have been found 1,500 miles away, scattered over eight states and three Canadian provinces. Mazama has not stirred for nearly a thousand years.

At night, when the blue disappears and the stars press through the dark ceiling and all the motor homes have turned off their generators, campers walk through the forest to a small outdoor theater run by the National Park Service. Some of the visitors clearly miss television; they bring potato chips and beer to listen to the story of how Crater Lake was formed. Tonight's narrator is a small, elderly ranger, Carrol Abbott, a native of Pittsburgh. He talks about the volcano the way you'd expect somebody from an old city in the East to explain the odd landscape of the West, and it makes sense. The eruption here was like indigestion, says Abbott: "When I was a little boy, a long time ago, we would always have a big picnic on the Fourth of July. I remember one time I played a little baseball and then ate half-a-dozen hotdogs, a whole bunch of sauerkraut and then went out and played some more baseball, came back and ate a few more hotdogs. Then I topped it off with a whole lot of ice cream.

When I got home, I exploded." Pause. Chuckle. "That's sorta like what happened here."

He urges everyone to step outside the cocoon of their motor homes and spend at least an hour walking somewhere in the park, "trying to read the landscape." They will find pumice deserts where the volcanic deposits are so thick that nothing has grown back; they will find wild-flowers growing from the insides of ancient, gnarled trees called *Krumm-holz*, a German word meaning "twisted wood"; they will see in Wizard Island, a hood that rises eight hundred feet from the surface of the lake, the shell of the magma chamber. What's more, he concludes, if they walk the mile-long trail down the steep, pumiced slopes from the rim to Crater Lake, they will find "the tenth wonder of the world—a place without a Coke machine."

Early morning, sun just over the eastern crater rim. Atop Garfield Peak, two thousand feet above the surface of the lake. Timberline follows the steep grade right up to the eight-thousand-foot summit. With a growing season of about seven weeks, clusters of weather-harassed, soil-deprived, crabby alpine fir are holding tight to volcanic afterthought like a dying man clutching his photo album. Life springs from the past. A few thousand years down the road, the summit of St. Helens may look much the same. Older, more broken down, but alive—inside and out. This morning, in a demonstration designed to back its case that an industrial plant would not harm the national park, the California energy company has set up a pair of hundred-watt speakers on the park border and floated a host of balloons above the treetops. They are trying to simulate a 120-megawatt geothermal power plant to show that the project won't be much of an obstruction.

I turn to the south, where the cone of Mount Shasta is undergoing the slow turn from rose to white, 106 miles away and clear as the neighbor's apple tree. I think of the three prospectors who fell upon the rim in the year that Winthrop visited southern Oregon. They never found the lost goldmine in the country of ice-covered cones, but they discovered this treasure: air so clean the eye can wander for a hundred miles or more, and a volcano transformed from beast to beauty. For now.

Chapter 9

THE WOOD
WARS

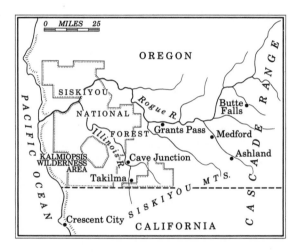

OREGON

PACIFIC OCEAN

SISKIYOU

NATIONAL

Rogue R.

Butte
Falls

FOREST   Grants Pass   Medford

Illinois R.

KALMIOPSIS
WILDERNESS
AREA

Cave Junction   Ashland

Takilma

SISKIYOU   MTS.

Crescent City

CALIFORNIA

CASCADE RANGE

B oundary Springs boils up from the ground just west of
Crater Lake and quickly forms the headwaters of a legendary river. Such turbulence from birth is appropriate,
for the Rogue River, on its way to the Pacific, drains a country
that is at war over its resources. To save a forest with a botanical
gene pool older than any other living thing in the Northwest,
men who call themselves Doug Fir and Bald Mountain Bill
are perched in trees, ready to fall with the front line of the
wilderness. In strategic places throughout the million acres of
the Siskiyou National Forest, ancient evergreens are spiked
with steel to sabotage mill saws, and bulldozer gas tanks are
filled with sugar to foul the engines. At night, in the valleys
shared by pot-growers and tree-fellers, gunshots are fired, windows are smashed. "Somebody's gonna get killed," mutters
the old man on the porch in the timber town of Cave Junction.

In court, pricey lawyers from the city try to answer the question: whose life is more endangered, the spotted owl's or the logger's? Victims of mutual incompatibility, both owl and logger are disappearing in Oregon, a state that once had enough standing timber to rebuild every house in America. And so men with braided beards sit in tall hemlocks trying to block the advance of loggers, and timber companies cut at an ever-faster rate, hoping to get the centuries-old giants before court injunctions on behalf of a small bird that can live only in the ancient coastal evergreens get at them.

Following the Rogue west from its source in the soft shoulders of the Oregon Cascades, I have trouble staying with this river as it hurls itself through deep basaltic trenches and forests congested with green life. The banks of the Rogue are a tribute to the imagination of nature—rain forest ferns mingle at the same party with blossoming azaleas, and dry-country pines tangle with the boughs of moisture-loving spruce. An oddity among the wet woods in the temperate zone that runs along the coast from Northern California to British Columbia, the Siskiyous bake under hundred-degree temperatures in summer, but take in enough rain during the dark season to boost the conifers to astonishing heights. The Ice Age glaciers which buried the rest of the Northwest, effectively killing all plant life and then carving the U-shaped valleys as they retreated, never made it this far south; the buckled clumps of red earth here are remnants of a forest that predates all life to the north by several million years. While most of the Pacific Northwest, covered by an ice sheet a mile thick, was unveiled a mere twelve thousand years ago, the Siskiyous have lived uninterrupted for perhaps 40 million years. Twenty different conifers and 1,400 plant species thrive in the Siskiyous, home forest for the greatest biological gene pool of the West, much as the Smokies are for the East. Three times as old as the Cascades and the Sierras, these mountains are resonant with life from the adaptations of those many centuries. They are not craggy or sharp or even particularly high. There are no glaciers, no granite spires, no volcanic cones, and only a few alpine lakes.

Like a stranger who defies stereotype upon first acquaintance, the Siskiyous are hard to figure. A little incongruent, at times spooky. Bigfoot, in this part of the country, is known as the Hermit of the Siskiyous— just under seven feet in size, smelling of body sweat and sticky hair, with yellow-tinged fur. He's been spotted by loggers and prospectors for years, but their cameras have always failed them when the beast came within focusing range.

Before the Rogue cuts its gorge in the Siskiyous, the river courses through the western slope of the Oregon Cascades, changing its look with the frequency of a fickle teen on an extended trip to the mall. In the higher reaches, the river is clogged with boulders that were tossed in its path by the eruption of Mount Mazama nearly seven thousand years ago. Even in midday, late summer, sunlight does not penetrate the canopy here, which is overwhelmed by the green of chlorophyll. Gathering strength from the waterfalls squeezed out of the upper woods, the Rogue roars through a dark canyon farther west of Crater Lake. I find salmon jumping from the Rogue's torrents—big chinooks, throwing themselves against the current. Farther down, light cuts through the thinning tree-tops, and the perfume of ponderosa pine predominates, carried by the wind. All is sweet and cleanly cluttered in the way of a pine forest. But then the lovely scent disappears, and the Rogue turns sluggish and flat and quiet. The only dam to block the river's 212-mile path to the Pacific appears here, backing up a reservoir surrounded by brutally shaved hill-sides. Now I'm on private land, out of the national forest. Nearby is Butte Falls, a timber town on the way down.

Logging trucks, carrying pine and fir of a girth that says the trees have lived three centuries or more, crowd the roadway. Walking up the hills, I can't find a trace of the original forest, the lungs of this land. All is gone—cut and bulldozed into slash heaps. In the hamlet of Butte Falls, population 428, there is confusion and anger. Residents of fifty years do not recognize the hills around their town. Lost in their own backyard, they talk as if collective Alzheimer's disease had taken over Butte Falls— like the Pretenders' song about a native daughter's return to Ohio: "but my city was gone." The favorite hunting spots have disappeared. The picnic meadow that used to be . . . here—gone. The woods where they first made love—a sunburned junkyard. The winds kick up dust instead of tossing evergreen branches against each other, and it seems much hotter than ever before. When it rains hard, water cuts new channels in the bare earth, clouding salmon streams. People shake their heads, sad as hell, and then trudge off to cut the remaining trees left near Butte Falls.

Global economics is wiping the green and the shade away from this timber town. For three generations the Medford Corporation has been the lifeblood of this community, gradually cutting away the old-growth trees on its ninety thousand acres. Historically, the company always logged just enough to make a profit and keep the town alive, ensuring a steady supply of trees. Then, in 1984, a corporate raider named Harold Simmons from the treeless canyons of Dallas paid $110 million for Medco, as it's called here, an acquisition added to a $2 billion empire of sugar, petroleum, chemicals and fast-food restaurants. Because the buyout ate up so much capital, the Texan ordered all the old-growth trees near Butte Falls to be cut as fast as possible while the market for timber was still hot. Old conifers from the Northwest, straight and fine-grained, make the best building wood, any lumberman will tell you. But they take a few centuries to reach the astonishing heights and level of strength so valued in world markets. Patience is not a virtue of late-twentieth-century corporate raiders. Before the sale, about 80 logging trucks a day rolled out of this town with Medco timber. Now, the pace is nearly 130 trucks a day. Off to Japan and Taiwan go the woods around Butte Falls, a third of an acre with every truck. Throughout the Northwest, 170 acres a day of ancient forest are being cut, 62,000 acres a year. In a few years, the residents of Butte Falls say, all the trees on Medco's 90,000 acres will be gone.

And what will become of Butte Falls? To survive, the loggers who live here on a wage of eight dollars an hour will have to look farther west and down the Rogue to the million acres of the Siskiyou National Forest— dry and wild and mostly uncut, home of the last big unprotected roadless area of forest left in continental America. A few groves of redwoods, the tallest trees on earth, some in excess of two thousand years old, live in the Siskiyous. Every timber company in the Northwest has its eyes on this public land, which is managed by the Forest Service, a branch of the Department of Agriculture. In a typical timber sale, the government builds roads into primeval forests, logging companies buy rights to use the roads and cut all the trees. In time, Smokey the Bear has become the nation's foremost road-builder, as the Forest Service has punched 343,000 miles of logging roads into the vast stands of public trees—more than seven times the 44,000 miles of road built by the national highway system.

Of late, Forest Service land managers have been treating their public trust in the Northwest like a tree farm—annual harvests reflecting market demand, and then reforesting with only one or two varieties of softwood seedlings—a process which is leading to the gradual elimination of many kinds of plant species. Few things are uglier than a fresh clearcut, with its scabbed earth, raw stumps, slash piles of debris and roads to nowhere. But a national forest replanted in the style preferred by the timber industry—corn rows of commercial trees—resembles nothing in nature. Ashamed of what the former friend of the forest had become, Jeff DeBonis, a longtime employee of the Willamette National Forest north of here, recently wrote a letter to his boss, F. Dale Robertson, Chief of the Forest Service. "Our basic problem right now is that we are much too biased toward the resource-extraction industries, particularly the timber industry," he wrote. "We support their narrowly focused, short-sighted agenda to the point that we are perceived by much of the public as being dupes of the resource extraction industries."

It takes up to a thousand years for a natural forest to become the rich rot of diversity known as the climax phase of the tree-growing cycle. Only a generation ago they said Oregon had so many overgrown trees that you could stretch a sixteen-mile-wide swath of this state's old growth from the Pacific Coast to the Atlantic. No more. Less than a tenth remains of the original 30 million acres of virgin forest in Oregon. The biggest chunk of that, roughly 440,000 acres, is in the north part of the Siskiyous, the oldest living area in the state. Although 1.2 million acres of wilderness have been set aside in Oregon, only 200,000 acres is lowland timberland. Wilderness in Oregon, as in Washington and British Columbia, is mostly rock-and-ice high-alpine country. Pressed by the demands of timber companies, which have exhausted all the old growth on private land, the Forest Service has announced plans to begin clearcutting much of the remaining unprotected public forest in the Siskiyous. In the hamlets around the Rogue River, clusters of people say they will die to prevent that from happening. Few people doubt them.

In morning light, before the sun washes away the mysteries of landscape and makes the country go flat, the hills in the central Rogue Valley look Tuscan: vineyards wear a coat of late summer mist, pears hang from orchards thriving on irrigation water, and the land rolls and folds in undulations of bright beige. Summer has been dry, leaving the madrona bark curled and the river much lower than usual. I'm on my way to the timber war zone, but curiosity slows me. In this corner of the Northwest, a place Oregon Territory promoter Hall Jackson Kelly called "the loveliest country on earth" in 1831, before he'd even seen it, people say things like "Allrighty" and wave to you as you drive by. They root for the football 49ers, because San Francisco, about 350 miles to the south, is closer than Seattle, 470 miles to the north, but urban influences are minimal, even with the advent of satellite dish television receivers. A handful of homesteaders keep dairy farms alive on small plots of land. Backcountry, away from the farms and vineyards, some of those who don't cut trees for a living grow pot. For several years, marijuana has been the number-one cash crop in Rogue River country.

It wasn't logging that first brought crowds to these mountains. The Siskiyous, then as now, are a chore to reach. But greed has always been a terrific trailblazer; when gold was found in 1853, roads were carved from the hills in a hurry. Prospectors, up from California over the Siskiyou Trail, and across the Plains and Rockies via the Oregon Trail, soon clogged the Rogue River basin. These were not the families of Protestant farmers who'd fled the depression of the Ohio River Valley to settle in the Willamette during the previous decade. These Rogue Valley newcomers arrived without wife or kids or a past. They needed whores and precious metal, in short order, to stay alive. By the end of 1853, the Rogue River Valley had great supplies of both. Overnight, towns such as Jacksonville and Ashland sprang up, a saloon and bordello for every two dozen prospectors.

The Indians were randomly murdered, sometimes shot for target practice. For centuries, the natives had lived well off the abundant salmon runs of the Trinity, the Chetco, the Illinois and Rogue rivers. Like most Northwest tribes, they were superb woodworkers, building perfectly symmetrical canoes, split-cedar houses, sanded and painted pottery, and furniture—all without benefit of axe, saw or any other metal tool. The great forest god provided them with a prolific source of waterproof wood, the western red cedar, which was used for everything from clothing to housing. As pioneers of the concept of sustained yield—now the seldom-followed but constantly stated forest-industry policy of never cutting more trees at any one time than would grow back to replace them—the natives were conservationists to a fault, even setting fires to encourage new growth in decaying areas. They called themselves the Takilmas and Tututnis, but the whites who came in the 1850s lumped them into a generic category which was thought to be descriptive of their behavior: the Rogue Indians. The main river and lifeline for the tribes was given the same name.

To protect them from further slaughter by renegade whites, the government opened up nearby Fort Lane for the tribes shortly after the waves of prospectors arrived. As the women and children were leaving the village for the safety of the fort, they were ambushed by a group of Oregon volunteers, who killed two dozen defenseless natives. In retaliation, the Indians killed twenty-seven whites. The war that followed lasted five years. Defeated, the Rogues nonetheless held out against removal to the arid wasteland of Oklahoma, which was the official Indian Territory and dumping ground for all tribes whose homelands had been pre-empted during the great western land-grab. Instead, the Rogues were sent north, to the Siletz reservation west of Portland, which was itself later taken by whites when the local timber was deemed valuable.

Young Theodore Winthrop, looking for acid-tongued pioneer Jesse Applegate, visited southern Oregon in 1853. Six thousand people moved to Oregon that year, drawn by gold and the Donation Land Act, which gave each male white citizen the right to own 320 acres and his wife 320 acres if they stayed on the land for four years. By the time the act was repealed in 1855, more than 2.5 million acres of Oregon were in private ownership. Winthrop was uncharacteristically silent on the hordes of prospectors panning the deep canyons of the Rogue for gold, perhaps because they didn't fit his prophecy of the Oregon Country's becoming a New England of the West, whose people would be ennobled by the stunning landscape. Yet he had plenty to say about the deep forests and rich river country. Surely, man would never conquer the biggest trees on earth, he said.

Wading through the tangle on the west side of the Cascades, Winthrop offered a typical reaction of the time. "These giants with their rough plate armor were masters here," he wrote. "One of human stature was unmeaning and incapable. With an axe, a man of muscle might succeed in smiting off a flake or a chip, but his slight fibres seemed naught to battle, with any chance of victory, the time-hardened sinews of these Goliaths."

Forty-three years after Winthrop wrote those words, a young German immigrant was hobo-hopping his way around the country when his travels took him to the Illinois Valley, named for the river that flows north from the California border into the Rogue in the heart of the Siskiyous. The trees towered higher than anything he'd ever seen in the Black Forest or along the Rhine. Even Switzerland's alpine valleys couldn't compare with the jumble of mountain country in the Pacific Northwest. He wrote his brother in Germany about the free land, the opportunity for quick money, the swift-flowing rivers. When Frederick Krauss received the letter in 1896, he promptly left Germany with his wife and two kids and headed for the Siskiyous. He had a small stake, and didn't speak the language. The rain could be a bit much, sixty inches a year on average. Summers tended to dry everything out and bring fire to the woods. But overall, this Oregon country agreed with Krauss.

During the time Frederick Krauss was establishing a hardscrabble home in the Northwest, another German-American, Frederick Weyerhaeuser, moved into a new mansion at 266 Summit Avenue in an exclusive neighborhood of St. Paul, Minnesota. His next-door neighbor at 244 Summit was James Hill, the Great Northern Railroad tycoon. Weyerhaeuser, by then the dominant lumberman of his day, had made his fortune stripping the trees of the Great Lakes area and the upper Mississippi Valley, and he knew that the mature white pine in that area was just about gone. Within his lifetime an area half the size of Europe—Michigan, Minnesota, Wisconsin and parts of bordering states—had been deforested. Paul Bunyan and his blue ox Babe sprang from mythology in the North Woods lumber camps, but by the turn of century big Paul and every other timberman was looking west at the greatest stands of softwood the world had ever known, on the west side of the Cascade Mountains. Problem was, how to get all that wood to market. Hill had an idea, and more land than he knew what to do with to back it up.

Although the first sawmill in the Northwest was a Hudson's Bay Company contraption built in 1827 and powered by water near the Gentlemen's fort on the Columbia River, commercial logging never took off on a big scale, because of the distance from forest to market. Timber was scooted downslope to a river or salt water bay, and then shipped to San Francisco. Getting a boatload of heavy logs around Cape Horn to reach the East Coast was financially prohibitive. The railroads changed everything. When President Lincoln signed legislation in 1864 which chartered the Northern Pacific Railroad Company, he authorized a giveaway of vast sections of the West as incentive to complete a line from Lake Superior to Puget Sound. The company would get a checkerboard land grant of ten square miles for every mile of track completed in Oregon and Minnesota. In Washington Territory, they would get twice as much. All told, the Northern Pacific was deeded 38.5 million acres of public land. By the time Frederick Weyerhaeuser moved into the house on Summit Avenue, his neighbor James Hill controlled the Northern Pacific and all the western land which the government had given away. Hill offered this proposition: Weyerhaeuser would get 900,000 acres of Northern Pacific land grant property for $7 an acre. Weyerhaeuser, a shy man whose only hobby was beekeeping, thought this over, and then offered $5 an acre. They settled on $6. On January 3, 1900, Weyerhaeuser took title to 900,000 acres in Washington for a price of $5.4 million—the biggest private land sale in the country at the time. He paid about ten cents per thousand board feet—a dime per tree, on average—for timber that now sells for five hundred dollars per thousand board feet. The land was choice: the forested slopes around Mount Rainier and Mount St. Helens; acreage from the Cascade Crest to Puget Sound; the lowland woods near the Columbia in southwest Washington, and the temperate jungle near Naches Pass above the Yakima Valley, the spot where Winthrop had written that the forests of the Northwest were thick enough to keep man at bay.

By 1914, when the first Krauss boys born in the Siskiyous were working odd jobs in the woods, the Weyerhaeuser Company had expanded its empire in the Northwest to just under two million acres—about twice the size of the state of Delaware—and was well on its way to the claim of world's largest forest-products firm. There were howls of outrage from populist stump speakers and radical union leaders. Teddy Roosevelt called Weyerhaeuser a "curse." In reaction to the land-gobbling, Roosevelt established the national forest system in 1905, putting 150 million acres in public trust, to be managed by a corps of professional conservationists, the Forest Service.

Of course, some still believed that the dark, brooding stands of timber on steep mountain sides were protected by their very size. The supply was inexhaustible; at times, it even seemed to rain timber. During the summer of Winthrop's visit, a settler named Ezra Meeker built a cabin near the Columbia River town of Kalama, Washington. A spring freshet carried a load of lightning-felled logs down from the hillsides to his homestead. Meeker guided his manna down the Columbia to a mill, where he was paid six dollars per thousand board feet.

But such stories were rare. More typical was the logger, a missing finger or two on each hand, who drifted west as the Great Lakes timber disappeared and found he had to work six days in the woods to pay for a one-night drunk. Weyerhaeuser lumber camps were run like prison yards. No conversation was allowed at meal times, no booze, no women, and, for several bloody decades, no unions. Until the labor revolts of 1917, the average pay was no more than two dollars for a ten-hour workday. Men were fired without prior warning. Pay was deducted for use of boots, blankets and bunkhouses, most of which were not heated. Little wonder that membership in the radical Industrial Workers of the World spread like jug whiskey through the logging camps. The constitution of the Wobblies didn't mince any words: "The working class and the employing class have nothing in common." Their black cat symbol, emblazoned with the words BEWARE! SABOTAGE! and WE NEVER FORGET, began to pop up at scenes of industrial sabotage. When Longview, the world's biggest planned timber town, opened on the banks of the Columbia with a company band playing "Nearer My God to Thee," the headline in the Wob newspaper was: LONG-BELL HIRES JESUS MAN TO QUIET SLAVES.

The turbulence was not as bad in the Siskiyous, where most of the mills were small, family-run affairs. Lew Krauss, grandson of the poor farmer who left Germany in 1896, began work at his father's mill as soon as he came of age. When he started a mill of his own—the Rough and Ready Lumber Company in Cave Junction, the principal hamlet in the Illinois Valley—there were more than twenty-five small timber operations. Krauss loved the Illinois Valley; he climbed the hills of the Kalmiopsis, fished the Rogue and the Illinois, panned for gold. As playground or income source, the natural world of the Siskiyous seemed to have no limits; as long as people used wood to build homes, the Krauss family would live well, and so Lew Krauss never gave a thought of going into anything but the timber business. He married, moved into a home not far from the house of his grandfather, and raised seven children. As the timber industry grew with the postwar construction boom, Rough and Ready prospered and expanded. By the standards of the Illinois Valley, where seasonal work was the norm, the Krauss family was rich.

In time, the small mills were consolidated or folded and the construction boom tapered off. By the 1970s, Rough and Ready was the only mill left in the Illinois Valley and was the chief source of income for residents of Cave Junction, employing more than two hundred people. By then others had moved to the red-earth hills and deep valleys of the ancient Siskiyous. They lived in communes around the old Indian village site of Takilma, just a stone's throw from the California border, but their lifestyle did not sit well with the loggers of Cave Junction. They ran nude in the woods, smoked prodigious amounts of dope, gathered for mystic chants and grew organic vegetables. What particularly bothered some residents of Cave Junction was the new land ethic of these mostly well-educated residents of the Takilma communes, who revered the practices of the all-but-forgotten Rogue River Indians. Some of the younger residents of the Illinois Valley, however, sons and daughters of loggers, who didn't want to work at Rough and Ready or be married to somebody who did, were attracted to the Takilma communes.

While the back-to-earth movement faded in other parts of America, it flourished here. Even when some of the young Cave Junction residents became disillusioned with commune life and returned to conventional society, their attitude toward the bountiful resources of the Siskiyous had changed. The vast tracts of old evergreens, they realized, were fast disappearing. "It's the last great buffalo hunt," said Lou Gold, a former Portland college professor who took up tree-sitting on behalf of the ancient forest.

As the timber companies cut all the trees on their private land, the pressure on the national forest reserves increased. Forest Service logging roads into the sanctuaries set up by Teddy Roosevelt tripled in the thirty years following World War II. The thousand-year-old trees were considered dead and useless by the people who ran the national forests. "One of my major initiatives has been to speed up harvest of the slow-growing or decadent, overmature timber stands in the Pacific Northwest, the old growth," said John Crowell, the chief of the Forest Service, in 1982. At the same time, visitors started showing up from Europe and Southern California and Florida asking to see the old trees, the ones with trunks as wide as garage doors and canopies that blocked the sky. As interest in the old forest increased, Dr. Jerry Franklin, a forester, the son of a Columbia River mill worker, was asked by the Forest Service in the early 1980s to do a study of the old growth. Contrary to the conventional view at the time, Franklin found that these forests were not biological deserts, but unique ecosystems, the jungles of America, whose rotted snags provided homes for the spotted owl and fuel for the next generation of thousand-year-old trees.

Some of the younger residents of Cave Junction saw in the forests of the Siskiyous and the torrents of the Rogue and Illinois rivers another future: tourism. Sons and daughters of third-generation logging families, they set up whitewater rafting outfits or took the family homesteads and converted them to bed-and-breakfast guest houses. Their livelihood became dependent on the very scenery which their neighbors and brothers were tearing up. Battle lines were drawn, as clear as the physical difference between one side of the Illinois River and the other. East of the river is a patchwork of logging roads and clearcuts, and the red earth is warm to the touch on large sections of denuded land. West of the river is the only big wilderness area in the Siskiyous, the 200,000 acres of the Kalmiopsis, where no roads penetrate a crowd of madronas, conifers, wild rhododendrons and the rare, pink-flowered Kalmiopsis plant, a cousin of the azalea which was thought to be extinct before it was discovered here.

For the last decade, the fight here has been over a roadless 400,000 acres just north of the formal wilderness. Conservationists want that section of land and the wilderness lumped into a 700,000-acre Siskiyou National Park—all of it off limits to the chain saw. Timber companies, including Medco of Butte Falls, and Rough and Ready of Cave Junction, asked the Forest Service to build 214 miles of roads into the area and allow them to cut nearly six thousand acres annually. When the Forest Service announced plans to do just that, some Oregonians said that punching a road through the sacred heart of the Siskiyous and stripping all the trees on either side of it in order to save a few hundred jobs would be no different than trashing a cathedral to get at the candle wax. A lawsuit, filed on behalf of the endangered spotted owl, blocked the immediate cutting. Some of those who filed the suit received death threats.

"You may not like living with us now," said Andy Kerr, a leader of the conservationists. "But we make great ancestors."

Between court injunctions, when bits and pieces of the wilderness area were nibbled up by the loggers, acts of sabotage increased. Near Holcomb Peak, for example, a zigzag pattern of spikes was nailed through dozens of ancient trees. Few noticed the ironic reappearance of a symbol not seen in these woods for half a century. Sheriff's deputies found posters of a screeching black cat with the words: BEWARE! SABOTAGE! And in smaller type, "We never sleep. . . . We never forget. . . ."

At the Rough and Ready mill in Cave Junction, Lew Krauss can barely control himself when he tries to talk about the conflict raging outside his office window. In his late fifties, Krauss is a tall, angular man dressed in plaid shirt and workboots. Nothing corporate or stuffy about him. Jimmy Stewart would fit in those clothes. He is likable, as Stewart is when he holds his finger up and says, "Now, wait just a minute. . . ." His grandfather would not understand this fight, Krauss says. In fact, as he talks, the land of his grandfather is enmeshed in a struggle brought by the Green Movement, whose members in Germany speak much the same language as the young residents of the communes outside Cave Junction. The planet is exhausted, they say; nothing short of direct action will save it. Krauss blames those who live in the communes and shacks down the river for holding up a timber sale in the national forest which he needs to keep the 220 workers at the Rough and Ready mill employed. Working with lawyers from the city, conservationists have held up numerous timber sales on the Siskiyous, claiming the spotted owl is being killed off by the loss of its old-growth-forest habitat. The owls, which nest in pairs, need up to five thousand acres per pair to live. The species is a barometer of the ancient forest; when spotted owls disappear from an area, it's a sign that the world of the forest is in deep trouble. Citing government studies that showed clearcutting the old trees has caused a steep decline in the population of the spotted owl, environmentalists in the 1980s found their best legal tool yet to slow logging in the national forests. In the parking lot at the Rough and Ready mill, some of the pickup trucks have bumper stickers which read, "Save a Logger. Kill a Spotted Owl." Inflatable owls are hung by their necks with ropes attached to the trucks. And when a convoy of logging trucks blocked the roads to protest Forest Service consideration for the spotted owl, a sign appeared in a local cafe which read: "Today's Special: Spotted Owl Stew."

The smell of fresh-sliced pine fills the air at the Rough and Ready mill. Two-by-fours and two-by-sixes are stacked thirty feet high for a quarter-mile in the lot outside the mill. After a long recession, times are good again. Never before have so many trees been cut at one time from the national forests of the Northwest. Lumber prices are approaching an all-time high. But Krauss can see the future.

"Spotted owl! Dammit, what'll it be next time? Because of that owl, they're holding up a billion board feet of timber on nineteen national forests."

Outside of court, more danger lurks. In California, a logger's saw exploded after hitting a spike in an old tree. He nearly died. Bad enough that a third of all loggers in the Northwest will be seriously injured at some time during their careers: Trees fall the wrong way. Chokers don't hold. Boughs snap when they aren't supposed to. Logs fall off trucks. Trucks fall off cliffs. Then there's the after-work hazards, like eight beers and a long drive home down the winding road. According to medical-insurance records in Washington and Oregon, only two lines of work are more dangerous than logging—professional football and crop-dusting. Krauss, afraid of losing a man to a tree-spiker, recently ordered that all trees be screened with a giant magnet before they are run through the mill.

On his wall are black-and-white pictures from the early days of logging, an era without limits, when seventy-two men once posed atop a cedar stump. Every timber town on the west side of the Cascades has a similar picture, or a stump. Few trees of such size are left in the woods of the Northwest. The first tree farm in America was planted in 1941 on the Olympic Peninsula. Should the trees from that plantation be cut today, their stumps would barely hold the boots of a single logger. Krauss realizes the big trees are fast disappearing, going to Japan, colonial masters of these woods. In the late 1980s, about 4 billion board feet of raw logs from the Northwest were sent overseas every year—almost a third of all the wood cut on private and public land in Washington, Oregon and northern

California, timber worth $2 billion. For every log sent overseas, four jobs go with it. And so in Coos Bay, the harbor is full of raw logs, and trucks bring a steady stream of fresh-cut timber into port from Weyerhaeuser's Millacoma Tree Farm, all of it consigned for shipment to Asia. But for the first time in memory, not a single plywood or lumber mill is operating in Coos Bay, because all the local wood is going overseas. The Philippines, Indonesia, Burma—these countries have long since stopped exporting raw logs from their declining hardwood forests. Only the Pacific Northwest continues to do so. The owners of these exporting timber companies blame the spotted owl for the log shortage. The small mill proprietors know better.

Timber is king in Oregon, the number-one industry in the number-one lumber-producing state in the country. Same in British Columbia. Not so in Washington, where the economy has diversified considerably, and less than one percent of the jobs are directly tied to wood products. During the last recession, the timber towns of the Northwest were full of heartbreak—thirty percent unemployment, boarded-up stores, foreclosed homes, divorce, alcoholism, child abuse. Around Aberdeen and Darrington and Forks and Morton and Sweet Home and Coos Bay and Butte Falls and here in Cave Junction, happy families were in short supply. The woods bordering these towns were all used up, just like the people.

When the industry bounced back, more roads were built deeper into the national forests, and record profits were reported, but the timber towns remained depressed, with some of the highest unemployment rates in the country. The spotted owl had nothing to do with this. After the recession, the timber companies thinned their operations down, turning to automation and getting wage concessions from the unions. It wasn't so long ago that Stewart Holbrook wrote: "Our classic symbol is a man with an axe. The sounds that have influenced us are not those of the oboes and strings of symphony groups, but the savage music of the whining headsaws down on the sandspit. The aroma that moves us most is that of sawdust wild on the wind." But now the man with the axe has been replaced by the latest tool of the timber-cutting trade, the massive Treepower FB-1, which can move up seventy-degree slopes, snipping twenty-inch-thick trees at their base. The FB-1, lumberjack of the future, sells for $300,000.

Now, in the best of timber-industry times, the companies are employing twenty thousand fewer people in Washington and Oregon than ten years ago, during the last boom period, and they are stripping public land of old-growth trees at a rate that will deplete the remaining stands within a few decades. The plates of armor which Winthrop thought so impenetrable are falling like a retreating army in midwinter. And the Forest Service, set up to protect against the avarice of timber companies, has become the industry's best friend.

What to do? Stop acting like a Third World country, says Krauss. As long as the Northwest is a resource colony for other countries, it will never get out of the cycle of heartbreak. What of the Kalmiopsis, the last big stand of unprotected woodland? All the previous battles, beginning with Teddy Roosevelt's creation of the national forests and continuing through the fight to create the Olympic, Rainier, North Cascades and Crater Lake national parks, have led up to this, the struggle for the Siskiyous. Should the big trees just up the hill from Cave Junction be cut because companies like Medco have used up all their private land around Butte Falls and Weyerhaeuser ships all its logs from Coos Bay overseas? Should the capital demands of a Texas billionaire determine the rate at which public forests are cut?

In the town of Ashland, population 16,000, just over the mountains from the Rough and Ready mill, the regular sunset staging of *Henry IV* is getting underway. The moon has started to cross the sky over the ridge. Stars are pressing through. The crowd quiets, and for the next three hours this part of the Siskiyous is alive with the old truths and shopworn jokes of Shakespeare. Every year, a quarter-million people visit this town at the edge of the mountains. In the winter they come to ski and watch Shakespeare indoors; in the summer they come to hike and watch Shakespeare under the stars in the clear nights of the southern Oregon summer. The fifth-largest theater company in the country is based in Ashland. Here is Winthrop's vision in full technicolor, the best product of the human heart on display in a natural setting that adds rich tones to the production. Like food eaten around the campfire, Shakespeare is better in the outdoors. Ever since this former mining town hooked its economic destiny to Shakespeare, there have been few of the economic downturns that have so decimated other towns in the Siskiyous. Just like the warm springs that bubble up in the center of Ashland, the Bard seems an eternal resource.

Cave Junction and Butte Falls will never be Ashland. Loggers do not become thespians, at least not overnight. But Ashland has shown the depressed timber towns of the Siskiyous that there is a way to stay alive other than turning the countryside to stumplands. When I ask Krauss about that, he says some towns belong to Shakespeare, others belong to the mill. If the remaining open forest of the Siskiyous were turned into a national park, Krauss is certain that Cave Junction, population 1,175, would fold up and die. Anybody who tells you otherwise has probably been smoking dope in those communes near the state border, he says. "Fugitives," he calls them, with a sneer that overwhelms the Jimmy Stewart face, and then adds the ultimate insult. "Fugitives from California."

One of those fugitives who came here during the early commune days was a young University of California graduate student named Robert Brothers, a slight, balding man with spindly legs who changed his name to Bobcat and took up with the tree-sitters. He grew up in Chicago, the son of a state worker, and moved west for college. While at Berkeley, he counseled people with psychological problems, but soon developed a distrust of his chosen field. When a patient would complain about his job being the source of his malaise, Bobcat would say, "Quit your job. That's what I'd do." Fifteen years ago he moved to Siskiyou country, which was full of change as the communes swelled with expatriates from the cities. Some lived for free on public land, setting up small lean-tos near summer marijuana farms. Others took up organic gardening, or tended small orchards, or sold handmade crafts at local markets, or started vineyards. Nobody needed very much money to get by. Bobcat lived off the income he got from family rental property in Chicago. The loggers and the back-to-earthers in the Illinois Valley coexisted—sometimes off the same, shared marijuana farms—though mutual suspicion prevailed.

Then in the early 1980s some of the organic farmers started to get sick. They had always drunk the water from streams which poured out of the Siskiyous in early spring. Cleanest water in the world, it was called, but suddenly it was poisoning the valley residents. Much more than nausea, the illness caused headaches, blackouts, coughing spells. A few years went by, and then some of the seasonal forest workers developed cancer. One young man died. His death was caused by malignant lymphoma, and his doctor blamed it on his continued exposure to a herbicide, 2,4-D, developed by Dow Chemical Company to kill vegetation in Vietnam. For years the Forest Service had hired teenagers to clear unwanted brush in the woods and near roads—summer work, clean and healthy. Then government officials in Washington, D.C., came up with another idea, and the Forest Service switched from handheld clippers to a program of spraying massive amounts of 2,4-D—a fast, effective way to defoliate certain areas, and, the Forest Service officials pointed out, cheaper than hiring teenagers to clear brush. But the chemical product of American war research often landed on blackberry bushes, poisoning berry-pickers, and with heavy rains it trickled down the streams and into the makeshift homes of the organic gardeners.

Joined by older farmers whose families had lived in the Siskiyous for generations, Bobcat and others in the valleys started asking questions:

Why was the Government spraying public lands with herbicides?

To control unwanted brush.

Why was the natural ground layer of the forest unwanted?

Because it slows the growth of trees planted for commercial timber harvesting, competing for nutrients.

That led to questions about the Forest Service itself:

You mean you're managing this forest, through chemicals and costly road building and replanting of a monoculture, for private industry? Doesn't every citizen of the country own the national forest?

At demonstrations, some of the valley residents would perform skits, acting out what happens to an unwanted conifer when it comes in contact with the herbicide. By 1984, under legal pressure, the Forest Service declared a moratorium on the use of 2,4-D. It has not been used since. But the Siskiyous would never be the same.

Some of the organic farmers and marijuana growers and urban drop-outs began to show up at timber sales, which used to be routine exchanges between Forest Service land managers and their friends in the industry. The slogans, tactics and pamphlets from Earth First!, a militant environmental group whose motto is "No compromise in defense of Mother Earth," became influential. Earth First!, with its hammer-and-monkey-wrench symbol, espouses a hybrid philosophy of Wobbly sabotage tactics and suggestions from writer Edward Abbey. Tree-sitting, gate-blocking, timber-spiking—the tactics of *ecotage*, as they call it—are used when court injunctions and media pressure do not produce the desired results. The ecoteurs flooded Cave Junction with newsletters telling people the proper way to chain themselves to a bulldozer or sit in a tree.

CLIMB TREES! screamed the headline on Earth First! publications. They also urged the climbers to bring along little plastic bags in which to store their body wastes. When metal detectors were used to trace tree spikes, some of the Earth Firsters shifted to ceramic nails.

In an Earth First! column by someone with the byline Budworm, the writer noted the dangers of tree-spiking. "If you are spiking, assume your ass has a big green target on it. You are wanted. Don't tell me or anyone else what you're up to (exception: if you're willing to be an anonymous spiker on a tv news documentary, get in touch with me for details)." Other stories carried tips for the serious monkeywrencher: "Spray paint, though environmentally destructive even without chlorofluorocarbons (weigh the cost benefits of your actions as always) still works best."

Earth First! put out a comic book featuring a revisionist history of the Forest Service's favorite mascot, Smokey the Bear—in the cartoons he became Stumpy the Bear, born in a clearcut. When the Earth Firsters were called terrorists, they countered that tree-spiking was an honorable tradition first used by the Wobs almost a hundred years ago.

"Tree-spiking is fine with me as long as nobody gets hurt," said Bobcat, who became the spokesman for Earth First! in southern Oregon.

The Earth Firsters quoted Bob Marshall, the Depression-era wilderness advocate who worked for the Forest Service. Marshall, raised in New York City, could walk thirty miles a day through rugged terrain, and still stay up half the night telling stories. In the 1930s, he proposed that a million-acre Kalmiopsis wilderness area be set aside. At the time, no roads penetrated the Siskiyous from Crescent City in Northern California up the coast to Coos Bay. A small wilderness was established in 1946, and later enlarged in the late 1970s. That was it for wilderness. As the Forest Service moved toward a plan in the 1980s to sever the remaining roadless area with clearcutting through the untouched forest, people threw themselves in front of bulldozers and chained themselves to the road gate. The battle centered around the Forest Service road proposed for the wilderness. If they could stop the road, they figured the forest would be saved, since helicopter logging is far more expensive. Less-militant environmental groups—the Sierra Club, the Oregon Natural Resources Council—obtained court injunctions against the logging plan. Earlier this summer, the Forest Service had stopped construction of the road when it was nine miles into the wild forest, saying further study of the spotted owl was needed. For the moment, it looked as if the forest would not be cut.

"We thought we'd won," says Bobcat, sitting inside his ramshackle shed deep in the forest near Cave Junction. He has a braided beard that goes beyond his navel, which he strokes as he talks. At the shack where he lives, the walls are covered with pictures of clearcuts, Indian artifacts and sayings from David Foreman, one of the founders of Earth First! Foreman's book *Ecodefense: A Field Guide to Monkeywrenching* is on a table. The shack is at the end of a dirt road, overgrown with brush, and cluttered with junked cars which are pasted with bumper stickers that read, "We Are All One Species." Inside is a woodstove. I ask him if it isn't a conflict to burn wood and keep junk cars while advocating a litter-free habitat for the other creatures of the Siskiyous. "Not at all," says Bobcat. "We selectively cut the trees here for burning, without harm to the environment. And the junk cars out back? Yeah, somebody's supposed to do something about that."

Tree-spiking, blockades, ecotage—those kinds of things, says Bobcat, work as delaying tactics until the lawyers can move in with court injunctions. And all those loggers at the Rough and Ready mill, what are they supposed to do? He says the future of the Siskiyou valleys must be in orchards and vineyards and farming and tourism. It's time for the people of Cave Junction to adapt or die. In increasing numbers, tourists come to sample the local wines here and float down the wild water of the Rogue and Illinois. Californians, cashing in their home equity and using it to purchase houses here that cost a fraction of property farther south, have taken to the old ranch homes of the valley as a retirement haven. They have no interest in scarred ridges and debris-filled streams. By some measures, the most valuable resource in the West is land, and the fastest-growing Western counties are within a mile of wild areas. "We will win," says Bobcat.

In late August, Forest Service officials release their proposal for the roadless area of the Siskiyous. They're done studying the spotted owl and have made up their mind: the owl will get more land set aside than previously planned, but it's time to get on with the business of the Siskiyous. They call for a return to the previously announced logging schedule of six thousand acres a year, and construction of more than two hundred miles of roads, including completion of the symbolic main road, in the biggest tract of ancient forest up for grabs in the Northwest. Earth First! calls for battle. But two days later, in the midst of a long dry spell, on a night when the air is so still that a whisper travels far, a thunderstorm rumbles up from California.

The sky goes very dark, then explodes in a blitz of electricity. No rain comes with the storm, just thunderbolts fired down at the ancient forest. Boom! Crack! Followed by the smell, dry wood engulfed in a firestorm. Dogs howl, then retreat for cover. Birds screech across the sky. Horses stampede against sharp fences, panicky, looking for a way out. In Cave

Junction, the loggers run outside and stare at the sky; at road's end near the junked cars, the Earth Firsters do the same thing. The night is full of smoke and flames and desperate voices, awed by the force of nature. All the tree-spiking and lawsuits and detailed forest-management plans and blockades are meaningless: the Kalmiopsis wilderness is on fire, burning out of control. The wind pushes the flames north, making them leap from tree to tree, hopscotching over the giants. The inferno creates its own winds, and its own sound, the swoosh of oxygen being sucked out of the atmosphere and into the maw of the furnace.

The next day the sky is dark; smoke fills the Illinois Valley, blots out the sun, and drifts east up the Rogue River Valley to Crater Lake. From around the state, firefighters are mobilized. A few days later, some reserve units from the National Guard are flown in. But it looks hopeless; there is no way to get people into the steep roadless area, and the winds are racing at such a speed as to make firefighting a fatal mission. The Siskiyou fire burns for ten weeks, consuming nearly 100,000 acres of old forest in the north Kalmiopsis—Oregon's largest fire in half a century. When fall rains from the Pacific finally douse the great blaze, the two sides start arguing over whether the dead trees should be left as is to nurture the next forest, or harvested to keep the mills of the Rogue River basin running.

Chapter 10

SALMON

The secret of life in the Northwest runs in packs of silver; as with most mysteries, it lies just below the surface, evident to anyone who thinks it important enough to look. At Willamette Falls, this secret reveals itself in rare flashes amidst the industrial clutter of Oregon City. The river here is a beast of burden, powering the street lights of nearby Portland, grinding wood pulp to paper, settling into locks that lift ships on their way. Against this metallic frenzy a few chinook salmon hurry upstream, driven by a singular impulse to pass on the baton of life and then die. To the continued befuddlement of biologists, they return to the neighborhood of their youth after seeing the world. In the fall, as the ground goes cold and the fields die, they bring a dose of fertility in from the sea, carrying the collected natural history of the Willamette in their gene pool. Fornication, in the ritualized style of the Pacific salmon, is never more charitable—or fatal.

On a morning bundled in mist, I count eight chinooks scouting the overworked passage here at Oregon City. Their stomachs empty since they crossed the Columbia River Bar into fresh water, they seek a square foot of gravel in the natal stream. Once the female finds a home, she will drop a load of perhaps five thousand eggs. If not already attached, the males may compete for paternal rights. Usually the bigger fish win, but occasionally a small salmon darts out from hiding and quickly fertilizes the eggs before the slower-moving studs have finished their mano-a-mano routine. From there, the upstream struggle is over, the salmon's skin loses color and protective oil; death is a few days away. The carcass is eaten by eagles or is washed downstream to somebody's farm—the salmon's death is one of nature's principal ways of bringing nutrients from the sea to the land of the Northwest.

This trickle of spawners in the Willamette is nothing, of course, compared to what used to be. "At the time of our visit to the falls of the Willamette the salmon fishery was at its height, and was to us a novel as well as amusing scene," wrote Captain Charles Wilkes during his exploration of the area in 1841. "The salmon leap the falls; and it would be inconceivable, if not actually witnessed, how they can force themselves up, and after a leap of ten to twelve feet retain strength enough to stem the force of the water above. . . . I never saw so many fish collected together before."

Most of the salmon that come up this way today are hatchery-bred, with a Northwest background no more extensive than that of the newcomers who fill the three-level homes in the orchard country east of Portland. But a few native kings, descendants of Ice Age pioneers who brought new life back to the glacier-ripped landscape, still make it through. With the reappearance this fall of these last few wild chinook, the chain remains unbroken.

A hundred and fifty years ago the expectations of a nation directed themselves into this hamlet at the confluence of the Clackamas and Willamette rivers, site of the first American city west of the Rockies to incorporate. Leaving debt and dubious backgrounds behind, the wagon travelers crossed the Plains, struggled over the notch in the Rockies, floated down the white water of the lower Columbia and ended up in the Willamette Valley. Usually, it was raining. The land was green and fertile, shadowed by the hulk of Mount Hood. The great cataract in the Willamette provided more than enough power to cut logs. The first paper mill and the first hydroelectric power plant in the Northwest were built around Willamette Falls. Down went the trees that shaded the riverbank, and up went a forest of smokestacks. In no time, Oregon City looked more like Pittsburgh than a new metropolis built under the sublime influence of nature. By the middle of the twentieth century, after enduring a diet of sludge and pulp effluents and logging debris, the Willamette River was nearly dead. A muscled mannequin, it looked like a river and snaked like a river, but beneath the surface the pulse of life was faint.

In the Northwest, a river without salmon is a body without a soul. From the Sacramento to the Yukon, every waterway pulled by gravity to the Pacific has, at one time, been full of the silver flash of life. During certain times of the year, you could walk under any rain-country waterfall and get hit over the head by a leaping forty-pound fish. Lakes ran red with sockeye, streams were crowded with coho, and the Columbia was the main highway for the biggest chinook run the world had ever known. It was a bounty that tested the limits of greed. By midcentury, the handful of fish which made it through the wall of nets, hooks, seines and wheels at the Columbia's mouth returned to the Willamette only to choke to death in water starved of oxygen. They died with eggs and sperm still inside them, belly-up in a rust-colored river.

Had he not died in the Civil War, Winthrop would have been forced to rewrite his Northwest descriptions if he'd seen what his New England brothers were doing to the Willamette. While Winthrop feasted on Pacific salmon throughout his journey in 1853—he talked of "feeling the exquisiteness of his coloring, grilling him delicately and eating him daintily"—the wild Atlantic salmon runs of his homeland were being wiped out by the excesses of the expanding industrial age. The new inhabitants of the Oregon Country would treat their natural bounty much better, Winthrop prophesied. How could they do otherwise? He had called the area from Portland down to the center of the state, "the sweet arcadian valley," a place "charming with meadow, park and grove." And it was upon reflection on what could be in the region of the Willamette that Winthrop repeated his central prophecy for this last frontier corner of mainland America:

> In no older world where men have in all their happiest moods recreated themselves for generations in taming earth to orderly beauty have they achieved a fairer garden than Nature's simple labor of love has made there, giving to rough pioneers the bless-

ings and possible education of a refined and finished landscape, in the presence of landscape strong, savage and majestic.

The lesson from the land nearly came too late. In the midst of the Depression, when less than a hundred wild chinook were returning to the Willamette, a cry went up to save the river. At the time, another wave of Americans was spilling into the Northwest, Dust Bowl refugees from Arkansas and Texas and Oklahoma. Hollow-eyed, with strange accents, they knew little about the area except that it was supposed to have in great abundance something they had lost—water. Yes, they had water in Oregon, enough to wash all the tears from the drought out to sea. But they were poisoning it. So, as one generation was happy merely to have a raw element, another generation said it was not enough. To be a North-westerner was to be a salmon-eater. In 1938, Oregonians, who were among the first people in the nation to give themselves the power of legislation by popular initiative at the ballot box, voted to clean up the Willamette River and save the salmon run. The buffalo had disappeared from the Plains, the caribou had long vanished from the Upper Mississippi Valley, the wild Atlantic salmon runs in New England were mostly memory. The Pacific king, also known as chinook or tyee, a fish which can grow to five feet in length and 125 pounds in weight, was one of the last of the true marvel creatures left in the New World.

Cleanup came slowly. The forest-products industry is king of the political heap in Oregon, and no politician who stands up to foul logging practices will last long in office. It wasn't until the late 1960s and the election of Governor Tom McCall that Oregon got serious about backing up what the voters had approved in 1938. Under McCall, a zealot with a droll sense of humor and an unshakable sense of destiny, the Willamette was treated like the main artery of the Pope. Without a flow of clean water down the center of the state, Oregon might well kill itself. The state took over the riverbank and started regulating how much poison from Portland's sprawl could be dumped into the stream. McCall made Oregonians ashamed of what they had done with their Promised Land. His entire government philosophy was built on the simple axiom that people should leave the earth—especially their patch of earth—a better place than they found it. He backed it up with jail sentences for offenders. Over time, the chinooks came back to the river. A trickle, at first, but gradually the runs increased. And by the 1970s, a city sophisticate in Portland, with a few hours to spare in the early morning before business, could fish for the same silver prize as the natives who used to congregate at Willamette Falls. After a bitter separation, nature and man were back together in the arcadian valley.

Oregon City still looks like Pittsburgh, and that is not all bad. I walk along the sturdy row of century-old brick buildings next to the river, smokestacks puffing across the way. Grim-faced men in soiled hats change shifts at the James River Company paper mill. Army Corps of Engineers bureaucrats, with all the efficiency of high school hall monitors, check visitors who come to the locks in search of salmon.

"You mean you just wanna see the fish ladders?"

"Yeah."

"The hell for?"

John McLoughlin, the Hudson's Bay Company factor who founded this city and solidified the English trading empire on the Columbia, is buried here on a bluff. I leave the falls, content with the eight chinook who've brightened the gray morning, and walk up the hill to McLoughlin's grave. The father of the modern Northwest is buried next to his wife in a simple mound. I stand under maple and oak trees that weep the colors of New England, wet wind on my face. Kicking at the leaves reminds me of a day, some time ago, when a silk-skinned girl of sixteen in a Catholic uniform kissed me in the park, and I drove home so full of glow that I ran a red light and totaled out my family car. Another scent carries me back to a cross-country foot race and the last hill with one guy to pass, and failure. Inhaling the mist, I remember the time we drove the night into the ground in drunken anger after Richard Nixon carried every state in the union except one. We kicked in the faces of all the sodden Halloween pumpkins that looked back at us. My past is imprinted on me, a tattoo of sensory dimensions, released by a breath of fog-dampened air or the sight of a leaf of faded color. So it is with the Pacific salmon, who are guided home by the smells from their juvenile days. The Willamette is alive today because of them.

After fishing for chinook in the Columbia River, Rudyard Kipling wrote, "I have lived! The American continent may now sink under the sea, for I have taken the best it yields and the best was neither dollars nor love nor real estate."

When you pull a fish like a king salmon out of water, it overwhelms you: the size, the fight, the color, the connection between a landbound two-legger and sea-touring giant. An outsider has trouble understanding this infatuation with salmon. They're just fish, or lox on a bagel. But then you go to a waterfall deep in British Columbia's high country and see leaping sockeyes, worn and battered, with long green snouts, struggling the final miles to their alpine lake. Now you think of them as athletes. You check the elevation, nearly 3,500 feet above sea level in the Chilko River, and they become alpinists. What kind of fish climbs a mountain? A Pacific salmon, of course. And then you slow-cook one in foil over a fire, the meat rich with oil that provides sustenance for the long spawning journey, and they are delicacies. The flesh, rosy orange, pulls away from filament-thin bones and needs nothing to enhance the taste.

"You throw a hook into some ordinary-looking creek and pull out a twelve-pound salmon," said Thomas Wolfe, the writer, upon his visit to the Pacific Northwest in 1938. A picture of the author shows him in the kind of pose that has made Westerners howl for decades. Dressed in a three-piece suit, he's out in the woods somewhere along the riverbank, holding his catch—a salmon twice as long as his tie. "This is a country fit for Gods," Wolfe wrote home.

Talk to any native elder from Northern California to Alaska, and you hear the story of a god that lives deep in the middle of the ocean. It's the same story, this mythic explanation of salmon, that's been told in a thousand different tongues around campfires along the Northwest Coast. The Great God Salmon exists in spiritual form deep at sea. Once a year, the spirit puts on salmon skin to return to the land—the god's sacrifice to man. If offended, the salmon will not return. Thus, the fish are never molested; the eyes are never poked out. When the first salmon show up in the spring, a single fish is taken to an altar, where the spirit inside him is given thanks for returning.

It took only one generation of Oregon Country whites to offend the salmon, to the point of near-extinction in the case of some species. When Winthrop came up the Columbia, the river had an annual run of about sixteen million fish. Perhaps two million will return this year. The sins of our fathers were no mere venial lapses; they wiped out whole runs, and in some places, killed the rivers with them. A trail of lawsuits, international treaties, expensive gear and multimillion-dollar hatchery programs precedes the fish I can catch in the Columbia this month, if I can catch one.

Not so long ago, hooking a chinook in midrun was an elemental thrill. Winthrop described a typical scene in 1853:

Over the shoots between boulders and rifts of rock, the Indians rig a scaffolding, and sweep down stream with a scoop-net. Salmon, working their way up in high exhilaration, are taken twenty an hour, by every scooper. He lifts them out, brilliantly sheeny, and giving them with a blow from a billet of wood a hint to be peaceable, hands over each thirty-pounder to fusty attaches who in turn lug them away to the squaws to be cleaned and dried.

Like Lewis and Clark before him, Winthrop could not get over the size of the Indian fishery. Dried and flavored for the winter, the fish were packed into hundred-pound baskets and then traded as currency or used as food supply for the rest of the year. The newcomers, those Scots and Brits and French-Canadians in the employ of the Hudson's Bay Company, were astonished. They came with a farmer's view of the world. Here were these people who knew nothing about growing vegetables or raising cattle, and yet they had all the food they needed. The first group of white traders had arrived at the fort at Astoria with their own salted Atlantic salmon. They threw it away when they saw what could be taken from the Columbia. For $60, the Hudson's Bay Company purchased 7,500 pounds of dried salmon from the natives during their first year on the Columbia. In no time, they jumped into the industry themselves, salting barrels of Pacific salmon for discriminating diners in London and Boston. When Seattle was just a whorehouse and a sawmill huddled on Elliott Bay, Doc Maynard asked Chief Sealth to show him how to catch fish coming up the Duwamish River. The chief gladly shared his skill, after which Maynard started a small export business of salted salmon. By the time of Winthrop's visit, the first gillnet was introduced on the Columbia, brought over from Maine's Kennebec River. Rectangular like a long volleyball net, it was used to catch fish as they swam into openings in the net just large enough to snare their gills.

The first salmon cannery on the Columbia went into operation in 1867, after the process had been pioneering on the Sacramento River. One year after it opened, the Columbia cannery was packing eighteen thousand cases of salmon a year, each case containing 48 one-pound cans. The world took a big bite of Columbia River chinook and clamored for more. Soon, every river outlet had a cannery; every pilgrim who'd gone belly-up in a goldrush had a boat of some sort, and horses and mules were hooked to seines which were dragged across the shallows. Chinese immigrants, fresh from the slave-labor of building railroad tracks, were put to work inside the foul-smelling slaughterhouses, earning about a dollar a day. They were prohibited from fishing, that being the work of Scandinavians, who quickly monopolized the industry. By 1883, Columbia River canneries were packing 43 million pounds of salmon a year. But from that point on, the fishery was in decline. Nearly a hundred years later, only 1.2 million pounds of salmon would be taken from the Columbia.

What could have been a productive industry with plenty for everybody turned into a feeding frenzy, Klondike on the Columbia. Riverfront towns were born and died within a few years' time. Cause of death: salmon greed. The chinook used to be taken at man's doorstep, at the waterfalls. As salmon became a valued commodity, they were caught farther and farther away from their spawning grounds. Whoever got to the fish first took home the biggest prize, a race that has reached the extreme edge of avarice with today's Asian driftnet fleets. These ships from Taiwan and Korea and Japan—countries that do not have a single wild salmon returning to their shores—drag the middle of the North Pacific every night with up to thirty thousand miles of nearly invisible plastic net. This wall of death—strip mining the sea, as it's called—takes everything in its path, including dolphins and whales and shorebirds, but also millions of young Pacific salmon who are in the middle of their migratory journey from river to far side of the ocean and back again. It is an immoral fishery, bound to kill one of the great renewable sources of food in the ocean if not stopped within the next decade. But it has its roots in American salmon-mining schemes.

The first fishwheel was introduced in the Northwest in 1879, a scooper that churned with the current, grabbing salmon at every turn. Most returning Columbia River chinook are headed for journeys of up to a thousand miles—through the Snake to the desert of southern Idaho, up to the Okanogan River in Canada, and all points in between. By grabbing the salmon downriver with mechanical efficiency, the fishwheels wiped out entire upriver runs. Twenty years after they were introduced, seventy-nine fishwheels were operating day and night on the Columbia. When the contraptions were outlawed in the 1930s, unique gene pools of fish that only spawned in distant streams were gone, never to be replaced. Coastal trolling began in 1912, a way of getting the fish before they even entered fresh water. At the time, Columbia River canneries packed enough salmon to feed every person on earth four pounds a year. Old-timers like to point out that canned salmon, loaded into the knapsacks of American soldiers who fought in the trenches of World War I, fed the war machine of the Allies. By war's end, there was precious little salmon left to can.

But, not to worry, said the biologists whose ideas were paid for by the cannery owners. A new word was floating down the Columbia near the turn of the century—*hatcheries*. We'll do the spawning for them. Create our own fish. The concept was not local in origin; long after the River Thames had become too sick with industrial sludge to support a natural salmon run, the British were experimenting with artificial procreation, with limited success. In the Pacific Northwest, the idea caught fire: to people who saw resources as unlimited, hatchery production was an intoxicating concept. Salmon need cold (about fifty degrees or less), clean water running over a gravel bed to reproduce. Loggers were fast clogging and suffocating those channels with silt and debris. With hatcheries, only a few fish needed to return to keep the species alive; since they were pulled from the water before spawning, there was less reason to keep the rivers clean. The first Northwest hatchery was built in 1877, just downriver from Willamette Falls on the Clackamas River. By 1888, the United States Fish Commission was fully committed to an artificial spawning program. It was so modern. So efficient. So much more like farming. Plant a seed and harvest a crop. If enough seeds were planted, the fishwheels could churn forever.

Factory conception at hatcheries was simple: a ripe female was cut open and her eggs dumped into a bucket. Then the milt of the male was squeezed over the eggs. Quick sex, but it worked. In the spring, millions of newly hatched fry were dumped into a pond near the hatchery, where they were imprinted with the smells of the twentieth century. Downriver and out to sea they went, freshly minted, and in a few years' time they returned. Dealt to the counties as government patronage, hatcheries sprouted up and down the Columbia. But the runs never returned to the old glory days. Not even close. These hatchery fish—they were different. Strange, the Indians said. A little smaller. A little dumber. A little slower on the draw when predators came near. When millions of hatchery fry were put into the river, they overwhelmed the wild fish and spread disease on a mass scale. Interbreeding diluted the gene pool of the native fish. The nets at the mouth of the Columbia and the fishwheels upriver made no distinction between artificially spawned fish and natural runs. Thus, the introductions of hatcheries only accelerated the annihilation of wild fish.

Then came the dams, the biggest harvesters of salmon. In 1933, the federal government inaugurated the greatest public-works plan in history—a scheme to tame the Columbia and bring electricity to farms in the three-state basin of the river. The Dust Bowl refugees would be tilling green land, with an unlimited supply of water, and dinner tables in crowded homestead shacks would be lit by dirt-cheap hydropower. Within a half-century, 14 major dams were built on the Columbia and 13 on the Snake. All told, the River of the West and all its tributaries are now pinched by 136 dams, most used for irrigation to water 25 million acres of farmland in the inland Northwest. The price was the loss of more than half the natural salmon spawning grounds.

The big dams raised concrete curtains, twenty to fifty stories high, through which salmon could not penetrate. Fish ladders were built, but only on certain dams. Many of those did not work. Scaling a three-hundred-foot dam is not easy; the fish need little pools to rest in before continuing to leap up the stairs of the ladder. Some dams were too high for any kind of ladder. More than a thousand miles of upriver spawning grounds were lost forever with the construction of the Grand Coulee Dam, for example. On the Snake, the Hells Canyon Dam ended a desert chinook run on such tributaries as the Owyhee, Malheur, Boise and Payette rivers. The Bureau of Reclamation's dams on the Yakima River, built without fish ladders, wiped out a sockeye run that used to number 600,000 fish a year of the rich, lake-spawning salmon. For every loss of a run, a new hatchery was built downstream. They called these swap products "mitigation hatcheries," because they were supposed to mitigate the loss—kill a salmon run and gain a hatchery. Dams became the new symbols of the Northwest—cheap power for the people—but they nearly killed the old symbol.

By the 1960s, everybody in the Northwest could warm their ovens for pennies, but few could afford to cook salmon inside them. The big, beautiful Pacific chinook has always been considered an indigenous right. Like sea otters and timber, this resource was thought to be inexhaustible, a part of the landscape. It was only when the wild runs were nearly gone, when the museum staffers and university archaeologists came sniffing around the the few remaining fish camps like undertakers with measuring tapes, that emergency steps were initiated. In 1980, Congress gave the salmon equal footing with the network of dams, a historic move. After a half-century of dam-building and channel-dredging, the government did something for Nature: the act directed four states of the Northwest to try and restore the Columbia River salmon runs by whatever means possible. Fish ladders that could actually be ascended by salmon were built. Spawning areas were protected from further dredging. And some attention was finally given to the fish going the other way, the young. What these fingerlings need more than anything is a little help getting downstream and back to the ocean. Most of them die because there isn't enough flow in the river to move them on toward the ocean in time. It's a simple matter of meeting a biological deadline: their bodies are fast changing from creatures of fresh water to creatures of the sea; if they don't make it to the salt water within a few months, they die—a young Pacific salmon stuck in a river full of dams.

To help the fry on their way, the Army Corps of Engineers was told to release bursts of water during the spring runoff, essentially creating a fake river flow. But for several years running they have refused to release much water at all. Water is fuel for hydropower, say the Corps managers, who are slow to respond to the new law of the land and forever at war with the river. They came up with an alternative idea to transport the small fish downstream in Corps of Engineer highway caravans; for the last decade, trucking young fish has been the Army's solution to the loss of the world's greatest wild king salmon run.

From the towers of academia to the councils of Indian fishermen, screams of outrage have been directed at the Corps plan. Young chinook rely on a long swim downstream to gain smarts and maturity. Trucking them through this crucial period in their lives leaves them naïve and more vulnerable to predators. Their clocks are thrown off; they don't know precisely when to move on. More important, as University of Washington fisheries professor Norman Quinn points out, when young salmon swim downstream they pick up the biological map which will later guide them home. Each bend in the river, each outlet, triggers a hormonal reaction which will later lead the returning fish to their spawning grounds. If you send them toward the Pacific over an interstate highway, the only smell they pick up is from the inside of a Corp of Engineers truck.

Crossing the Columbia from Oregon into Washington, I'm surrounded by boats packed with anglers. For a few days this September, several thousand people will get to feel the way Rudyard Kipling felt. The fish are running hard this fall, hordes of chinook and coho heading for the interior, for mountain tarns and desert creeks and valley irrigation ditches. The lawsuits, the official acts of idiocy, the Rube Goldberg schemes of the Corps, the racist insults between Indians and whites—all are forgotten for a few days of fishing.

For Billy Frank, Jr., the fall fish run makes his heart race. That guy, the salmon, he's coming back. Goddamn! He's made it through a period of near-extermination. What's more, so have the Indians. Billy Frank's father used to say, "When the salmon are gone, there will be no more Indians." A Nisqually tribal member, approaching his sixtieth birthday, with long gray-black hair tied in a ponytail, Billy Frank, Jr., says, "Hey, I'm here. I'm alive. So are the salmon."

He's still jumpy around white fishermen. Because of salmon, he's been beaten and shot at and arrested more than ninety times. His boat has been sunk, his nets ripped, his car tires slashed, his children insulted, his home sprayed with graffiti. But as the twentieth century draws to a close, this American native feels as if he can finally walk into a room full of blond gillnetters without the fear that somebody's going to take a punch at him, or spit on him, or call him a drunk.

"I have this measuring stick I keep at home," he says. "If I can go into a sportsman's club and come out alive, I put a notch on it."

He lives near the mouth of the Nisqually River, just off the wildlife refuge and not far from the tree where his tribal ancestors signed a treaty with the American government that was supposed to give them access to their salmon run for eternity. Once, all six species of Pacific salmon returned to the Nisqually. Now, only the coho—also known as silver—and the chum return.

Citing the treaty of 1854, Billy and his father would paddle out into the Nisqually in cedar dugouts in front of their home at Frank's Landing, where they would hang nets during the fall coho runs. No sooner would they pull their first fish from the water than Washington State game wardens would arrest them as poachers. Billy Frank, Jr., said he was not just another angler, but a member of a sovereign nation with specific property rights to one river's fish runs. The first time Billy Frank, Jr., was hauled into jail for fishing, he was thirteen years old. Back and forth it went for nearly forty years. In time, most of the Nisquallies moved away from the river's mouth, forgot about the conservation culture of the salmon, went on welfare, died young, or killed themselves with alcohol. The salmon born in the Nisqually in south Puget Sound were caught by fleets of American fishermen off the Washington coast, by Canadians off Vancouver Island, by Russians off Siberia, and by Japanese dragging forty-mile-long driftnets. Fish that used to be taken at the Nisquallies' doorstep were snatched from the middle of the ocean. The few salmon that would make it all the way across the Pacific, down along the North American coast, into Puget Sound and up the Nisqually River were supposed to belong to Billy Frank, Jr., and his father and a handful of other Nisquallies who were trying to make a living as they'd always made a living. The Puget Sound runs dwindled, from ten million fish a year, to two million, to less than one million, to a few hundred thousand.

"The golden egg of the Northwest was this guy, the salmon, and they were destroying the golden egg," says Frank, a small man with a perpetually furrowed brow, wrinkled from woe. "They talk about cheap electricity. Hydropower. It's not cheap. It's all been paid for by the salmon. When these lights come on, a salmon comes flying out."

Frank fingers a gold salmon medallion around his neck. "That guy, the salmon, he just wants a little breather."

In 1970, Frank and other Indians whose ancestors had signed the original treaty with Governor Isaac Stevens sued the state of Washington in federal court. The judge was an appointee of President Nixon's, George Boldt, who had gained a reputation as a hardball conservative after he presided over the trial of student antiwar activists known as the Seattle Seven. For three years, Boldt heard testimony about the salmon as god, the salmon as food, the salmon as cultural icon, the salmon as the source of all things good in the Northwest. Ostensibly, it was a trial about numbers—who gets what. But it turned into a trial about broken treaties and a way of life ten thousand years old. What Billy Frank, Jr., remembers from the case was the hatred he saw in the eyes of state prosecutors. One assistant state attorney general broke his fist when he slammed it down while thundering against the Indian fishermen. When it was all over, Judge Boldt ruled that the Indians were entitled, by treaty, to take half the fish that returned to Washington waters—a stunning victory for the tribes. It was this court decision, which is to Northwest Coastal Indians what *Brown* v. *Board of Education* was to blacks in the American school system, that ended the fish wars for the Puyallups. A similar ruling extended the principle to Oregon treaty tribes.

At the time of the decision, Indians were taking only about five percent of the returning salmon. They now take half. The court decision caused widespread violence, battles between whites and natives not seen since the Indian wars of the 1850s. Boats were bombed. Nets were cut. Indians were shot at. About half the white fishermen went into bankruptcy. The state of Washington refused to enforce the court decision, a position which the Ninth Circuit Court of Appeals in San Francisco called "the most concerted official effort to frustrate a decree of a federal court witnessed in this century." Despite the continued struggle to overturn the decision led by Attorney General Slade Gorton—who came from a fish-processing family in Massachusetts but never understood the salmon culture of the Northwest—the United States Supreme Court upheld the Boldt decision. In their ruling, the justices referred to an earlier High Court decision in which Judge Joseph McKenna said salmon were as necessary to natives of the Northwest as the air they breathed.

The tribes had always felt they had a traditional right to a clean environment; with the Boldt decision, they gained a legal right. They hailed the ruling as a belated but honorable tribute to American justice. Beyond its political implications, what the court ruling did was bring Indians into the management game, which forced all parties to look hard at how to conserve the great original resource of the Northwest. A treaty was signed with Canada to protect fish bound for American waters. Fish managers started looking at the whole picture—logging, dams, pollution—and not just hatchery patronage numbers. Using the Boldt decision to protect the entire salmon habitat, the tribes had a legal tool to keep the rivers clean and Puget Sound from choking on its own excess. As passions died down and salmon runs started to improve, the decision was starting to look like a gift from the salmon god—the divine hand of the land.

And Billy Frank, Jr., the habitué of jail cells, hunted and harassed at night by game wardens, has become a close adviser of Washington Governor Booth Gardner. As chairman of the Northwest Indian Fisheries Commission, he now tells game wardens what to do. But he seems a man unsuited to vengeance. He looks at the coho hurrying up the Nisqually River and sees the spirit wearing the salmon skin—the silver flash of life. The Coastal Salish Indians, Winthrop said, had eyes for the sustenance of their lives which the whites had yet to develop. "In muddy streams, where Boston eyes would detect nothing, Indian sees a ripple and divines a fish," he wrote.

Frank says more whites have learned to see. And the natives who'd gone blind? Many are looking at the river again, looking without tears. "We just about got this thing turned around now," he says of the Puget Sound salmon runs. "It's taken more than a hundred years. But I tell my people to get ready. Get your smokehouses back in shape. Don't forget the ceremonies. That guy, the salmon, he's coming back."

East of the city of Seattle, nearly 100,000 people crowd the banks of tiny Issaquah Creek on a Sunday afternoon to look at battered chinook making their way to a spawning pond behind the shopping malls of suburbia. The creek is shallow, perhaps two feet deep at most, and no more than twenty feet wide. In places, it looks like nothing more than runoff from a lawn sprinkler. These foothills of the Cascades belong to the New Northwesterners now, young families who live in planned communities with Indian names like Klahanie Ridge. About twenty thousand people a year move into this part of the state, pushing the limits of Seattle's sprawl to the vertical edge of the Cascades. They profess wonderment at these big chinooks in their new neighborhood. It's certainly something to show the folks from Chicago. The Issaquah Salmon Festival brings everybody out of the new developments to look at the magic in their stream. Most of them don't connect the fish to their new homes, except as part of the scenery of this green corner of America. When the rains come in a few weeks, the Snoqualmie River, which flows through this part of King County, will swell up overnight and flood its banks, washing away thousands of salmon eggs. The river never used to flood with such force and regularity; the soggy lowland would soak it all up. Now, the wetlands are paved over for Hyundai dealers and Toys 'R' Us stores. The rain, instead of sitting in the natural reservoirs, runs off the pavement of the new suburbs with Indian names and floods the river, killing much of the next generation of fish.

Lining the banks of Issaquah Creek today are young women in leather mini-skirts and old men in Budweiser hats. The sun is out, the creek is thick with salmon. Children tell their parents the story of the life cycle of the fish.

All over the Northwest, the scene is repeated in the early days of autumn. At the University of Washington, the only college campus in the nation with its own salmon run, about four thousand chinook and coho are coming back again this year to a pond off Lake Union. A dentist across the lake from Seattle has imprinted enough fish to return to his backyard. If you wanted to, you could get Pacific salmon to return to your living room, says Jack de Yonge, a newspaperman who writes about salmon the way the French write about food. In Lake Washington, surrounded by a million people, 600,000 sockeye salmon have passed through on their way to the Cedar River, providing a big city fishery for the tastiest of all salmon. Like the chinook anglers in Portland, the sockeye fishermen present a picture of an urban oxymoron: while thousands of cars are stuck in commuter traffic on their way across the bridge into Seattle, boats bob along the lake angling for the big sockeyes. City stress on one side, country relief on the other. Most of the small boats are outfitted with $1,200 digital fish-finders—sonar—to help them track the schools of sockeye. There are so many salmon coming back through the locks that connect Puget Sound to Lake Washington this year that the daily limit has been upped from two to six fish a person. In retail markets, that fish sells for twelve dollars a pound.

Farther north, in the city of Everett, a group of children from the Jackson Elementary School patrol the little drainage ditch that runs from behind their playground to Puget Sound. For five years they've been trying to keep Pigeon Creek free of lawn fertilizer, industrial runoff, old tires and other enemies of salmon. Their teacher, Brandon King, came to Everett as a child from western Pennsylvania. His father used to take him to Pigeon Creek in the fall to show him the secret of life in the Pacific Northwest. Big wild cohos filled the creek then; it has not had a run for more than a decade. Under King's direction, the children have been planting salmon fry in the creek, hoping something might happen. This year, it did. While scouting around the creek, a fifth-grader spotted several silvers returning up the ditch. A miracle, they all said.

The rains have arrived. The roses of late summer look like melted wax on long stems. The sky is in a rage; no weak little mist is this. I'm in the green closet of the Stillaguamish River valley, about sixty miles northeast of Seattle at the western edge of the Cascades. Zane Grey, one of the originators of the Western novel, once said the Stilly was the best steelhead-fishing river in the world. If I could see the river, I might be able to judge for myself. The sky is too thick with horizontal rain to allow much deciphering of the water.

This is no place to get lost; it's full of hungry people who've been on strike at the Simpson Timber Mill in Darrington for most of the year. Various scarecrows in white collars hang in effigy along the main road. Tar Heel country, the valley here is populated by third-generation refugees from cut-over forest lands of Southern Appalachia. Some of them still make moonshine behind their tree-shrouded homesteads. I see a few stooped-over figures draped in camouflaged rain gear out in the cow fields picking magic mushrooms, psilocybin, which sprout in great abundance in the rain country. They call this valley the Bluegrass Capital of the Northwest, but all I can think of are the toothless hillbillies in *Deliverance*.

I find the little village of the Stillaguamish Tribe, about a hundred Indians living in new houses surrounded by a forest of dripping evergreens. Long ago, the federal government said they were no longer a legally recognized tribe. In trying to restore their treaty status, an old Stillaguamish woman named Esther Ross stood in front of a bicentennial wagon train in 1976, making headlines across the nation, and she once threw the bones of a dead ancestor on the desk of Governor Dan Evans. They are now a legally recognized tribe. This morning, about two dozen Stillaguamish gillnetters have been out on the raging river fishing for chum salmon. They display their catch, about three thousand fish, in front of the village this morning. Everybody comes out of the homes, smelling of wood smoke, and stands in the rain to look at the fish. Been a long time since this many salmon have been seen by these people.

An old Chevrolet pulls up, full of kids. A man without front teeth, eyes heavy from little sleep, steps out of the car and opens his trunk. He has another two hundred pounds of fish to add to the haul. They weigh the fish and laugh in the rain. Japanese wholesale buyers will pay them the best price they've ever received for their chum catch.

"What're you going to do with your money?" I ask the man.

"Buy some food."

"And?"

"Maybe some tires for my car. Got my eye on a pair down in Arlington."

Zane Grey would not recognize the Stilly today; it runs brown like 7–11 coffee. I've come up here not to see the Indians but to look at the biggest threat to the silver flash of life in all the years the Stillaguamish River has carried salmon. State biologists estimate the fishery, including crab beds in the Puget Sound bay into which this river empties, is losing $3 million a year because so much logging debris is clogging the river and smothering spawning channels. With every passing hour of this storm, the river rises another foot, knocking out the resting pools for upstream-bound salmon, scooping up the freshly fertilized eggs. The reason for this carnage lies upstream.

I climb into a van with Pat Stevenson, biologist for the Stillaguamish Tribe. The rain intensifies. It's about 9:30 in the morning, but the sky seems as dark as an earthen ceiling. The ditches on either side of the road resemble small streams. We drive for about an hour, winding up a mountain road, until we reach the bridge over Deer Creek, one of the main tributaries of the Stilly and a world-class steelhead river—that's wild steelhead, not hatchery-bred. Though technically not salmon, the winter-running steelhead trout look just like salmon and act just like salmon. They weigh up to forty pounds and can grow to fifty inches in length. Catching one with fly rod and reel is an angler's dream. What happened to Deer Creek is the steelhead's worst nightmare.

"Sure you wanna cross this?" Stevenson asks me. "Bridge may not be here when we come back."

The river roars downstream in boiling, brown rapids, four and five feet high. "A few weeks ago, this was your basic babbling brook," he says.

We cross the bridge and continue another few miles to road's end. We then hike a few hundred yards in cut-over forest land, large cedar stumps all around.

"Hope you're ready for this," he says.

I thought I would be, but I am not. We edge up to a vast canyon, where the earth cracks in layers. I feel as if I'm watching a slow-motion earthquake. Streams of mud and clay and gravel slide down from all sides of the canyon, funneled into Deer Creek. The debris backs up, fills with water during storms such as today's downpour, then explodes, scooping out every steelhead and salmon spawning nest in its path.

"Don't get too close," Stevenson warns me. I've never seen anything like this—a cancerous canyon five hundred feet across, two thousand feet long and eight hundred feet deep. More than a million cubic yards of debris have slid into the river. Five years ago, this was a gentle forest slope. Then, the Georgia Pacific Timber Company clearcut most of the trees in the watershed. Now, the land will not hold water. The logging company says it's nature's fault, not theirs.

When you press timber-industry leaders about the effect of land-savaging logging practices, they sometimes deflect the main question and talk about the future of salmon: just like the Japanese, we'll raise them on farms and breed them in hatcheries, they say. British Columbia is already headed in that direction. Once, the Fraser River used to support a sockeye run of up to 40 million salmon. This year, about 2 million fish will return. Log-clogged channels and debris-covered spawning grounds strangled the run. Within a few years, however, British Columbia is expected to pass the Japanese in number of salmon raised in the netted pens of fish farms. These small, odd hybrids never know the ocean depths or the cold gravel of a mountain stream. They are raised like cattle, frequently diseased by bacteria from their cluttered feces. The Weyerhaeuser Company tried to get into salmon ranching in Oregon in the 1980s. They spent $40 million to create a hardy breed of trained coho. It didn't work, and this year the timber company threw in the towel on fish farming and went back to clearcutting.

"Salmon are more than just Burger King sandwiches," Norman Quinn, born and raised in New York City, told me one day at the University of Washington. "They are the canary in the mine shaft, an indicator of the health of everything we care about here."

In the pouring rain above the Stillaguamish, land crumbling all around me, I feel dizzy and disoriented, as if one misstep is going to send me stumbling into the Deer Creek slide. There is no silver flash of life here, only the color of destruction. If all the salmon of the Northwest were raised on farms and bred in hatcheries, slides like this would be common, children would have few reasons to care about drainage ditches behind their schools, and visitors from Chicago would have less to marvel at on a fall day. The land above the rivers would be more prone to lose the thin layer of green life that has been attached to it since the glaciers melted away. What's more, it would lose the resonance of spirit.

Chapter 11

HARVEST

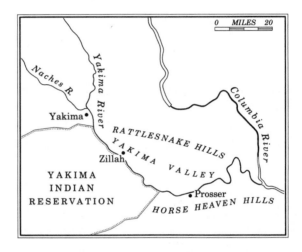

I'm freezing; the forest floor has given up the day's heat, and the pine needles are stiff with cold. I'm hungry, my stomach a hollow melon. I'm alone—just a few minutes ago, I started talking to myself. Dangerous stuff, this gibberish without the brake of contention. In the valley below, there is warmth and food and company. There are calories in all colors and grapes of joy growing from earth as rich as German chocolate cake. Not yet, not yet. I'm on a diet of cold air and barren ground to prepare for the harvest. Food tastes better after a fast. Wet fruit finds a welcome home in a dry mouth. The sober head is more receptive to the spin of champagne. So I walk along the cold shallows of the Little Naches River, muttering like a politician in an echo chamber, stomach on empty, head full of tomorrow and the valley. The Yakima Valley. Eden with irrigation.

I started walking just east of the Cascade Crest, intending to follow gravity's groove through the pine forests down to the valley. Up here, after years of spring runoff and wind-ripping, the surface holds nothing but a few generations of alpine mulch. The Naches is a cocky little stream, darting through rock cleavages and around downed timber, quicker and deeper than it should be. It drains the country where William O. Douglas recovered his strength after a childhood bout with polio, the fall elk-hunting ground of Yakima warriors. The Naches pulls the Bumping and American Rivers with it down a chasm to the valley, where the snowmelt of the Cascades arrives at the doorstep of the desert with a promise of life. Once there, the Naches joins the Yakima River. About seven inches of rain a year falls in the Valley, a home for rattlesnakes and ground squirrels that don't need fresh drinking water to stay alive; they metabolize moisture from desert plants.

In two days of wandering the Naches all I've had is water laced with powdered lemonade—sugar with food coloring. When I take a long pull from the lemonade, it gives me a quick boost, causing me to speed up, followed by the inevitable letdown. The sun has now passed beyond the crest and the massif of Rainier, which knocks down most of the storms from the west and leaves this area parched in its shadow. Daydreaming, I'm startled by a splash in the river, as if a big stick had been thrown nearby. I look downstream and see the surface break with trout, big guys, leaping for late season dragonflies, those oddly intertwined bugs who always seem to fly in tandem. Watching the trout jump has a Pavlovian effect on me; they are a suggestive tease to the stomach. I've never looked at a fly-covered cow and thought of cheeseburgers; but as I watch these rainbows, I think of white flesh, moist, cooked just right over a fire.

I do some quick rationalizing and conclude that it wouldn't be cheating to break my fast with a native fish. After all, they're part of the natural bounty. I set my pack down and rig up my portable Zebco rod, two pieces with a spinner reel. Grandpa would never forgive me for this, using a lazy man's tool for a sporting test. I tie on a goofy-looking fly, something that might pass for an earring in West Hollywood, and float the little sucker downstream. The current carries my fly to a pool created by downed logs. Then—*splash!* The line goes taut. The Zebco whines. Hot damn, I've got one of the little bastards! He goes for cover under the logs, but I cross over the stream and reel him in on the other side. I flop him onto the rocks—a beauty, about thirteen inches, a fine rainbow. I'm so hungry I'm ready to sample trout sushi. I cut him open to see what he's been eating; the guts don't tell me much. In ten minutes, as the last of the light slips away, I catch two more trout. Now, I'm ready to feast.

On the riverbank, I start a fire in a clearing. I rustle through my pack and find a single beer—cold from the free-falling temperatures. Now, I've got two pieces of a paradise pie. I put the beer in the Naches for an extra chill. When the fire settles down into hot coals, I take out my little Boy Scout frying pan, squeeze a bit of olive oil on the bottom, and balance it over the edges of two rocks near the fire. In a few minutes, the oil starts to sizzle, and I put the three trout in the pan, which is too small to hold them. I suspect they'll shrink up into a fine fit. There's no wind in this alpine valley tonight, just the roar of the river. A moon-sliver pokes through the woods to the south. I retrieve my beer, take my fish out of the pan and flop 'em on a plate. I say to my stomach, Gentlemen, start your engines.

Afterward, I light a cigar and lie back against my pack. I think of something Winthrop said when he was camped with two Indians and three horses on the banks of this river in 1853, a few months before it became a wagon trail so steep that oxen were lowered down by tether. "I fed my soul with sublimity," he wrote. After a dinner by campfire in the Cascades, there is no better dessert than sublimity. Tomorrow, I plan to consume the bounty of the Yakima Valley. Despite my repast of trout and cold beer, I can't quell a rising food lust. I think of apples so big they barely fit in the palm of your hand. Grapes the color of passion. Quail and duck fresh from the irrigation swamplands. A sip of Chardonnay to wash down the duck, or maybe one of the three-year-old Merlots from the upper valley. Or a thick, rust-colored beer brewed with Yakima hops. Pears, or a few cherries left in cold storage from the summer harvest. Late peaches. I've orchestrated a stampede of anticipation, but I've still got fifty miles of river to follow.

Along the banks of this river, Winthrop treated his horses to a patch of wild pea vines and himself to a grouse which he shot and slow-cooked over the fire. His head sated with sublimity, his stomach full of grouse, he fell asleep next to the cold river. Later, he concluded, "There are things to be said in behalf of cobblestone beds by rivers of the Northwest. I was soft to the rocks, if not they to me."

I wake up shivering, the top of my sleeping bag covered with frost. It's not quite morning. I try to return to a dream, just to see how it turns out, but I can't get back in. I get up, dress, fold my bag and continue downstream. At a junction of the Naches and the Bumping, a road leads down to the Yakima Valley from Chinook Pass. By plan, I'm supposed to follow the river to the valley, just as Winthrop did. It's the late twentieth century, no reason to stay on two feet; Winthrop didn't have the benefit of the interstate highway system. I stick my thumb out. An hour goes by, three cars pass. Then a logging truck stops, and a man with a baseball cap emblazoned with the slogan "We Interrupt this Marriage to Bring You Deer-Hunting Season," leans over and says, "Hop in." He's heavily into deforestation, carrying a load of old-growth ponderosa pine down to the mill in Yakima. His cargo looks a lot like the trees I slept next to, two-hundred-year-old beauties. With the casualties in back and me in front we wind down the road along the Naches.

Coming into the Yakima Valley, we pass a few orchards in the high country, sloped rows of trees clinging to hillsides and bluffs. The earth is overcooked, seared of any late season vegetation, but huge patches of green are grafted to this quilt of brown. Sprinkler heads spit water above the treetops. The blades of giant windmills rotate slowly, trying to mix the cold air of the orchard floor with the warmer air ten feet above ground. The Naches widens and slows, changing from mountain stream to valley irrigation artery. Along the river, before we enter the sprawl of the town of Yakima, shacks of corrugated tin, plywood and cardboard appear, the homes of migrants. An army of forty-five thousand Mexicans picks the hops that are brewed into three-dollar-a-glass ales, the spearmint that becomes gum for sluggers in the World Series, the Rainier cherries that so delight, the grapes that ferment to fine white wine, the asparagus of spring, the peaches and pears and prunes for summer tables, the apples for the world.

According to natural law, nothing should grow here but sage and scrub brush and those creatures of the desert that don't need drinking water to stay alive. On the floor of the Yakima Valley I do a 360-degree head turn, and all I see are fruit trees and vineyards and hop fields at the height of life. The wind carries the scents of the season, fresh-pressed cider, grapes under crush. Beyond the hillsides of irrigated green are the desert tops of two ranges which rise above the valley, Rattlesnake Hills and Horse Heaven Hills. Floating above the horizon on the western skyline is the 12,225-foot volcano of Mount Adams, a suspended snow cone.

The apples on Jim Doornink's farm have reached climax. Ripe. Sweet. Full-colored. Firm. I pick a Golden Delicious, the color of winter sun. I polish it on the nap of my jeans and then bite into the fruit Eve used to tempt Adam, the ancient Greek symbol of love and fecundity. All that fiber and potassium and Vitamin C in a sweet orb of eighty calories.

"This is the best day of the year to pick these apples," says Doornink, a big man in his late thirties with massive forearms who looks somewhat like his brother Dan, a onetime fullback for the Seattle Seahawks. He takes out a small handheld pressurizer and tries to punch through an apple.

"Look at that," says Doornink. It takes eighteen pounds of pressure per square inch before the apple breaks, more than enough to meet the minimum Washington State apple firmness standard of eleven pounds per square inch. Nowhere else in the world are farmers required to poke eleven pounds of pressure against their apples before they're allowed to sell them. He cuts open a few Red D's and sprays them with iodine. The fruit goes black before it lightens in the center—the proof of maximum sweetness, another state requirement. But I don't need the pressurizer or iodine to tell me that.

Ever since Doornink unleashed the bees of April for a pollination orgy, he's been waiting for this—peak week. Every apple farmer in the Yakima Valley is jacked. Nobody sleeps more than a few hours at a time. The trees are dripping red and gold and a dozen shades in between. Following the blossom, the apples absorbed a summer of desert sun, sixteen hours of light every day, and then a month of cool night temperatures. An apple that hasn't experienced the hard times of cold is flat, tasteless, bland. But an apple that's hung in the hundred-degree temperatures of day and held through the thirty-five-degree nips of night is a fruit with experience. Cold helps to brings out acid, which makes an apple tart. Color is painted by warmth. When they connected snowmelt to the sun a hundred years ago here, they created a valley of plenty: The farmers of Washington will harvest half the apples grown in America this year—about 12 billion pieces of fruit, and more cherries than anyplace on earth.

Bouncing in the seat of Doornink's truck, we listen as the radio picks up traffic reports from across the Cascades in Seattle. Here, we're looking at a seventy-five-degree day, the sun reflecting back off the snows of Mount Adams, the air full of harvest and free of clouds. In Seattle, traffic is backed up practically to the Canadian border and drizzle is falling. They haven't seen the sun for two weeks. I pick up a Yakima station, all Spanish, and another local one, all John Bircher, the broadcaster warning about the danger of a civilian population not sufficiently armed with AK-47s and other semiautomatic fruits of the Constitution. Doornink and I drop off a load of apples at the cold-storage facility, a warehouse of dark manipulation. Used to be, all apples were sold fresh until about Christmas, when they started to go mushy. Then came cold storage—or "controlled atmosphere," as they call it here. All but about one percent of the oxygen is sucked from the air inside these blackened rooms, and the temperature is maintained at thirty-one degrees. The conditions keep the fruit suspended, as is, for about a year, allowing farmers to sell a crisp apple twelve months after it was picked from the tree. A marvel of technology, controlled atmosphere has one drawback: every year, says Doornink, they lose a worker or two who mistakenly steps into the vacuum without his bottled oxygen.

Back at the Doornink family farm, I sample the Rome Beauties—my favorite, midsized, almost perfectly round. Doornink owns sixty acres, mostly Red and Golden Delicious, but he grows pears and cherries for diversity. Last year, he lost about fifty dollars for every bin of apples he sold. Too much sun. Too many apples. The fruit looked bad. Throughout the valley, millions of pounds were left to rot on the trees or poured into canyons. Farmers paid juice processors to take them off their hands. This year, the the volume is down, the fruit looks good, and Doornink and his wife, Rena, are hoping to go to Europe on the proceeds from the harvest.

Jim Doornink wanted to be a doctor like his father, Glenn, the patriarch. Side by side, they look Dutch Calvinist and mean, Gothic farmers, big-boned, slow to laugh, with massive hands. The vagaries of working the land shape a country face so differently from a city face. Usually, it's an edge-of-bankruptcy look, neck and brow wrinkled by sun and worry. The doctor's father was a dairy farmer who came to the valley in 1928 and then went bust. The doctor bought the orchard in 1957. Jim started working in the fields at the age of six. Today, with the fruit plump and full-colored, the Doorninks are lighthearted and generous of spirit. Those Dutch faces shine.

The surgeon inside Jim Doornink has never left. He is a practical doctor of horticulture. In the yard next to the eighty-year-old house where Jim and Rena Doornink live are rows of experimental trees. Doornink is constantly grafting one species to another, toying with taste and look. The average American eats nineteen pounds of apples every year, mostly Red Delicious, a species almost unheard of fifty years ago. Tastes change. If the consumer ditches the Red Delicious for one of the new boutique apples growing on small farms throughout the Northwest, then what? Some growers think the Red Delicious has already reached its peak. Doornink does not want to be left high and dry with yesterday's fruit fad. The great thing about apples is that they lend themselves so easily to genetic alteration. A well-read amateur can play fruit god, adding a touch of tart here, a douse of pink there, grafting to make smaller sizes for smaller appetites. The aerobic apple is all the rage now, a cute, eight-bite snack that fits into the purse or the suit pocket of a fat-phobic urbanite.

"Apples are kind of like kids," says Doornink. "They all come from the same human family, but they all look slightly different. If you were to take ten thousand seeds cut of this orchard, you'd get ten thousand different apples."

"A valley bare and broad," is the way Winthrop described this desert floor of the Yakima Valley. His prophetic powers were missing here; bothered by heat and conflicts with his Indian guides, he turned surly and short-sighted. Taking shelter at a Jesuit mission, he dined on local potatoes and salmon from the river, and argued philosophy with the blackrobes from the Society of Jesus. He poked fun at their attempts to wean the Indians away from polygamy and fishing. The Yakimas might take to potato farming, said Winthrop, but giving up spousal variety was another thing. He noted that the native women of the valley were gorgeous, much different from the round-faced, squat coastal tribes. "A strange and un-lovely spot for religion to have chosen for its home of influence," Winthrop wrote of his overnight stay in the mission. "It needed all the transfiguring power of sunset to make this desolate scene endurable."

The sign in the upper Yakima Valley says: WELCOME TO YAKIMA—THE PALM SPRINGS OF WASHINGTON. The desolate scene is more than en-durable, thanks to the transfiguring power of water, but Palm Springs it's not. Five mountain dams provide water for a half-million acres of farmland in the valley. The Yakima River, birthed in snowmelt just east of Snoqualmie Pass, is held back by the turn-of-the-century dams of Keechelus, Kachess and Cle Elum. Two other forks, Tieton and Bumping, are also pinched by reservoirs. Every winter the farmers of the Yakima Valley watch the snow pile up in the Cascades; if the white tops disappear too early, as they did this year, water battles break out. The irrigation system here is an Old West anachronism: first grab, first served. If you were given irrigation access eighty years ago, you still get first shot at the water in a drought year, even if your farm is of marginal importance. Not only farmers are bound by the old rule; the tribes of the 1.3-million-acre Yakima Indian Reservation were promised by treaty adequate stream flow for their salmon runs. This spring saw the largest downstream migration of young salmon in thirty-five years. The Yakimas wanted enough water released from the irrigation dams to help those fish get down to the Columbia, and then out the gorge to the Pacific.

The adult salmon, four- and five-year chinooks, are going upstream today. At an irrigation canal juncture, I watch them flop and leap up through a fish ladder. The same water that will fatten Jim Doornink's apples is helping the big kings return to spawning grounds in the upper valley. Nature brought every taste of the human palate together here. Once, it was all covered by water, an Ice Age lake which shrank to a river that left behind twenty stories of rich sediment. Now it brings food to the tables of the world.

At the county fair, the 4-H Clubbers say if all of this year's harvest were placed in boxcars of a single train, that train would stretch from here to Chicago. The fair is a celebration of fertility, a Yellow Brick Road of produce. The pumpkins dance. The squash gator. The gourds crawl. Japanese pear-apples—small and round, light beige in color. Firm like an apple, but sweet like a pear. An after-dinner fruit. And here's grapes—four shades of purple.

Over a dinner of peppercorn duck, slices of scarlet tomatoes, cucumbers, squash, bread and a bottle of Sémillon—all Yakima Valley bounty, of course—I'm told the story of the Red Delicious apple, which is relayed like the narrative of the Nativity. In the midnineteenth century, a farmer in Peru, Iowa, noticed a renegade seedling growing among the apple trees he'd been raising in neat rows. He mowed the fledgling tree down twice, and twice it reappeared, more vigorous than ever. Finally, impressed with the tree's fight, the farmer let it grow. In ten years' time, it blossomed and bore a single apple—the first Red Delicious. Grafts from that tree were eventually brought to the Yakima Valley.

"And every damn Red Delicious apple grown in this valley is a descendant of that one tree," says Lowell Lancaster, an oversized orchardist who is sitting across from me at the dinner table. He looks like Hoss from *Bonanza*. Everything in this valley—produce and people—seems big. The fruit at the county fair was of extraordinary size. Surely, the apples of the Yakima Valley get some boost from the lab.

"Just one," says Lancaster. "Ethylene gas."

These huge apple farmers wait for me to react, expecting some lecture on chemicals in fruit. They hold grins and food in their mouths, and then laugh all around. One of them gets a piece of green bean stuck on his front teeth.

"Yeah, ethylene gas, that's what the apples themselves produce as they start to get ripe," says Lancaster. "It's like a dog in heat. Tells the fruit it's time to get ripe. If it's late in the season, with a frost on the way, we spray ethylene to help get everybody going. Puts 'em in the mood to get ripe."

The dirty word here is Alar, trade name for a growth-regulator that brings a brighter touch of red to apples and gives them a longer shelf life. A decade ago, no one had heard of Alar in the Yakima Valley. Apples, like tomatoes of thirty years ago, were raised fresh and fat without uniform size or look. Then the packagers and mass marketers started to influence the growers. They wanted all the fruit to look the same, factory-painted, firm enough to hide the scars from transportation. The supermarket chains, with their demands for color conformity, became one of the worst enemies of the small grower. Around the same time, an innovative Wenatchee Valley farmer named Grady Auvil started raising the biggest and best-tasting sweet cherry every produced—the Rainier, nearly as big as a plum, light yellow in appearance, with a blush of pink—but he couldn't sell it to the big fruit wholesalers because it shows its bruises rather than hiding them as Bing cherries do. As a result, only a few thousand acres of Washington grow what has to be the best cherry in the world.

With apples, the buyers from Safeway and A & P wanted a deep red that would hold its color for months past the harvest. Such a thing is impossible, unless helped along by chemicals. In time, like a coach secretly giving his best runner steroids, and feeling guilty whenever the athlete broke a record, the apple farmers of Washington started using Alar, and they experienced years of tremendous growth and prosperity. Salesmen from the chemical companies and big food chains convinced the farmers they couldn't live without it, saying the consumer wanted a red that was nearly artificial in appearance instead of the duller, natural tone. Alar turned farmer against farmer; those who used it had a competitive edge over those who did not.

When researchers found that massive doses of Alar could cause cancer in lab rats, the market for Washington apples crashed, no matter the color or background of the fruit. Many of the small growers, some of the last of the nation's family farmers, most of whom had never used Alar, were forced into bankruptcy. Others dumped their fruit or gave it to the homeless. They blamed a concerted media attack—"television terrorism," they called it—for their bad times. Never before had the apple, the very embodiment of good health, taken such a hit. Nobody claims to use Alar now. Mention of the word is like bringing up an old girlfriend in the presence of a new wife.

I pick through the rest of my duck, which has a pear glazing atop it. More fruit stories pour forth from the farmers. The first apple tree was brought to the Northwest by the Hudson's Bay Company. The tree, planted at Fort Vancouver on the Columbia in 1825, still bears fruit.

"Betcha didn't know that apples and roses come from the same family? You can even graft a rose onto an apple tree."

The table goes silent. We pick at our teeth and food for a few minutes. A farmer sitting at the far end of the table speaks up for the first time tonight. "The Golden Delicious came from cow shit," he says.

"No shit."

"Cow shit," says the fellow. "What happened was, a cow ate an apple and shit the seeds out. One of those seeds, carrying the strains of other apples, grew into the the first Golden Delicious."

Granny Smith apples are the product of the garbage of a New Zealand woman who dumped rotting fruit in a creekbed. They grew up into trees which produced a tart, freckled green apple. She gave them away to her friends, who referred to the treat as "Granny Smith's apples."

It's getting near bedtime for big Lowell. He's expecting to make good money this year, after the disaster of last year, and is just scratching to get at the dawn. The only thing worse than the loss from overabundance was a long-ago freeze. Early November, twenty years ago, an arctic breeze scampered down through Canada along the Okanogan Valley into Washington, freezing up all the fruit trees while they still had sap in their veins. The sugar flow went hard, and expanded, causing the trees to literally explode.

"You could hear them pop, one after another—pop, pop, pop," says Lowell. "Never seen anything like it. Lost most of the orchard."

Following the Yakima River downstream toward the Columbia, I enter the wine country and a culture far removed from that of the apple growers. A person who harvests *vinifera* grapes for premium wine is not a farmer but an alchemist. Among the trellised vineyards, I hear music today, the sound of crush. At the Hogue family farms, across the railroad tracks along the river, the hops are recently in, the asparagus has been pickled, and now it's time to make some wine. Great bunches of Cabernet Sauvignon grapes are dumped into a vat, where they are crushed and the juice drained. From there, the juice goes to stainless steel storage and then to oak barrels and, in two years' time, to the market—about three hundred cases of the most eagerly sought-after red wine in the Northwest. What sets the Hogue family vino off from the other wines of the world— aside from the taste, a high-acid Cabernet so crisp some people drink it with seafood—has to do with the volcanoes to the east, the snow atop them, and the far northern latitudes of this valley that was dismissed by Winthrop and other nineteenth-century prophets as useless.

Here, a few fruit farmers looking for crop diversification, aided by a handful of young hotshots from California, have gilded the Yakima Valley.

There are no stone cottages or elegant chateaus or pseudorustic tasting cellars in this part of the valley. For that matter, there is no history. This is a place of concrete apple juice warehouses and dry hills carved up by dirt-bike trails. On the same day that winemaker Rob Griffin is overseeing the crush of red grapes out in back, he has bottled a small rattlesnake which he found slithering around the front. Griffin slaps a Hogue Cellars label on the jar of the rattler's new home. "It'll be a good year for snakes," he says.

In less than twenty years, the Pacific Northwest has become the greatest premium-wine-producing area in North America outside California. The wine growers here are not the peasants of Tuscany or the Ph.D. farmers of the Napa Valley. They are people like Wayne Hogue, a onetime sharecropper, then a hop farmer, now a genius. After working years for other people, he went out on his own with forty acres of hops in 1949. Over the decades he added spearmint, selling the mint oil to Wrigley's, and Concord grapes, which he sold to Welch's, and potatoes, which he sold to burger chains. Around the family dinner table at Christmas, the Hogues used to drink jug wine made by Mateus and toasted the new year with Andre's Cold Duck champagne.

By the mid-1960s, a few small growers in the valley were starting to experiment with *Vitis vinifera*, the grapes that produce the world's great wines. As a hedge against the highs and lows of crop prices, the Hogues planted ten acres of premium wine grapes in 1972, thinking maybe they could sell a few to the Californians during a down year for hops. The climate was right, with more than seventeen hours of daylight in June, a critical grape development period. The Yakima Valley has two more hours a day of sunlight than the Napa Valley during peak growing season. Looking at the globe, the growers noted that the Yakima Valley was located between the 46th and 48th Parallels, the same northerly latitude

as Burgundy and Bordeaux. With irrigation water, and the sun predictable, growing conditions can be tightly controlled, the grapes receiving
the same amount of water as the French areas would receive naturally.
Grapes ripened to full color in the long hot days, and gained enough acid
for flavor in the cold nights.

The shot heard around the wine-producing world was fired in 1966 by
André Tchelistcheff, considered the dean of California winemaking. He
tasted a Washington Gewurztraminer and pronounced it the best in
America. From then on, young graduates of the oenology school at the
University of California at Davis began to look north.

"I came here with a genuine sense of mission," says Griffin. "Everybody
said, 'Don't go up there, Rob. It's too cold in the winter for grapes to stay
alive.' I showed up in 1977, and there wasn't much to look at. But all the
ingredients for world-class winemaking were here—the soil, the climate,
the water." He started work at Preston Wine Cellars, down the valley
near Pasco, seeking to develop a crisp, dry white. He came up with a
Chardonnay and a Sauvignon Blanc that won so many admirers that
when young Griffin showed up at the Dom Perignon cellars in Reims for
a visit, he was welcomed at the champagne shrine as a celebrity from
the wine-growing frontier.

"They'd actually heard of me, Rob Griffin from the Yakima Valley," he
says.

The Hogues hired Griffin in 1984, when the family decided to get
serious about winemaking. The brothers, Gary and Mike, and their father,
Wayne, sold their first vintages in the early 1980s from a roadside card
table. Then a Chenin Blanc from that period won a gold medal at an
international contest, and the Hogues were on their way. At first, they
were uncertain about what to call their wine and how to market it. They
were farmers, after all, not lawyers on a lark or urban exiles looking for
a hobby and a tax haven. As Gary Hogue says, "I grew up with shit on
my shoes." The role model at the time was Chateau Ste. Michelle, a
pioneer Washington winery known mainly for its Riesling, sold in all fifty
states and throughout Europe and Japan. Recently, it was named the
best vintner in America. But the Hogues were uncomfortable with
French-sounding pretense for a Washington wine.

"There aren't any chateaus here," says Gary Hogue. "I doubt if there's
a building older than a hundred years in this valley. We didn't want to
be something we weren't, some Euro-winery or whatnot. We figured what
we had here was crisp and clean and fresh, like the country here. Finally,
we just put our names on it—Hogue Cellars, Yakima Valley wine. Wine

is such an ego thing; it's the only crop where you can follow it all the way through the chain and stand in front of people and say, 'How do you feel about this?' "

At the same time, up the river from Hogue, a former New York attorney named David Staton was starting to turn out Chardonnays and Rieslings that were beating all California whites in national wine-tasting contests. The Riesling of Washington has enough acidity to balance the grape's natural sweetness, an original taste. In Oregon, the Pinot Noirs from the Willamette Valley were causing Frenchmen to scramble to their maps of North America. Staton, with winemaker Rob Stuart, another Cal Davis graduate, pioneered a vineyard trellising method that allowed more air to circulate around the grapes and gave them maximum sun exposure. As a hedge against winter freezing, he came up with a drip irrigation system that forced the roots to go deep for water rather than spread out along the surface. In the alluvial Yakima Valley, he found that roots could go thirty feet down and still be in rich soil. At one time, he thought the best hope for American winemaking was in California. No more. The temperature variations of the Yakima Valley—a fifty-degree drop from noon to midnight is not uncommon in the spring and fall—were perfect for full-flavored grapes. By comparison, he says, California wines are flat and overripe.

The future is in red grapes. The biggest problem the Hogues had with their Merlot and Cabernet Sauvignon last year was keeping it in stock. Recently, the hop farmer's 1985 Cabernet Sauvignon Reserve was chosen the Best of the Show from among two thousand entries at the largest international wine competition in the country. A few years earlier, when the brothers tried to peddle their wine at the finer restaurants in Seattle, they were told to go away and take their stinking fruit and berry wine with 'em.

Griffin talks like a true evangelist. "Everybody thought the Mount St. Helens eruption was going to kill the Yakima Valley wine industry. We got three inches of ash on the ground here. The sky went completely dark. But the best grapes are planted in the worst soil. They'll tell you that in France. Volcanic soil drains better than anything. It's not fertile. It's sterile. It's silica, what they use to make glass. But all you need is a good medium."

As the color of an October day gives way to the soft tones of night, Gary Hogue cracks a year-old Chardonnay. We sit outside and watch the light shrink on the Rattlesnake Hills, and listen to the last sounds of harvest. We are surrounded by the best products of the earth at this latitude, under the benign influence of these volcanoes and the life-giving water from the Naches and the Yakima. Theodore Winthrop looked around and saw a fallow basin; I think of the Yakima Valley as a young bride at the altar, about to begin a full life. Hogue, dressed in plaid shirt and workboots, keeps asking me what I think of his Chardonnay. The bottle is nearly empty now, and I'm not sure how to describe it. I review all those wine terms: should I say it has a delicate aroma, with a complex but subtle bouquet, outstanding clarity, well-shaped body with just the right touch of vinosity, or should I talk up the acidity and residual sugar? We drain the bottle, and I turn to Hogue.

"It tastes like the Northwest."

Chapter 12

GOD'S
COUNTRY
CANCER

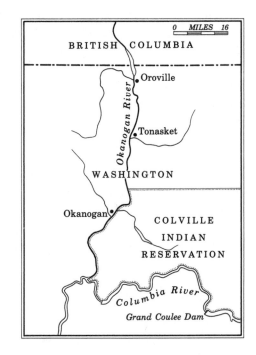

0   MILES   16

BRITISH   COLUMBIA

Oroville

Okanogan River

Tonasket

WASHINGTON

Okanogan

COLVILLE
INDIAN
RESERVATION

Columbia River

Grand Coulee Dam

A hard wind from the north delivers the first blast of winter
to the Okanogan Valley this morning, a few days into
November. Along the road that follows the river, migrants
hitchhike for rides south. The apples have all been picked;
those that remain belong to the deer and the frost. I follow the
Okanogan River north from its confluence with the Columbia,
searching for people who were here in the fall of 1963, when
much of the world looked to the apple farmers and ranchers
of this remote country to render judgment on a time of hysteria. Many of the people I want to see are dead. Others have
moved away. To live in this valley, bordered by the dry edge
of the North Cascades on one side and the forested expanse
of the Colville Indian Reservation on the other, where the
summers burn hot all day and the winters bring isolation,

requires an emotional commitment that few people can remain faithful to for life.

When I start to knock on doors and introduce myself, people smile and tell their dogs to stop barking. But when I say I'd like to talk about what happened to the Goldmark family—John and Sally and the kids—the response is the same: We'd rather not discuss that. At one home in Malott, a riverside village of perhaps two dozen people, the old woman I wish to speak with slams the door in my face.

I continue upstream toward the Canadian border. The river, banked by aspens holding a last shock of gold, still looks much as it did when Hudson's Bay Company voyageurs canoed its waters, loaded with trading goods for the inland tribes. However, there is one big difference: the land on either side of the river is full of fruit trees now. The first white homesteaders, who came to the Okanogan barely a hundred years ago, quickly realized they had found ideal orchard country. Farther north, where the river drains central British Columbia, the valley serves as the breadbasket of Western Canada. The problem was, you couldn't get water uphill to the trees without the help of windmill-powered pump, or mule, or human shoulders. So, most of the early farmers went under; their crumbling shacks can be seen throughout the valley, abandoned to gravity and the weather. With completion of the Grand Coulee Dam in 1941 came the promise of public power—dirt-cheap electricity for every apple grower and rancher in Okanogan, a county twice the size of Connecticut with a population of about thirty thousand. On the face of an old clock in the center of the town of Okanogan is a slogan that tells the story of this valley: Live Better Electrically. For a long time, the clock didn't work. It does now.

For the first third of the twentieth century, electric power was a privilege, controlled by private monopolies; President Franklin Delano Roosevelt, using the Columbia River just south of the Okanogan Country, made it a right. Water, the most basic and plentiful resource of the Pacific Northwest, belonged to every citizen of the region, Roosevelt said. Among intellectuals and poor folk alike, the idea of public power—the baton of progress—was enormously popular. In this sentiment, Roosevelt echoed Winthrop, an Eastern blueblood from another era. Winthrop said the land would set future inhabitants of this area free. Roosevelt showed them how to do it. The snowmelt of the high Cascades and the western flank of the Rockies would power turbines to provide electricity so cheap and plentiful it would make prosperous landowners out of sharecroppers. In most of the small valleys and farm hamlets of the inland Northwest, this transition went fairly smoothly.

A few hundred yards from the Canadian border, I look for the home of Gerald Thompson, who grows apples on ninety acres of hillside above the valley floor. Even with the wind tossing dust and leaves and tumbleweeds throughout the bowl of the Okanogan, this country is astonishingly beautiful. Open sky. Clean water. Ice-covered mountains rising to the west, rusted mesas to the east, each level covered with bigger pines. And down the center of the valley, grafted to either side of the river, are nothing but miles and miles of fruit orchards. Thompson's house has no address; he had said I could find it by looking for green shake siding and a white roof. He greets me at the porch, frowning.

"I don't think you're gonna like me," he says.

"Why not?"

"I changed my mind. Not sure I want to talk to you."

Outsiders find either suspicion or open arms in this community, same as elsewhere. In the tradition of the American West, new arrivals have no past; tolerance is a high virtue, just as nosiness is a low crime. Usually, that holds for the Okanogan Country. For a hundred years, highbrows and hicks have lived side by side. The town of Winthrop, one valley to the east, was founded by a Boston-bred Harvard graduate, Guy Waring, and named for Theodore Winthrop's ancestor, the first governor of the Massachusetts Bay Colony. Another Harvard graduate, Waring's college classmate Owen Wister, spent his honeymoon here in 1898, a visit which he drew upon to write the first popular western novel, *The Virginian*.

Thompson is missing a few teeth up front, his gut hangs over his waistband and his face is blasted red from the wind and sun. I say I'm interested in getting a few things straight about the Goldmark trial of 1963. Thompson was one of twelve jurors who sat in a courtroom of linoleum floors and rough plywood doors while the idea of the international Communist conspiracy was put on trial. In passing judgment on themselves, they delivered a verdict on the rest of the country. For two months, they pondered the thesis that Communists could take over a farm community just as sure as a virus could invade a healthy cow. It was the only time that the postwar Red Scare was put up against the legal test of truth. Historians view the case as the turning point against the loose libels and conspiracy theories which coursed through much of American thought from 1945 to the early 1960s.

Beyond the historical implications, a man's reputation was at stake, a man who had embraced the Okanogan Country only to have it turn on him. John Goldmark, a war hero who'd given up the promise of his Harvard Law School credentials to become a cattle rancher and citizen politician here, had been driven out of state office by a campaign that labeled him a tool of the Communist conspiracy. If anything, Goldmark was a product of the New West—that which would blossom under irrigation and prosper with cheap public power. Tall, athletic, a voracious reader and superb outdoorsman, he became a sort of Northwest archetype of the American Dream: a man who thought the land could enrich the spirit and harden the body. Delivering on Roosevelt's promise, he helped to put water to work producing electricity that freed farmers from burdens dating back to the Stone Age. Like timber and fish, public power was soon looked upon as a regional right. But those who had controlled electricity in the Okanogan Country did everything they could to hold on to it. In the dying days of a losing fight, they targeted John Goldmark, calling him a Communist and a traitor. His life in ruins following the 1962 smear campaign, he sued for libel. Witnesses flew in from all over the country to help the twelve Okanogan Valley jurors decide.

"Well, by God, I was a witness, all right," says Thompson, slowly warming to the topic. "As a juror, I spent the winter in that courtroom when I coulda been pruning my trees."

He has no trouble remembering the trial. The question is whether he *wants* to remember. The Big Lie of 1962 has yet to die; he is scared of what could still happen.

"You saw what they did in Seattle," he says, shaking his head.

On Christmas Eve 1985, Annie Goldmark was baking a ham for a holiday dinner of close friends and family. The dining table inside her Seattle home, a two-story Tudor overlooking Lake Washington, was set for ten. A thick fog which had covered the city for most of the week obscured any view of the lake or the Christmas ships which cruised near the shore. It was a few minutes before 7 P.M., and the guests were due to arrive in half an hour. Her dinner on schedule, Annie went upstairs to take a shower. A minute later there came a knock on the door. Her son Colin, a ten-year-old who spoke fluent French just like his Paris-born mother and fluent English like his Okanogan County father, answered the door and was greeted by a man with a dark beard and stocking cap over his greasy hair. He held a white box in one hand and a tiny black gun in the other. It was a toy gun, but looked authentic enough. When David

Lewis Rice knocked on the door covered by a Christmas wreath, he had not expected a child to greet him. Inside, stockings hung over the fireplace and presents were piled high around a tree. Rice had planned this visit for six months; it was to be the act of a soldier against the imagined villain behind all that had gone wrong during his twenty-seven years. Rice blamed Communists for trying to subvert the country from within; he was part of the flotsam of urban castoffs who bounced from city to city, light-years removed from a fantasy such as Morning in America.

"Charles Goldmark, please," said Rice as the boy answered the door.

Born a month before his father went to fight the Japanese in the South Pacific, Charles Goldmark grew up on the Okanogan ranch. At first, the family had no electricity, and only a rough, deep-rutted twenty-five-mile road connected the Goldmark home to the handful of stores in the valley below. Chuck Goldmark eventually went to Yale Law School, served as an Army intelligence officer and started a legal practice in Seattle. He used to say that the days of growing up on the remote ranch east of the Cascades provided the best education a boy could ever get: the eerie stillness before a thunderstorm, bunchgrass poking up through old snow in early spring, helping an infant calf get through the first days of life. No book could teach such things. It was an exalted life in new land.

When Chuck Goldmark greeted the stranger at the door of his Seattle house, both sons now at his side, David Rice was momentarily confused. Chuck was handsome, with sandy hair and a build befitting his hobby of mountaineering. He seemed no older than thirty-five or thirty-six. Rice was looking for another man, somebody much older, the Okanogan Valley Communist he'd read about. Rice flashed the small black pistol and ordered them inside. One boy ran into another room. Rice told Goldmark to call for him. He directed them all upstairs. Hearing the shower, Rice told Goldmark to ask for his wife.

"Honey, can you come out here?" Annie put on a robe and walked into the bedroom. Rice ordered them to get down on the floor, face down. The two children, scared as they dropped to their knees at the foot of the bed, rattled him. Kids—this wasn't part of the plan. He pulled the sweaters of the two boys up over their heads so their arms would be bound. Then he handcuffed Chuck and Annie.

"Do you need money?" Chuck asked.

"Yes, I can use all you got."

Rice had pawned the cheap television set belonging to a woman he was in love with and used the proceeds to pay for the tools of his Christmas Eve plan—the toy gun, chloroform and handcuffs. Searching Goldmark's wallet, he found an automated bank card and asked for the identification number. Chuck gave the number of his law firm's bank card. Rice had intended to interrogate Goldmark about Communists in Seattle, but he didn't have time. Dinner guests were on the way over, he was told. He opened the white box and proceeded to apply chloroform to each of the family members. One by one, they lost consciousness. Annie struggled at the smell, but quickly went out like the others. Hurrying now, Rice went downstairs looking for a weapon. He found a small filleting knife and a heavy steam iron, then went back to the upstairs bedroom. Starting with Chuck, he bashed in the heads of each of the four people on the floor, using the sharp end of the iron. After hitting Annie several times, he saw her start to move, so he hit her again. The two children were bludgeoned in the same way. Checking the pulse of Chuck and Annie, he found they were still alive, "So I decided to complete the job with the knife," he said later, in describing how he plunged the weapon into their brains. Wiping his feet of blood, he walked downstairs and left the house.

The first dinner guests arrived a few minutes later. The lights were on, the table was set, but nobody was there.

They called out. "Chuck? Annie?" No answer. One neighbor went next door to call the house. No answer. Then they called police, who arrived within a few minutes. Upstairs, officer Bane Bean found blood all over the walls, and the moaning, labored breathing of four people: Charles Goldmark, age forty-one; his wife, Annie, forty-three; and their two sons, Derek, twelve, and Colin, ten. Annie died that night; over the next thirty-seven days, the three remaining Goldmarks died one after the other.

On Christmas Day, David Rice showed up at the front porch of one of his political mentors, a Boeing Company electrician named Homer Brand who had founded the Seattle chapter of an odd little right-wing group called the Duck Club. At their meetings at a smorgasbord diner in Seattle's Scandinavian community of Ballard, they talked about Jewish banking conspiracies and how paper money wasn't worth anything because it was no longer backed by gold. Somebody had to do something about the goddamn lawyers, one of the members would say, and everybody would roar in approval. And what about the federal income tax—it's unconstitutional. Goddamn right. Rice, a drifter, newly unemployed, took it all in. "Shut your mouth and open your eyes—that's what I always say," was a favorite phrase of his. At one of these meetings, Rice heard about the Goldmarks—not the family that he later slaughtered, but the first generation, the post–World War II pioneers of the Okanogan high country. What did he hear? An old story, a lie. Brand said something about

Goldmark—living right here in Seattle—being the "regional director" of the Communist Party. As the target took shape in Rice's mind, he read some yellowed news clips about John and Sally Goldmark, who had been labeled tools of the kind of conspiracy in which Rice had come to believe. The voices inside his head told him to take direct action.

"Hey, Homer," Rice said excitedly to Brand on Christmas morning. "I've just dumped the top Communist!"

"Oh, yeah," Brand replied, skeptical. "So what else is new?"

Rice was caught the next day, after police were tipped off by another acquaintance. In the spring of 1986 he was found guilty of four counts of aggravated first-degree murder, the only crime in Washington State punishable by death. He had confessed to the killings. In a failed effort to save his life, defense attorney Tony Savage said Rice was mentally ill and easily influenced by talk that most people would consider irrational. "The extreme right wing did not cause his illness," said Savage. "But his illness provided fertile ground for their philosophy." After a short deliberation, the jury sentenced Rice to be executed. The jury foreman, Joel Babcock, said whoever planted the original thought that Goldmark was a Communist was as much to blame for the death of the family as was Rice. A grocery store clerk, age twenty-five, Babcock said the trial made him think hard about things he'd never thought about before. "This whole thing started with something that wasn't true," he said after the trial. "Whoever started such slander should feel a little embarrassed right now—a little guilt."

The seed that landed in the head of David Lewis Rice blew over the Cascade Mountains twenty-three years after it was shaken from the weeds of Okanogan County. When Gerald Thompson heard about the Christmas Eve carnage at the Goldmark house, he knew right away what was behind it.

Now, his face angry, his eyes watching the wind rip dead leaves from his apple trees, Thompson snaps his fingers.

"Just like that I made the connection," he says. "It came from these guys who first made up all these lies about John Goldmark. That was what killed Chuck's family."

John Goldmark first came to the Okanogan Country in 1946, looking for a fresh life in a land unencumbered by the rust of his native East Coast. As one of the most remote areas in America, the Okanogan fit the bill. While still at war in the Philippines, the young Navy ensign wrote his wife, Sally, about his urge to move west, "where people are less twisted up in traditions, class and inhibitions." After scouting the apple valleys of central Washington, he bought the ranch on the high plateau of the Colville Indian Reservation. From the house, a homestead structure in a grove of aspens, you could look across the plateau to wheat fields and pine in one direction and away to the blue curtain of the Cascades in the other. John, Sally and their infant son Chuck moved onto the ranch in early spring, when the ground was still covered with snow. He put his Navy officer's sword over the fireplace and set out to become a man of the land. Harvard Law School and a stint as a New Deal administrator in Washington had not prepared him for the life of frontier cattle rancher. But he listened. He applied pure logic and science to the sometimes illogical trade of farming. In time, he established a healthy herd, grew wheat and grain, and built an airstrip on his property so he could land a small plane. The boys, Chuck and Peter, learned about ranch life at home and the rest of the world at a one-room schoolhouse on the Indian reservation, a million-acre trust for nine tribes from the central Columbia River region. They both learned to fly the family plane, herd cattle, build fences and climb mountains.

At first, John Goldmark was not trusted by many ranchers in the valley, who were suspicious of his Ivy League credentials and his move from New York to the Okanogan. "People always wondered what a guy like him was doing in a place like this," says R. E. Mansfield, the oldest practicing attorney in the Okanogan Valley. The flip side of small-town security is a type of gossip that can be as lethal as big-city crime. John and Sally Goldmark were assaulted with the worst of this rural specialty. Rumors circulated that John was running a secret operation with his primitive airstrip up there on the plateau. And his wife, Sally—what sort of past had she dragged out from Brooklyn to the Okanogan?

John could be hardnosed—he did not suffer fools easily—and was always trying to do things differently. Initially, most of the other ranchers laughed at him. But over the years, they paid him the ultimate form of respect: imitating some of his ingenuities. Ten years of ranch life changed his look to that of a typical cowboy—lean, with a weathered face and crew-cut hair, always dressed in jeans and boots and plaid shirts. Yet, he could move just as easily inside a courtroom or a legislative hall as he could on the range. "John Goldmark was the only person I ever knew who made me think: 'There goes a great man,'" says Stimson Bullitt, a prominent Seattle attorney from the family that founded the KING Broadcasting empire. Others said he was too stubborn to like. In later years, he reminded some friends of Hank Stamper, the tough-nutted timberman in Ken Kesey's novel *Sometimes a Great Notion*.

In the mid-1950s, John served on the Rural Electrification Board, where he was an early proponent of public power, in part to help bring the twentieth century to his ranch and in part to help his neighbors. At the time, even though the Grand Coulee Dam had been operating for more than a decade, electricity in this part of the state was controlled by a private utility, the Washington Water Power Company, based in Spokane, 150 miles to the east. Most of the farmers couldn't afford its rates. Even those with money had difficulty convincing the company to connect power lines to their remote locations. With construction of the Grand Coulee Dam, then the biggest public-works project in American history, Roosevelt had said, "We are going to see with our own eyes electricity and power made so cheap that they will become a standard article of use." Such a thought seemed far-fetched. During the Depression, less than half the farmers of Washington had electricity, and only a third in Idaho and Oregon had it. Irrigation water was carried by horse, or hand, or primitive pump. Kitchen tables were lit by kerosene lamps. Homes were heated by wood-burning stove. Roosevelt looked at large sections of the dried-out American Midwest, where the earth was stripped of fertility by savage windstorms, and directed the blank-faced and bankrupt farmers to the area drained by the Columbia, new land holding the promise of accessible water and cheap power, with every farmer a shareholder.

Washington Water Power, through the faithfully supportive Spokane *Spokesman-Review*, fought public power and the Grand Coulee Dam as if they were a plague that would wipe out every community in the inland Northwest. The campaign was so relentless that for many years public power was kept out of the hands of the people whose rivers were being dammed for such purposes. Eric Nalder, growing up in the small desert town of Ephrata in the early 1950s, was ashamed to mention that his father was an engineer on the Coulee Dam for fear of being taunted by his neighbors. Advocates of the dam were called "Coulee Communists."

John Goldmark maintained that the ranchers and poor farmers of the Columbia had a God-given right to affordable electricity from hydropower, a campaign theme that helped him get elected to the state legislature in 1956, as a Democrat in a heavily Republican district. He was twice reelected. By his third term, he was chairman of the key House Ways and Means Committee, and used his position to push for increased public power, more park space, libraries, better roads. By the time 1962 rolled around, John's reelection seemed like a sure thing. But right from the start, things were different in this campaign. In announcing John's intention to run for a fourth term in the legislature, the local Tonasket *Tribune* carried a story in which it was said that "Goldmark is a member of the American Civil Liberties Union, an organization closely affiliated with the Communist movement in the United States." The story mentioned that Goldmark's oldest son, Chuck, was a freshman at Reed College in Portland, "the only school in the Northwest where Gus Hall, secretary of the Communist Party, was invited to speak." John knew some people in the valley didn't like him; but this was poison.

The Tonasket paper was owned and edited by Ashley Holden, who for many years had been political editor of the *Spokesman-Review*, where he helped direct the long, losing fight against public power. "His hatred of anybody who advocated publicly owned electricity was so strong, it was almost like a mental illness with him," said Bob Dellwo, a lifelong Democratic Party activist from Spokane and an ex-FBI agent who spent decades fighting Holden and the *Spokesman-Review*, "If you were in favor of public power, the *Review* and the Washington Water Power Company considered you the closest thing to a Communist." However, one by one, the rural counties of eastern Washington shook off the Washington Water Power Company and set up public utility districts, which they used to provide their neighbors with some of the cheapest electrical rates in the world. In his sixties, Ashley Holden left Spokane for the small-town bully pulpit of the Okanogan Valley paper, which he endowed with the masthead slogan, THIS IS A REPUBLIC, NOT A DEMOCRACY— LET'S KEEP IT THAT WAY!

The second shot against Goldmark came from Albert Canwell, an embittered former legislator who operated as a self-described expert on international Communism from his home on the Little Spokane River. Some men play golf for a hobby, Canwell once said, "I collect information on the Communists." With Holden's help, Canwell circulated a tape in the valley, a question-and-answer session in which the expert, Canwell, answered his own questions. In the tape, Canwell mentioned John Goldmark's affiliation with the ACLU, "one of the most effective Communist fronts in America." Next, he and Holden published part of that tape in a private newsletter, where they questioned why Goldmark, "a brilliant young lawyer, a graduate of Harvard Law School, a nephew of Justice Brandeis of the Supreme Court," had chosen to become a rancher in the distant Okanogan.

In late summer, Canwell and Holden took their campaign to a packed meeting at the American Legion post in Okanogan. Goldmark and his friend, local state senator Wilbur Hallauer, asked to speak, and were told they could not. The ACLU was the stated topic of the night, but Goldmark was the evening's true target. As several hundred people filed into the overheated Legion post on a summer night, Canwell handed out an open letter addressed to Sally Goldmark, in which he asked her if the Communist Party, "knowing your secret," had pressured her into drafting left-wing legislation for the state of Washington.

The Depression had been very hard on the family of Sally Ringe. The daughter of German immigrants, she was forced to give up her studies at medical school after her father went into bankruptcy. She worked in a New York soup kitchen for a while, seeing the faces of the broken men and women of the 1930s, day in and day out. Idealistic and outspoken, she joined the Communist Party in 1935. She paid her dues and attended meetings for six years. Shortly after she met John Goldmark, she lost interest in the party—Hitler's alliance with Stalin had changed the minds of millions in America and Europe—and she quit. She later cooperated with the FBI when two men came to the ranch in 1949 to ask about her background. She was found to be so harmless that her husband, who had remained active in the Navy Reserve as a commander, was twice given top officer security clearances. In the Okanogan Country, she was active in the Grange, the PTA, the 4–H Club and the county-fair board. But Sally's years as a Communist would haunt her for the rest of her life.

At the Legion meeting on that summer night in 1962, Canwell preached against the Communist in their midst with the vigor of a tel-evangelist reaching for a ratings point. He handed out a Washington ACLU chapter newsletter with Goldmark's name on the masthead, and then told the farmers and ranchers that the ACLU was "the major Communist front operating in the state of Washington." In those days, calling somebody a Communist was the same as branding him a traitor; it was a word effortlessly hurled at many prominent citizens. For nearly an hour Canwell spun tales about hidden agents and threats from within. You couldn't trust anyone. Communists were gaining force on both borders, and operated "both within and without," he said, "like an octopus." He sat down to thundering applause. Then John Goldmark tried to speak for five minutes, saying the ACLU reflected the principles of the Declaration of Independence. He was hooted down. When his friend Wilbur Hallauer tried to speak, the mob turned mad. "Get him out of here!" they yelled at their longtime state senator, and he was pushed off the stage.

Goldmark later said that looking into the enraged eyes of the people who had been his friends and neighbors for sixteen years sent a chill down his spine. He felt as though he were surrounded by a lynch mob. Who were these people? What had happened to the tolerant Westerners, free-thinking and independent, who would help you fix your fence if you bucked bales in return, who judged you by what you did instead of what was said about you, who never asked where you went to school or what your father did for a living? In the Okanogan Country, there was no hint of the restrictive class system of some circles of the East, where school ties and family connections could bind or exclude for life. But there was this, the noose of the rural West.

The Canwell speech was summarized that week in Ashley Holden's newspaper, under the headline COMMIE FRONT EXPOSED BY AL CANWELL IN LEGION TALK. In the same issue, he wrote an editorial in which he said John Goldmark "is a tool of a monstrous conspiracy to remake America into a totalitarian state which would throttle freedom and crush individual initiative. . . ." Two weeks later, John Goldmark was defeated for a fourth term in the state legislature by a three-to-one margin. In a newsletter published after the election, Canwell described his Legion Hall talk as "the bullet that got Goldmark."

Shunned by neighbors, thrown out of office, his family tortured by further gossip, John called on his friend Bill Dwyer, who at thirty-three was just coming into his own as one of the best young lawyers in the Northwest. Goldmark wanted to sue for libel. Dwyer said it would be tough. Goldmark had never directly been called a Communist—just a stooge, dupe and tool of their invisible conspiracy. Goldmark decided to press forward. On November 4, 1963, more than a year after the smear campaign, the trial opened. Twelve jurors—three sawmill workers, two apple farmers, an unemployed construction worker, a beekeeper, an Indian, two wives of cattlemen, a state employee and a cook at the local chow house—were impaneled to pass judgment on the claims of their neighbor, who had since become a stranger. They filed into court dressed in overalls and stained shirts and worn workshoes. The same type of folks who were ready to hang John Goldmark in the Legion meeting one year earlier were now asked to examine the truth behind their community's hysteria.

For two months, they heard from a range of national experts—United States Senators and prominent ex-Communists among them. A witness for Goldmark was Sterling Hayden, the actor, who said, "I was perhaps the only person who ever bought a yacht and joined the Communist Party in the same week."

Three weeks into the trial came some startling news—the young President, John F. Kennedy, had been shot.

"Who shot him?" Canwell asked Richard Larsen, a reporter for the Wenatchee *World.*

"Whoever it was, I hope he was a good shot," Ashley Holden replied.

Kennedy's accused killer had been to Moscow and Cuba, and was a professed Marxist. What would this do to Dwyer's careful dismantling of the conspiracy theory? Goldmark feared the worst. But jurors were already with him, Thompson said later. "We knew he'd been screwed," he told me. "You can't do that to a guy, no matter what you think of him, and get away with it." For all the experts brought from distant cities to the small town covered by ice-fog in midwinter, nobody was ever able to connect the ACLU or John Goldmark to a conspiracy to remake America into a totalitarian state. Testimony from twenty years of government Red hunts failed to provide a single nugget to back the claims made against him.

In closing arguments, Joseph Wicks, a defense attorney, again raised the question of why an educated man would choose to live in such wild country. Said Wicks: "He, the brilliant student of government, of political science and of law, of human nature, settles for a cow ranch in Okanogan County where he didn't know whether apples grew on trees or on a vine, where he didn't know which end of the cow gave milk or which end of the cow ate the hay."

The vitriol pouring forth was so strong that Sally Goldmark started trembling. Wicks acknowledged that the smear had riled up the community. "Sure, it creates hatred. And isn't it about time that we had a little hatred for those people that declare that 'We will bury you?'" Wicks quoted Scripture, then pounded his fist down. "What is God to an atheistic Communist?" At that, Sally burst into tears and ran from the courtroom.

In rebuttal, Goldmark's attorneys played on the jurors' sense of decency. Just as a terrible lie could spring from this wide-open country to ruin a man, so could a judgment of simple wisdom and fairness. "Life is only good in a community where freedom and justice are preserved for everybody, not just for a few," said Dwyer. His colleague, R. E. Mansfield, responded to the venom of Wicks with a Biblical quote of his own. He chose his words from the Book of Proverbs: "A man that beareth false witness against his neighbor is a war club and a sword and a sharp arrow." Twenty-two years later, the verse would prove to be prophetic.

The Goldmarks won; the first part of this story is an American fable, where truth, justice and tolerance win out over evil. After five days of deliberation, the jury returned with a verdict against Ashley Holden and Albert Canwell—the largest libel verdict in state history at the time. Gerald Thompson remembers sitting up in the attic of the old concrete-covered Okanogan County courthouse, watching the snow bury his car down below. The jurors were angry at what their community had done to the Goldmarks, he said, and they wanted to make it right. With the verdict, Thompson went back to his orchard near the Canadian border, convinced that never again would anyone call a decent man a traitor in the Okanogan Valley and get away with it.

More than a quarter-century after the trial, R. E. Mansfield is still prac-ticing law in the Okanogan Valley, as he has done since 1937. In his law office hangs a poster-size picture of his hero, Franklin Roosevelt. The valley, slowing down for the winter, looks much the same as it did during the Goldmark trial. But some things have changed. The biggest employer, the timber mill in Omak, has just been purchased by its union employees, making it one of the largest businesses in the West owned by its workers. A worker-owned timber mill—in the old days of the Okanogan Valley such a move would surely be labeled a Communist takeover; today, the local newspaper hails the employee buyout as a bold stroke for community ownership and self-destiny. Mansfield, who faced some lean times after he represented Goldmark, is a beloved figure in the valley; he now plays cribbage with one of his worst enemies, "a guy who hated my guts and believed I was a dyed-in-the-wool Commie." The John Birch Society, whose members saw Communists behind every apple-storage bin, has all but vanished.

What happened to the Goldmarks—both generations—brings tears to the eyes of a man who is usually never without a joke. Mansfield has never stopped thinking about that family. After the 1963 trial, the Gold-marks recovered their reputation, but never put their lives completely back together. Four years after the verdict, on a cold winter day, John was bucked from a horse in a distant part of the ranch. When Mansfield and others finally found him, he was seriously injured and near death from the onset of hypothermia. Several hip operations failed to restore adequate movement. He moved to Seattle, where he practiced law for several years. After a long fight with cancer, he died in 1979. Six years later, Sally Goldmark died of emphysema just before her oldest son and his family were butchered.

Still, the libel trial had done to the Red Scare what the Scopes monkey trial had (at least temporarily) done to Creationism. Bill Dwyer wrote a thoughtful and moving account of it titled *The Goldmark Case: An American Libel Trial.* In 1988, after one of the longest delays for any judicial appointee in modern times, Dwyer was approved by Congress as a United States District Court judge in Seattle. During the nearly two years that elapsed after he was first nominated, critics said Dwyer was unqualified to be a federal judge because he had done volunteer work for the ACLU.

Mansfield believes that the Goldmark trial changed life in the Okanogan Valley forever. It had always been the type of open country, in appearance, that could stir poets from Winthrop to Wister. What has changed following the Goldmark trial is that the people opened up a bit, too.

"I don't think the home folks will rise up in ignorance quite like that ever again," he says.

But John Goldmark was smeared not so much because he was different, says Mansfield; his crime was that he helped to pry the Okanogan away from the grip of private power. The tragedy that befell him did not fulfill any prophecy of Winthrop's, though Goldmark was certainly drawn to this country for the very reason cited by the Yankee prophet as a magnet for future generations; rather, the case brought out a truth penned by Richard Neuberger in his 1939 book about the Northwest, *Our Promised Land.*

"Class warfare of a sort has rocked the northwest corner over the principal ways proposed for using America's greatest block of hydroelectric power," Neuberger wrote. There were sure to be casualties from the fight over who controls the most elemental resource of the Promised Land, he said, but even with that struggle, the Northwest represented the best hope of America during one of its darkest periods.

Mansfield has seen the promise fulfilled, but he will always be troubled by the price.

"They hated John Goldmark, these guys from the Washington Water Power Company and all their shills," says Mansfield. "He fought them every step of the way. Then public power came in, the rates came down, and the farmers could afford to pump plenty of water to their orchards. They'd never go back to the way it was. The monopoly days were gone for good. Just too bad a good family had to die for it."

Chapter 13

COLUMBIA

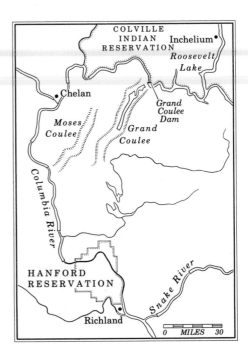

When the federal government decided to wrestle the Columbia River away from nature and place it in the permanent custody of the Army Corps of Engineers, it did so with some trepidation. Man as a geological force— this was a line that had never been crossed. The land could be altered, customized to human scale, but surely not controlled. And what a way to start: no river in North America except the Mississippi is more powerful than the Columbia; it carries a quarter-million cubic feet of water per second to the ocean, ten times the flow of the Colorado, twice the discharge of the Nile into the Mediterranean. The Corps planned nothing less than radical surgery, a fifty-year operation that would involve ripping open the chest of the Northwest and redirecting the main artery.

Elsewhere, the earth-movers had won a string of significant

victories, cutting a canal fifty miles across the Isthmus of Panama, blasting railroad tunnels through the Rockies and Cascades, stealing water from the High Sierra and the Colorado for delivery to the desert of Southern California. There was no reason scrubland could not be green, or forests leveled to plain, or long-dry coulees filled with fresh water, or dead seas resurrected from salty graves. By the time the West was old and the twentieth century was young, the men from the platoon of progress had little trouble playing God. And so a deity with sliderule and bulldozer took over the Columbia, expecting all mortal elements to fall in place.

Building is the great art of our time, it was said then. And technology, of the heavy-metal, grind-and-grunt school, was king. Salmon were caught in fishwheels and canned by an octo-armed machine called the Iron Chink. Seattle was lopping off its hills, filling in its tidelands and constructing the biggest skyscraper west of the Mississippi. Portland was drawing hydroelectric power from the Willamette and sending forth enough lumberjacks to fell a thousand acres of virgin forest a day. British Columbia was starting work on an ill-fated canal across its interior. The leading citizens of Vancouver, just a few years removed from the mines which made them rich, were planning to tailor their tidelands and gouge open the bordering mountains. Idaho had demonstrated that the unruly Snake River, which brings water from half of the intermountain West to the Columbia, could be dammed to satisfy the interests of a few powerful desert cattlemen and potato farmers. The geo-technicians of the early twentieth century approached the Columbia with the zeal of the first plastic surgeon in Beverly Hills. There was just so much potential.

Problem was, things could be a bit outsized in *the field*, as they called the world outside the drawing room. Take Beacon Rock, the largest monolith of stone on earth except for Gibraltar. Rising from the north shore of the lower Columbia, the rock is the basaltic core of a broken-down Cascade volcano, a piece of vertebra from the spine of the mountain range. Seeking the Pacific, the Columbia long ago smashed through this range, carving out the magnificent gorge and leaving chunks like this along the way. Lewis and Clark named Beacon Rock and admired its stark, vertical beauty. In a New World of magnificent proportions, it seemed to fit. The Corps of Engineers saw it as a nuisance. Although the rock never impeded river traffic, it was just sitting there, not doing anything for anybody, and therefore it was the Enemy. So, the Corps drew up a plan to pulverize the second-largest monolith in the world and use the shattered pieces to build a breakwater at the Columbia's mouth, thereby accomplishing two enormous tasks at once.

A man named Henry Biddle, a naturalist, new to the Northwest, tried to stop the Corps. He was a descendant of Nicholas Biddle, of Philadelphia, who had edited Lewis and Clark's journals and later became president of the United States Bank. Unable to dissuade the Corps, Henry Biddle bought Beacon Rock in 1915. The whole thing. For the next three years, he built a path of stone and wood from the base to the summit, a mile-long trail up the nine-hundred-foot vertical length of the rock. He then sold the rock to the state of Washington for one dollar on the provision that it remain a park—and a finger in the eye of the Corps—for eternity. Until recently, it was the only significant battle the Corps of Engineers had lost.

Atop Beacon Rock, the wind out of the west is warm this morning. The vine maple growing from the rock is drained of green and tinged in red, and a few Doug firs, dwarfed by the constant wind, cling to the edge of the monolith, their roots spread out in a pattern that reveals a strained scramble for soil. In a few weeks' time, the wind will shift the other way, as the colder desert air is sucked into the mild west side of the Cascades. Either way, there is always a breeze in the Columbia Gorge, stiff and new, blowing twenty or thirty miles an hour. The River of the West may have given up its current and most of its independence to the Corps, but the wind has never been touched; carrying the spirit of the old Columbia, it rushes through the Gorge, more dominant than ever.

From this view on Beacon Rock, the Columbia appears as a river of paradox, overwhelmed with responsibility but holding to a few wild quirks of character. To the west, the river is banked by steep, green walls from which pour the torrents of the Cascades. One of these waterfalls, Multnomah, drops 620 feet, pummeling rock and creating a misted mini-rain-forest all around. The Columbia flows these last 140 miles west unimpeded by man, picking up the Willamette, the Sandy, the Lewis, the Kalama, the Cowlitz, the Clatskanie and hundreds of smaller waterways on its final ride to the Pacific. The river below me is far different in appearance from the river an idealistic Franklin D. Roosevelt stared at while he chugged through the Columbia Gorge on a train ride in 1920. Scribbling a speech on the back of his breakfast menu—this was well before handlers scripted every breath for politicians—the young vice-presidential candidate thought about the future of this wild country, picking up where earlier dreamers had left off. In 1813, Jefferson had envisioned "a great, free and independent empire on the Columbia," the western edge of an America he called "Nature's nation." FDR saw a chance for the common man to live regally within the 250,000 square miles drained by the big river. He wasn't sure how that would come about, but he wrote that it might have something to do with "all that water running down unchecked to the sea."

Looking the other way, upriver to the east, I see Bonneville Dam, the first of the big harnesses on the Columbia, completed seventeen years after Roosevelt committed a rough draft of his thoughts to paper. The Gorge itself is about eighty-five miles long, a cleave in the Cascades that begins in the mist of the Sandy River near Portland and ends in the desert of The Dalles. After years of abuse, the Gorge is on the mend. I climb down Henry Biddle's rock for a closer look.

From here on out, I'm heading upstream, following the late salmon, the early winter windsurfers, and Winthrop. I have already paid my respects to Fort Vancouver, birthplace of the modern Pacific Northwest, which Winthrop visited three times in 1853. The fort was the center of a universe that stretched from Mexico to Russian America, and from the Rockies to Hawaii. For twenty years, Dr. John McLoughlin ruled this empire from the Hudson's Bay Company headquarters on a level bank across from the confluence of the Willamette and the Columbia. A Scot, he was six feet, four inches tall, with shoulder-length hair. The Indians called him the White Eagle. Under his direction, the Gentlemen Adventurers salted barrels of salmon, milled timber at a water-powered sawmill, grew vegetables and shipped these elemental products of the Northwest up to two thousand miles away. He never removed Indians from their land, but saw the value of keeping the tribes strong and their fishery alive. Capitalism needed healthy trading partners, not conquered serfs— a lesson lost on most of the American settlers and government agents who followed McLoughlin. Visitors to Fort Vancouver drank French wines from Waterford crystal glasses and picked at their sturgeon caviar with sterling silver. As the Americans began to pour in, McLoughlin directed them south of the Columbia, hoping he could keep Washington as part of what became British Columbia. The fort's setting, in the words of a young company man who first visited in 1833, was "The finest combination of beauty and grandeur I ever beheld." Across the river, Mount Hood rises from rumpled hills, enough water locked in its glaciers to feed the valleys that surround it. Behind the fort, Mount St. Helens floats on the northern horizon. But paradise lasted only a bit more than two decades; McLoughlin retired soon after the English gave up claims below the 49th Parallel in 1846. He moved to Oregon City, became an American citizen, and died shortly thereafter.

Nothing could be further from the Hudson's Bay Company idyll than the cluster of timber towns on the Washington side of the Columbia Gorge in Skamania County. Sasquatch, the photo-defying Bigfoot, is legally protected from hunters by order of the county council, but no similar resolution for the Gorge has come from local politicians. When I ask Arlene Johnson at the Chamber of Commerce what is unique about the area, she thinks for a long time and then brightens: "In the winter, we have the highest unemployment rate of any county in America—thirty-five percent."

The people of Skamania County fought to keep the Gorge from becoming a National Scenic Area. They grew up in the tail end of an era when the scenery belonged to whoever could get to it first and hold onto it. What they didn't like was the idea that you wouldn't be able to just mow down a swath of timber or put up a mini-mart without going through some kind of land-use committee made up of blue-hairs and birdwatchers. The American frontier may have been officially pronounced closed in 1890, but land-use laws and zoning remain foreign terms to many Western counties possessing some of the finest scenery in the country. It took an act of Congress in 1986 to force on the area a sentiment that Winthrop said would rise naturally. Following the legislation, citizens of Skamania County scorned the federal government and prepared for hard times. Pretty scenery won't pay the bills, they said. Like their union brothers downriver in Astoria at the Columbia's mouth, the loggers of the Columbia Gorge asked, What are we supposed to do now?

The river today is wall-to-wall windsurfers. It's midweek, cold in the morning, mild by noon, but nobody's talking about the temperature. All that matters is the wind. They come from Germany and Australia and Texas and Nova Scotia, the skin-cancer-be-damned set, lawyers and trust-funders and drifters and dropouts; on the Columbia, hopping five-foot swells with a forty-mile tail wind, they go by just one name: Boardheads.

Nearby, the last log flume in America hangs from the high walls of the Washington Cascades. A seven-mile-long wooden slide, it's built over thick-timbered trestles and runs from the forest to the Columbia. The cliffs of the Gorge are too steep for roads, so the timber companies devised these flumes over which logs scooted downhill. Lumberjacks used to bundle up their best clothes and slide down the flume into town for a Saturday night drunk, which was followed by the Sunday morning walk back up, with hangover. The flume here shut down in the mid-1980s' timber recession, for good. In a way, the last flume is a fitting symbol of the transition under way in the Gorge, and throughout much of the Northwest. The future has something to do with the squeal of delight on those Saturday night rides.

Farther upstream, at Hood River, the Columbia is sluggish from the brace of Bonneville Dam, but with the wind, it looks like a choppy cross section of the Pacific. Everybody's talking about "catching a blow" and "rigging up" and how great it is when rain falls in Portland because the cooler air gives the desert air a real yank. The radio news in the morning begins, not with bulletins from the Mideast, but with a wind report. The town of Hood River, named for the glacial stream that runs nearby, is surrounded by pear and cherry orchards that thrive on the east-Cascade sun and meltwater from the pyramid of Mount Hood. Walking the streets, I see few signs of the depression which was supposed to kill the Gorge economy once the scenery was protected. Carpenters are hammering away at new homes. Restaurants are full of people. Old houses with big gardens have converted to bed and breakfasts.

When word first got out among the international community of transient thrill-seekers that the best wind in the world blew through the Columbia River Gorge, most locals were suspicious. Bums on water, who needs 'em? There are Pacific beaches in Hawaii with stronger winds, but in no place is the wind more consistent than in the Gorge. A University of Oregon study found that the average windsurfer earns thirty thousand dollars a year and is twenty-eight to thirty years old. They contribute up to $20 million a year to the economy of the Gorge. I stroll into an old wooden building in Hood River, two stories and a loft that used to be a fruit warehouse, across the street from a long-deserted salmon cannery. The ground floor is cluttered with sailboards fresh off the assembly line. I talk wind with a salesgirl who moved from Salt Lake City because she can ski any day of the year on the eternal snows of Mount Hood, and windsurf the same day. In the back shop a dozen workers blend fiberglass and plastic into lean boards which sell for $1,500 and up. Three small manufacturing facilities like this one have opened in Hood River. They make the boards from scratch; at some of the shops, the craftsmen get a share of the overall sales. Wages are good, usually better than union timber jobs. At one of the shops, work stops on days when the wind is really howling, a consensual rule.

One man in his forties, still making the rough transition from timber beast to sailboarding hipster, says, "If you'd a told me ten years ago I could make a good living off windsurfing, I'd a said you were fucking-ay crazy. But hey, look at me. I just bought a new car. Windsurfing has done wonders for this town. They're even talking about putting in a second street light."

Unemployment is at six percent in Hood River, lower than in any timber town on the Columbia. Windsurfing has given the town back its pride. But now with new prosperity has also come the first signs of discontent: Californians. You expect to see their pictures in the post office. They take home-equity loans on overpriced bungalows in Santa Monica and buy sixty-thousand-dollar farmhouses here for summer playpens. The equity exiles talk about Hood River's becoming the Aspen of the windsurfing set. It already is. So why the anxiety? Flash and cash are not easily transplanted to Oregon, a state closer in spirit to its New England ancestors than to its neighbors in California.

Across the river, in Skamania County, timber is selling at an all-time high price, and still twenty-five percent of the county's work force is jobless. The logging companies, pouring profits into automated sawmills that cut wood with a minimum amount of human help, have been shedding workers by the thousands. But in the town of Stevenson, the riverside burg where the opposition to a Scenic Columbia Gorge bill was centered, a new business has opened up, the first new enterprise in more than a decade—a windsurfing shop. For 150 years the people of Skamania County never did anything but tear and gnaw at their natural resources, and nobody ever got rich but a few timber barons. Now, they're starting to feel the wind; it never stops blowing.

At dawn the next day, with the tufts of brown grass hardened by frost, I slip under barbed wire and scramble down basalt cliffs near The Dalles. In the desert 190 miles upstream from the river's mouth, there is no life without the Columbia. Everything looks baked and burnt, the river walls tiered by bath-rings from the prehistoric course of the Columbia. Winthrop called this area "the Devil's race course," the overland end of the Oregon Trail, a place where the river tumbled down Celilo Falls. From here, wagons were portaged around the falls, stripped of their wheels, then lashed to a barge for the final trip to the Willamette Valley. If I had been here with Winthrop, instead of following his ghost, we would not have been able to hear each other speak; the Columbia crashed down the stepped cliffs with such force as to drown all other sound. It was a place that moved the tongue-tied to fluid fits of poetry, the agnostic to divine reconsideration. Now it's gone forever, another casualty of the Corps. Today, somewhere around the bend, I hear a dog bark guarding a federal bureaucrat; I hear the bee-swarm sound of electricity sprinting along transmission lines that are strung from The Dalles Dam to Los Angeles, 846 miles to the south; I hear the morning—an oddly modern sound—and nothing else.

I come upon six abandoned shacks, sun-blasted to a deep brown and perched on level rock. Each dwelling is no bigger than an average bedroom; the roofs are perforated, and the floorboards are crumbling. One of these structures has a cross at its apex. When I walk inside, the smell of rats is overwhelming. Outside, I pick through old bottles and a rusted stove. More ghosts. Farther upstream, I find a couple of wooden planks, sun-peeled plywood nailed to poles of pine on the edge of the river. But unlike the long-deserted hamlet, these platforms show signs of recent life. One, covered by blue tarp, includes a bed mattress, rat-chewed and stained by mildew. It is indented from a human form. I look around and see beer cans, an old rocking chair, and everywhere, strings and wire. The smell of salmon is unmistakable. This Indian dipnet platform, little changed in style over centuries, surprises me; it's like a gramophone in a video store. I had thought that the Indians of the desert Columbia, like most of the whites, took their salmon from Safeway. A frightful contraption, the platform is bound to the rocks by two guy-wires. Another surprise: The river at this point is actually moving. Little swirls and eddies.

I scramble along more rocks, looking for the owners of these platforms, but find nothing more than the hum of transmission lines sending electricity out from the half-mile-long powerhouse of the Dalles Dam. No Celilo Falls, of course; they were buried when the dam opened in 1957. No spillway, even; the dams have become so efficient at channeling all water through deep turbines that a flow over the top is considered purely cosmetic. I climb around a turn and drop down, closer to shore, still on precariously vertical rock. There, on an enormous, wobbly platform is an Indian fisherman. He is wearing a wool cap and overalls, and his long hair is braided in matching pigtails. His body leashed to a climbing rope and harness, he leans way out over the river. Looking around, I see three twenty-foot-long dipnets near three different platforms. He jumps from pole to pole, pulling them through the water and coming up empty. He looks like a museum piece—the deep color of his face and hair, the traditional pine dipnet—set against the enormity of the dam. After ten thousand years, perhaps he is the end of the line. I ask him about the fishing. A late fall chinook run is still underway, and he had hoped to bring back a big catch for a tribal salmon feed. After three days of work at a spot where a single person used to take up to five hundred fish a day, he has a half-dozen salmon to show.

Thousands of Indians used to gather at Celilo Falls to spear chinook and coho or catch them in dipnets. Because of this salmon bounty, The Dalles was the great trade mart for all Northwest tribes, the center of a native network that spread out across the Rockies to the Plains, and far north into British Columbia. Here, the Klamaths of Northern California traded slaves for salmon, the Nez Perce brought horses and bighorn sheep horns, the nomadic Shoshoni swapped buffalo hides, the Makah came down from the rain forest of the Olympic Peninsula with sea otter pelts, the Vancouver Island tribes brought their trademark canoes to exchange, the Chinook bartered with dried clams and bright shells. On a fall morning, The Dalles was like an open-air shopping center, crowded with perhaps as many as fifty thousand people.

By the time of Winthrop's arrival, there were few hints of what used to be; a majority of the Columbia Plateau natives had died of disease. Fresh from the jungled forests of the Cascades, Winthrop considered these basalt walls and bristled fields to be the northwestern corner of hell.

"Before me was a region like the Valley of Death, rugged, bleak and severe," he wrote. "A tragical valley, where the fiery forces of Nature, impotent to attain majestic combination and build monuments of peace, had fallen into despair and ugly warfare." What bothered the Yankee traveler, aside from the fact that he contracted smallpox and was forced to spend his three-week convalescence quarantined inside Fort Dalles, was the lack of any vegetation, bare hills all around in the Sahara of the Northwest. How could this be in the land of the Big Green? Fifty miles from impenetrable forest, and not a stick of timber anywhere, not a fern or blade of grass.

"Racked and battered crags stood disorderly over all that rough waste," he wrote. "There were no trees, nor any masses of vegetation to soften the severities of landscape. All was harsh and desolate." He left a passage for us prophet-checkers. "The Dalles of the Columbia, upon which I was now looking, must be studied by the Yankee Dante, whenever he comes, for imagery to construct his Purgatory, if not his Inferno."

I find the place closer to limbo than hell. By harnessing the Columbia here to send power to Southern California, the Corps of Engineers ruined a place that has been called the greatest salmon fishery on earth. At Celilo Falls, the water used to crash down in a series of gradual drops, the stairs of a giant. Hurling themselves upstream, the fish would leap one section at a time, resting in little pools.

Long after the Indians were sent to reservations, tribal fishermen continued to catch salmon at Celilo Falls, holding out at what became a sort of aboriginal Alamo. When dam building began in earnest in the 1930s, Celilo Falls was spared, at first. Pictures from the early 1950s showed half-naked natives in cowboy hats tethered to ropes as they leaned out over the crashing water with their long nets. When somebody wanted to see what the West was like, they were shown these Real Life Indians who risked their lives at a place where the river narrowed and dropped, named *Le Dalle* ("The Trough") by the French. Right up to the end, in 1957, the desert daredevils pulled fish from Celilo Falls. They protested construction of the dam, of course, but were told to step aside; this was before Northwest Indian fishing rights had been upheld by the Supreme Court.

In the evening, I head for an Indian village, planning to sit in on a salmon ritual which the dipnet fisherman had told me about. I turn off the interstate that follows the Columbia and drive on a dusty road a few miles upstream from the graveyard of Celilo Falls. The desert, about twenty miles east of the green Gorge, is still and cold. About a hundred Indians have gathered for a salmon feed. Flames leap from a large firepit. Despite a sign warning against drinking alcohol, two women stagger over each other—and then fall to the ground. About thirty fish are pulled out of ice and cut into strips by several heavyset women. The fish meat is bright orange-red, full of oil and taste. One woman pinches off about two fingers' worth and holds it up in disgust: "You go to a restaurant and order salmon. This is what they give you."

Following the ancient recipe, they stretch fillets flat around cedar sticks and then cook them upright on thin poles placed in the ground near the fire. This keeps the juices in, while slow-cooking the fish. Some venison is cut by the men and placed on a grill. While waiting for the meal, we all eat potato chips and drink Cokes. I talk to an elder about the dam and what it did to Celilo Falls, but after a few minutes he gets angry and clouded up and can't go on. I leave before the food is cooked.

Early morning, threading through orchards in the hills above The Dalles, I'm dazzled by the late-season d'Anjou pears. Hitchcock-shaped, with a blush of pink, they are firm and sweet and full of juice which drips down your mouth when you take a bite. The cherries are long gone, most of them off to Japan, where they sell for ten times the price they retail for here, and the apples are all picked. Water from the Columbia, piped up from the reservoir of the dam that killed Celilo Falls, keeps these trees full of vigor. Without irrigation, nothing would grow. The desert here receives about six inches of rain a year—less than Phoenix—just an hour's drive from the hundred-inch annual rainfall in the west Cascade forests. Irrigation brings life to 7.2 million acres in the four states of the Columbia Basin. In the spring the orchards are convulsive with color, rolling rows of blossoms perfuming the desert air. In the fall, the trees are Impressionistic, bordered by the volcanoes of Mount Adams and Mount Hood. The perfect picture is broken only by the hangover of sorrow from the night before. I'm troubled by a puzzle of economics: chinook salmon were native to this area, and they are selling for ten to twelve dollars a pound this year, when you can find them. The fruit trees were brought in, and at harvest the growers practically give the crop away. If billion-dollar dams can help fruit grow in the desert and light boulevards in Los Angeles, surely salmon, which require nothing more than a river channel free of obstacles, can get some help from the geo-technicians.

By midafternoon on the third day, I'm ready to leave The Dalles. Before I go, I spend considerable time looking for the place where Winthrop recovered from smallpox, the old Fort Dalles site. I find it high on a bluff above town that still looks almost exactly as he described it. I go to the spot where he stared north to Mount Adams, his outlook soured by the desolate land below. "My heart sank within me as the landscape compelled me to be gloomy like itself," he wrote. "Nature harmonized discordantly with my feelings, and even forced her nobler aspects to grow sternly ominous."

The land could chill the soul just as easily as it could enlighten. Eighteen fifty-three was one of the worst years of the smallpox epidemic, which killed as much as ninety percent of the native population along the Columbia. Winthrop, suffering through three weeks of chill and fever, had a recurring dream that he'd caused the smallpox epidemic among the Indians. He must have wondered why his Yankee constitution could take the illness and the Indians could not. He hinted at the passing of orders, from the indigenous population to the New England transplants. It was not the hand of God that was at work, he concluded, but the random swing of nature.

Farther upriver: the air is drier, drained of all humidity, the land more barren. Few orchards cling to the hills of the Columbia in the hottest part of the Northwest, the northern end of the Great Basin. Less than twenty-five miles east of The Dalles, the river is pinched by the John Day Dam, a mile-long blockade across the water, the third Corps dam in less than a hundred miles. Man stands out here like asphalt in an alfalfa field. Up on the Washington bluff, a distant castle pokes in and out of view. Closer, it appears to be a mirage, a four-story stone mansion with a perfectly manicured green lawn set against the bony hills. There is no population center for miles. And yet, here's this castle, Sam Hill's mansion, the lawns of which are crowded with peacocks. Hill was an inspired lunatic, somewhat of a premature answer to Winthrop's prophecy. The son-in-law of railroad baron James J. Hill, Sam bought seven thousand acres of windswept scrubland above the Columbia in 1907, intending to erect a glorious home for his wife, Mary. After twenty years, it was still unfinished, but Hill, desperate to tie his life project to royalty, convinced Queen Marie of Rumania, a granddaughter of Queen Victoria, to come to America and take a train out west to his mansion, which she dedicated in a formal, black-comedic ceremony. Over the years, the mansion on the hill remained unoccupied and unfinished. People wandering through the Columbia desert would see the enormous castle and wonder, *What the Sam Hill?* After Hill's death, the mansion became Maryhill Museum, home for one of the most extensive collections of sculptures by Auguste Rodin. It's the oddest place for such a museum, but oddly fitting—through a sputtering evolution, it brought the better works of man near one of the better works of nature.

Another hundred miles upstream is the Big Bend, where the Columbia does a ninety-degree turn, flowing south through the barren home of some of the nation's darkest nuclear secrets before heading west. Here, the Columbia picks up the Snake River, which drains most of Idaho and parts of Wyoming, Utah, Nevada and Oregon. Though stapled by thirteen dams from its headwaters near Yellowstone Park to the confluence here, the Snake still has some power of menace. By the time it enters the Columbia, the Snake has carved out Hells Canyon, a slit in the earth more than eight thousand feet deep at its lowest point. The outsized landscape has inspired man to take extreme alteration measures. Egged on by merchants in the wheat towns of the Palouse, the Corps of Engineers dredged and dammed the Snake to allow passage of barge traffic all the way to Lewiston, Idaho, a Pacific port in the arid plateau.

In the vast desert here, the federal government built an instant city of fifty-five thousand during the World War II campaign to manufacture the atomic bomb. The sage and jackrabbit country around Hanford was declared a nuclear weapons reservation, an island of intrigue sealed from public view for nearly half a century. During the war, only a handful of the factory hands knew what they'd been working on. Then American planes dropped the first atomic bomb on Hiroshima, and a local paper screamed out the answer: IT'S ATOMIC BOMBS! PRESIDENT TRUMAN RELEASES SECRET OF HANFORD PRODUCT. After the war the area around the Snake and Columbia confluence, once a cluster of a few hundred subsistence farmers, caught atom fever. Nine primitive nuclear reactors were built, constructed virtually overnight. In just a few years' time, the main product of the Big Bend country went from peaches and asparagus to weapons-grade plutonium.

The Cold War was particularly prosperous. But during one 1949 experiment, the largest radioactive emissions ever documented drifted over the land here. It was kept secret for nearly forty years, while cancer deaths among young farmers and their children chilled the families of the high plateau. When documents about the emissions were finally released, they showed that people who lived downwind from the Hanford nuclear plants received doses of radiation—about 5,500 curies—ten times higher than Soviet citizens living near the scene of the Chernobyl nuclear disaster of 1986, and hundreds of times greater than the 15 to 24 curies released during the partial core meltdown at Three Mile Island. Perhaps twenty thousand children—because of their age, they were particularly vulnerable—were exposed to deadly levels of radiation which cause healthy cells to mutate. One fourth of the people living near the hardest-hit area have died of cancer since the 1960s.

All nine reactors are closed now—skeletons in the desert, they are frozen memorials to the infant nuclear age. Hanford, weaned on the bomb and all its by-products, is in steep decline, uncertain how to proceed in an ambiguous world. Cancer victims on the farms downwind petition the government for help, while most of their neighbors in the cities of Richland, Pasco and Kennewick ask for more nuclear-bomb-building contracts to keep their "Miracle in the Desert" from crumbling. They wonder why the market for plutonium has gone flat. News of better relations with the

Soviets is greeted with glum appraisals at Rotary lunches. Neighborhoods built along *Leave-It-to-Beaver* dreamlines are full of For Sale signs, many pasted over by foreclosure banners. The wagons have been circled; after some controversy, students at Richland High School have voted overwhelmingly to keep as their school logo a mushroom cloud from a nuclear bomb blast.

"You've heard of a family crest," says Marcia Cillan, the student body vice president at Richland High. "Our crest is a nuclear bomb." Once, years earlier, at commencement day ceremonies, the Army rigged a bomb of napalm and TNT and set off a mock atomic blast, a mushroomlike explosion which shattered the windows of nearby buildings.

Hanford boosters have placed one last hope in trying to get the government to convert a half-finished commercial nuclear reactor into a tritium producer. Warren Magnuson, the retired United States Senator who directed more government contracts to the state than any other man, said such a desperation move made no sense.

"The times have changed, and we must change with them," said Magnuson, whose influence brought highways and health centers and dams and bridges and military stations to the young Northwest during his forty-four years in Congress. He died in 1989, but he spoke for history. There are three great treasures in the Pacific Northwest, he said: Puget Sound, the Cascade Mountains and the Columbia. Each deserves respect, bordering on reverence. The desert can produce many things when watered, but nuclear bombs should not be a permanent product of the land, Magnuson said. What would Winthrop make of this nuclear-crazed community on the Columbia? A detour on the way to the Promised Land? An aberration of nature, perhaps? If so, its cycle was remarkably short: up from the dust to the City of Tomorrow, then back to the dust as the world realized the City of Tomorrow could not be trusted.

I want to see the last wild stretch of the Columbia River—the Hanford Reach, fifty-seven miles of freedom. It's a rumor I've never confirmed. Because this part of the river lies within the 560-square-mile Hanford Nuclear Reservation, it has been shielded from most of society, including the dam builders, since World War II. But with Hanford closing down, the river is coming out. I turn off a couple of lonely roads, pass Keep Out signs and fences of diminished authority, angle toward the river, and there it is: the only free-flowing stretch of the Columbia. Full of renewal, the river races through the desert here, pulling water past rust-colored cliffs and mesas untouched by irrigation or cattle grazing or roads. From the steep, eastern bank of exposed geology, I see mule deer and jack-rabbits and the ever-circling hawks. A coyote dashes from the brush, startling me. I walk along a cliff, three hundred feet above the river, and stare into a canyon with a fresh pulse, the wind in my face.

Now, down on the shoreline, I look out at the only slice of the Columbia which in any way resembles the river seen by Winthrop, and Lewis and Clark. I toss a piece of wood into the water, and it quickly disappears. Unlike the rest of the backed-up Columbia, the river here has a current of mystery and strength. Several generations of history haunt this place. On level ground next to the river is a trio of aging willows, planted for shade by homesteaders who were chased off the land when the bomb builders took over, a rough collision of two eras. Across the river, in the foreground, is a tree with nine blue herons perched on its limbs; in the background is an abandoned nuclear reactor.

Arrowheads and chipped tools from the Wanapums, who have lived in the upper Columbia for centuries, are littered on the beach of a small island separated from the shore by a shallow stretch. Undisturbed, never buried by water from the dams, the island looks as if the natives left just yesterday. They built pit houses here during the salmon season and crafted bowls and weapons while drying fish for the winter. I can still see the shelters carved into the bank of the island, and rock flakes near their encampments. Later, when I talk to a few members of the Wanapum tribe—there are only a handful left, clustered in a village upstream—they say the Hanford Reach is sacred country, full of burial sites. "I wish they would just leave it alone," says Patrick Wyena, as he sips beer with five other Wanapums.

The graveled river bottom here, unstirred by the earth-movers, is home to the biggest natural chinook spawning ground in continental America. About half a million fish a year return to the reach to spawn and die. There is no need for multi-million-dollar hatcheries; all that these big kings need to propagate is for the Hanford Reach to stay the way it's been. Also lurking in these depths are sturgeon. An Ice Age survivor, prehistoric in appearance and size, Columbia River sturgeon can grow to two thousand pounds or more and live for a century. When they break the surface of the water, it is as if the Loch Ness monster had arrived from Scotland.

The Corps of Engineers is moving fast to kill the salmon run and lasso the last stretch of freedom. For years they have been trying to get permission to dam the Hanford Reach, but nobody wanted the project. With that plan on hold, they are now proceeding with a scheme to gouge the river shallows of the reach for several miles, at a cost of $200 million, to benefit a few commercial interests in the upriver town of Wenatchee. The Port of Chelan dreamed up this idea and presented it to the Corps, whose members have never met a river that couldn't be dredged, dammed or rechanneled. Never mind that most of the apples grown around Wenatchee reach their markets in no time by trucks traveling the highways; the Corps thinks it would be nice for Wenatchee to have deep-water barge traffic. Typically, that's the way the Corps works: find a few Chamber of Commerce locals to put forth a pipe dream, then send the bill to the rest of the nation. The Army engineers estimate a half-million cubic yards of river bottom would have to be dredged, producing enough sediment to fill a football field to three hundred feet deep. Of course, they recognize that chiseling the reach into an industrial waterway would kill the last great natural salmon spawning ground on the Columbia and forever alter the final wild stretch. But the Corps says the natural salmon run could be replaced by an artificial one, created by manmade spawning channels.

With the rest of the Columbia already shackled, the Corps is running out of projects; hundreds of engineers are sitting around offices in the Northwest with no rivers to dam. "We are in the business of building dams and dredging channels," says Noel Gilbrough, the Corps project manager. "This is the last place on the Columbia where you could put a dam. But, we are having some trouble selling this project."

Now, the sky turns on me; thunderheads collide and dump ice marbles of hail. I look for shelter, but there is no place to duck out of the squall. If I were across the river, I could huddle under the roof of the abandoned nuclear reactor, a frightening thought. I trudge back uphill, drenched, and then continue upriver again. As I head toward Grand Coulee Dam—passing Priest Rapids Dam, Wanapum Dam, Rock Island Dam, Rocky Reach Dam, Wells Dam, Chief Joseph Dam—the Corps is dealt a stunning blow by Congress. The news out of Washington, D.C., is that the Hanford Reach has been placed off limits to the earth-movers for a three-year period of study to determine if it should receive permanent protection under the Wild and Scenic Rivers Act. When I hear the news I stop my car near a place called Dry Falls, site of the biggest waterfall the world has ever known, a prehistoric cataract forty times mightier than Niagara. Today, no water drops from this red-tinged basalt wall, four hundred feet high and nearly four miles across. A former channel of the Columbia, it has been dry for nearly a thousand years. When an ice dam broke at

Lake Missoula eighteen thousand years ago, a mountain of water was unleashed over the Columbia Plateau, cutting channels into the desert floor and flooding the lower Columbia valley from the Snake confluence to the ocean. The surging water of that flood comprised ten times the combined flow of all the rivers in the world today. When the water receded, the Columbia was a new river with at least three new arms: its main channel, the Moses Coulee, and the Grand Coulee, which included Dry Falls. In time, the water retreated to the original path of the river, leaving behind coulees up to 1,600 feet deep in parts.

Now the sky is heavy with darkness and fresh thunderheads. A wicked wind ricochets through the Dry Falls coulee. Alone as I stand with this trough of the ages, the narrative lines come through: without help, the earth can still tell a good story.

Like a tooth drilled clean and packed with silver, the Grand Coulee is full of water again, a twenty-seven-mile-long irrigation reservoir. But the Moses Coulee is empty. At the upper end of the old Indian hiding grounds, where Chief Moses sheltered his band from winter winds and marauding whites, I yell into the expanse; the sound bounces against the wrinkled walls and then falls away. Down below is a ranch of hay and alfalfa and cattle, where Bob Billingsley has been trying to scratch a living from the floor of the old Columbia River channel since 1928. He is the padrone of the Moses Coulee, a rancher of high humor and wind-buffed cheeks, eighty-five years old on the afternoon that I drop into his coulee. Bob's father homesteaded in scrubland above the Columbia in 1908, went bust, took a series of odd jobs, and then settled on a patch of bottom land in this coulee with his family. Bob knew that a geological tug-of-war had been waged in this prehistoric ditch. He found bones from the joint of an elephant, including a ball joint as big as a watermelon. He found petrified wood and Indian arrowheads. He drilled for a well in the middle of the coulee, four feet, ten, thirty, eighty, a hundred feet, and never reached clay. As far down as he could go, the soil was thick, nutrient-rich river sediment, a gift from the Pleistocene flood that carried bits and pieces of British Columbia, Montana, Idaho and Washington topsoil to this hidden coulee. His spring would only provide enough water for a hundred acres, so he figured out a way to back up the late winter floods and save the water for release over the summer. He hired Indians to work the fields with him, including a stepson of Chief Moses. They became fast friends, the Indian telling Billingsley about the horse races they used to have in the coulee and Billingsley giving him tips on how to deal with the government.

The coulee is lifeless in the low end where it meets the Columbia—a deep, wide gorge that looks like a Martian roadside park. At the high end is the Billingsley ranch, alive with galloping horses and orchards and cattle and grandkids.

Every day, Billingsley rises with the sun, puts a pinch of tobacco in his cheek, and works outside till the lunch hour. Then he kicks back, plays with his grandkids, helps his wife, Helen. Reads. Life is good in the Moses Coulee. He has a satellite dish out back which brings him 127 channels of television; when that bores him, he goes to his library of memories. He remembers the Woody Guthrie anthems to the Columbia— the socialist folksinger wrote twenty-six songs in twenty-six days of work for the Bonneville Power Administration—and all the Dust Bowl farmers and teachers and laborers who came to the desert of Central Washington because land was nearly free and water was just as cheap. "Most of these guys, they lasted until their sock ran dry," says Billingsley. For twenty-five years he went without power, and then came the Grand Coulee Dam.

"The farmer deserved electricity just the same as everybody else," he says. "What the Grand Coulee did was to make us no longer second-class citizens."

Deep inside the bowels of the dam, the walls shake and glass rattles. The noise is not from generators; they hum along in relatively quiet fashion, their turbines capable of producing 6.4 million kilowatts of power— enough juice to run most of New York City. The sound comes from the pumping action, water racing through pipes twelve feet in diameter, going three hundred feet uphill through bedrock to the formerly dry channel of the Grand Coulee. You stand inside this fortress and realize that nothing since that Ice Age flood has so reshaped the land; the Grand Coulee is the height of man's attempt to play God. I'm nearly six hundred river miles from the Pacific, inside one of the manmade wonders of the world. Yet, I feel a vague uneasiness. The most extensive hydroelectric power system ever built is on the upper part of this river. Water from the dams painted the desert green, lit up the inside of Indian shacks on the Columbia Plateau and dirt-farmer cabins in the Okanogan. With runoff under control, the dams gave a degree of assurance that the floods of spring would no longer wipe whole towns off the map. But this triumph of technology marked a surrender for the laws of the earth.

Conceived in a populist flurry as the largest of Roosevelt's New Deal programs, the Grand Coulee took eight years to build and provided a retort to a long-ago speech of Daniel Webster, who had said, "What do we want of this vast, worthless area, this region of savages and wild beasts, of shifting sands and whirlwinds of dust? To what use could we ever hope to put these great deserts or these great mountain ranges?" The idea for the dam was born in the coffee-table chit-chat of a country lawyer, Billy Clapp, and a young prospector, Paul Donaldson, who had just returned from a luckless reconnaissance in the dry coulee. Looking for news in the summer of 1918, a reporter from the Wenatchee *World* promoted their bull-session with an eight-column headline across the top of the front page, a description of the unharnessed power of the Columbia: TWO MILLION WILD HORSES. Following Roosevelt's election in 1932, the project gained favor as The People's Dam, an engine for agriculture and cheap power. In Murray Morgan's book, *The Dam*, he remembers what a fellow student at the University of Washington had told him when Grand Coulee was under construction. "If our generation has anything good to offer history, it's that dam. It's going to be our working pyramid."

Here on the Columbia Plateau, with the advent of the biggest public-works project ever undertaken, Roosevelt thought he had found the Dust Bowl solution. A half-million farmers would live near the lonely coulees within a generation's time, he predicted. With the Columbia set to provide half as much electricity as was generated by the rest of the country, industrial leaders made plans to bring manufacturing plants to its banks. But Roosevelt said he wanted farmers, not factories; he worried that smokestacks would sprout from the nutrients of cheap electricity, making the West too much like the East.

"There are many sections of the country where land has run out or been put to the wrong kind of use," he said during a trip to Grand Coulee in 1934. "Out here you have not just space, you have space that can be used by human beings—a wonderful land—a land of opportunity."

In scale and audacity, the dam was astonishing; engineers were going to anchor a mile-long wall of concrete in bedrock at the bottom of a steep canyon in the Columbia. They would excavate 45 million cubic yards of dirt and rock, and pour 24 million tons of concrete. Among the few dams in the Northwest not built by the Corps of Engineers, the Grand Coulee was the work of the Bureau of Reclamation. When completed, it was a mile across at the top, forty-six stories high, and heralded as the biggest thing ever built by man. The dam backed up the river for 151 miles, creating a lake with 600 miles of shoreline.

At the dam's dedication in 1941, Roosevelt said Grand Coulee would open the world to people who had been beat up by the elements, abused by the rich and plagued by poor luck. But a few months after it opened, Grand Coulee became the instrument of war. Suddenly, the country needed to build sixty thousand planes a year, made of aluminum, smelted by power from Columbia River water, and it needed to build ships—big ones—from the same power source. Near the end of the war, America needed to build an atomic bomb, whose plutonium was manufactured on the banks of the Columbia. Power from the Grand Coulee was used to break uranium into radioactive subelements to produce that plutonium. By war's end, only a handful of farms were drawing water from the Columbia's greatest dam. True, toasters in desert homes were warming bread with Grand Coulee juice, and Washington had the cheapest electrical rates of any state in the country, but most of that power for the people was being used by Reynolds Aluminum in Longview and Alcoa in Vancouver and Kaiser Aluminum in Spokane and Tacoma.

The Dust Bowl solution, the last gasp of agrarian idealism, had brought Industrial Age factories to the Northwest. Roosevelt didn't fully anticipate the vast shift from country to city that was underway. A hundred years ago, forty-three percent of all Americans lived on farms; today, less than four percent do. In 1939, there was not a single aluminum plant in the Northwest; ten years later nearly half of all the nation's aluminum was produced in an area served by two Columbia River dams. In 1935 there were eighty-five thousand individual farms in the state of Washington; thirty years later, there were only forty thousand. Many of the refugees from the fallow land of the interior ended up as factory hands.

Upstream, the Grand Coulee raised the river level more than three hundred feet, forcing the evacuation of three thousand people. Ten towns were buried by water. They were replaced by places with such names as Electric City and Elmore, futuristic villages that now look as dated as 1950s sci-fi films. The worst damage from the dam was to the upper Columbia River salmon. King salmon are among the most durable creatures of nature, strong-willed and singleminded when the spawning urge sends them upriver, but no fish can scale a five-hundred-foot-high dam. More than a thousand miles of spawning grounds were lost forever.

I'm looking for someone who can tell me what the upper Columbia used to be like before the Grand Coulee Dam changed the personality of this place where the desert gives way to gentle mountains and forests of tall ponderosa pine. Everybody says talk to Martin Louie. So I follow a road northeast of the dam until it dead-ends among rusted cars clustered in the "new" community of Inchelium. The old one is under water. I'm directed to the small, tattered trailer of Martin Louie. When I enter at midday, I find a tiny man lying on a cot, covered with flies. He wakes, lights a cigarette, and looks around as if he's lost. He has no teeth, and his lungs can barely hold a breath. He lives in squalor, an outhouse-size home in the dust along the banks of Roosevelt Lake, the 151-mile reservoir that is the upper end of the Columbia in Washington.

Louie can't remember how old he is; and that may be because he nips from a bottle more often than he should and is never without a cigarette. His dark face contrasts with the snow-white hair atop his head, a crew cut. Back issues of *True Detective* are piled up near his cot. On the wall is a brown picture of Inchelium before the flood. I introduce myself. Louie stares at me for a few minutes, silent.

"You're not another one of those Mormons?" he says at last. "'Cause if you are, you can leave right now."

"No, no, I'm not a missionary."

"What d'you want, then?"

"I want to know what it was like."

"You can't know."

Louie is a member of the Lakes Band of Indians, a small tribe which lived near the present Canadian border. In the summer and fall they pulled salmon from Kettle Falls, a Columbia River fishery second only to The Dalles in bounty. Twice in the last century, the Lakes people were decimated by smallpox. When Louie was born, sometime around the dawn of the twentieth century, they were recovering somewhat. They still had Kettle Falls, and as long as the water tumbled down those cliffs, the salmon would be easy to catch. Louie attended two schools, he says: white school and Indian. At white school, he learned about "the only two books you haven't got a chance against: the Bible and the law book." At Indian school, a classroom without walls, he learned about the land.

"The white creator lives up there. The Indian creator lives all around. You see the Indian creator every day, every night. You see him in the day, in the sun, and at night, in his brother the moon. But most of all you see him in that water. That river. It's never emptied out yet. It controls all life. It controls everything. The Indians call that Father."

Until the dam went up, Louie lived the life his ancestors had lived, a gentle routine on the upper Columbia. When the reservations were set up, the Indians were promised access to their salmon runs forever in a treaty backed by one of the two books which Louie is afraid of. At the dedication of the Grand Coulee Dam, much was made of the fact that the first electricity to go out was used to power the new washing machine of an Indian woman who lived not far from Louie. But she didn't need a washing machine as much as she needed a free river. When the dam went up, the fish stopped returning, and Louie lost his livelihood and his independence. When the Columbia became Lake Roosevelt, he was a man who didn't know his way around. He became a seasonal worker, a serf for somebody else. Now, in the last years of life, he is drowning in bitterness.

"When I want salmon now, you know what I have to do? I have to travel up to the Fraser River to buy it. And—here. . . ." He eases himself up, bites on the cigarette. ". . . I'll show you what I can buy for twenty dollars." He opens the door of a small refrigerator, the outside paint chipped away, and pulls out a small, heavily wrapped packet. He strips away the layers until he comes to a few pieces of smoked salmon. "This."

Kettle Falls, the salmon mother lode south of the Canadian border not far from Louie's home, is just another section of smooth water now. It stirs no sense of awe or aesthetic impulse unless the imagination goes to work. The Columbia used to fall thirty-three feet in less than half a mile here. I find an odd-looking rock on a bluff above the graveyard of the falls. It's a boulder full of slash marks, apparently a whetstone used by generations of Indians to sharpen their spear points. I close my eyes and imagine healthy men pulling salmon from the falls. I open my eyes and see the glass of a reservoir and the dying face of Martin Louie. For ten thousand years or more, people lived with the wind-tossed pines and turbulent river and never went without. When the river was dammed, it brought prosperity to one band of humans while forcing another to go hungry. I've seen the grapes and apples and wheat that grow in the new desert, but I will never experience Celilo or Kettle falls. I paid for a year's worth of college tuition by working the caldrons of the Kaiser Aluminum plant one summer, a factory powered by cheap hydroelectric energy, but my education about the once-free Columbia must come secondhand, from the soured memories of people like Martin Louie.

Standing above the Columbia today, the river that carries water from

all parts of the Pacific Northwest to the ocean, uniting deserts and glaciers, forests and farmland, cities and sage country, I'm troubled by this
paradox. Winthrop thought the land here would change a man, not the
other way around; still, at the ebb of the twentieth century, we have yet
to prove him entirely wrong.

Epilogue

PACIFIC NATION

S ometimes the wind along the Pacific shore blows so hard
it steals your breath before you can inhale it. At La Push,
a Quileute Indian village huddled amidst the sea stacks of
the Washington coast, the wind owns almost every other
breath. Few people live along the shore from San Francisco
to Vancouver Island; in those places where humans have settled in next to the raging surf, often there are more Indians
than whites. Such is the case here at La Push, where one must
have skin of cedar bark, or the sea otter's sense of humor, to
live with the theft of many breaths. Compliance with nature
is a virtue. And nobody in La Push thinks of this most northwestern edge of the lower forty-eight states as land's end.
Rather, it is land's start.

As a soundtrack to the task of sorting cluttered thoughts,
there is no better music than a winter storm on the Northwest
Coast. On one side of me is the darkest and thickest of American forests, an evergreen cushion between the ocean and a
nation in the early years of its third century. Great shanks of
wood, thrown against the beach by the muscular sea, are piled
in random disorder at the high edge of the tideline. The original
forest cover of this continent, like the native inhabitants, has
been pushed from Winthrop's home in Massachusetts to this
coastal strip in the far west. I wonder if these misted giants
of five centuries or more in age will survive the commercial
appetite of my generation.

Were I to follow Winthrop home, I'd have continued east
through the pine forests and high desert of Idaho, crossed the
Continental Divide in Montana, and traced the river drainages

to the Atlantic. But that was his world, the age of Europe, when all eyes looked east. I live at the dawn of the Century of the Pacific. At the end of *The Canoe and the Saddle*, Winthrop foresaw the start of this shift from east to west, a trickle of immigrants "moving away from the tame levels of Mid-America to regions of fresher and more dramatic life on the slopes toward the Western Sea." Along this coast, life is certainly more dramatic, made so by the elements and a sky that should never be taken for granted. The freshness is evident in a change of attitudes. Although the non-Indian Northwest was founded on Pacific Rim trade—the wealth that Captain Cook's men obtained from the Cantonese mandarins for the sea otter pelts they picked up during their 1778 trip to Vancouver Island— it is only now in the dying years of the twentieth century that people of this land have embraced Asia as their future.

When many Northwesterners hear talk about the decline of America, it means little to them; they see, in such talk, the diminished influence of Europe and those power centers in the American and Canadian East that look to Europe for identity. As the nations of Europe meld to a single continental unit, stagnant in population growth and new immigration— the "tribes of the setting sun," as West Coast author Joel Kotkin calls them—the Pacific Rim is bursting with fresh life and ideas and commerce. Since 1980, more immigrants have arrived on the West Coast, most of them from Asia, than came to the United States at any time after the last great European wave in the early twentieth century. A similar immigration trend has hit British Columbia, where a third of all Vancouver citizens trace their ancestry to China. Seattle led the nation in new job growth in the late 1980s, and one in three of those positions was tied to Pacific trade. Just as the Irish and Scandinavians and Russians and Italians brought new tastes to the North American table, the Pacific Rim immigrants bring ties from the old continent, a link of opportunity.

Thirty years ago, American trade with Asia was only half that of its trade with Europe. Those figures have reversed themselves, with European trade amounting to only fifty percent of the volume the United States does with Asia. About $3 billion a year in Asian money pours into Vancouver, the Hong Kong of North America, where financiers are building a new sort of Wall Street, a place for traders who will operate on a world clock. The new mandarins, instead of receiving sea otter pelts taken from Vancouver Island by English seamen, are becoming Canadian citizens and helping the port of Vancouver emerge as one of the Pacific Rim's new financial centers.

About 120 miles south of Vancouver, Seattle citizens who have had a taste of Manhattan or worked jobs in Europe are trying to reposition their fast-growing city as the Geneva of the Pacific, a home between the Cascades and the Olympics for dialogue in many languages. Long before the national networks and the broadcasting syndicates tried similar exchanges, the Seattle television station founded by Dorothy Bullitt, daughter of a pioneer Northwest mill family, was linking up citizens of Russia and America by satellite to talk about the differences that would kill us all. At the same time, Bob Walsh—born in Winthrop, Massachusetts— was working to bring some of the best athletes, dancers and artists in Russia and America together in Seattle during the summer of 1990. Walsh has since married a Russian, Nina, who lives with him on a bluff above Elliott Bay, where the windows look out at the Olympic Mountains and the water that connects Siberia to Seattle.

The new products of the Northwest—airplanes and medicine and wine and computer software—are in their way dependent on the old resource: the magnificent scenery. No industry is more damaging to that scenery, and none brings less good to fewer people, than the current timber business, a hangover of the exploitive early years. The most economically distressed counties in the Northwest are those that depend on logging for their livelihood. The most prosperous are those that have unchained themselves from their mills. Someday the Northwest will stop acting like a resource colony, stripping the last of its big trees from the mountains and shipping that wood abroad with little concern for the resulting job loss or the land scars. When that day comes, Northwest forests will be able to produce a profitable by-product—furniture—and the scenery will be far less threatened. By some estimates, tourism will be the number-one industry in the world by the year 2000. The newly prosperous people of Korea and Taiwan and Singapore will come to the Northwest to visit their relatives; if they are lucky, they will see a land not far removed from the cradle.

North Americans used to fear Asia, and some still do. A backlash against the Asian influx in Vancouver has developed. Some Vancouverites want harsh immigration restrictions and have begun to spread the type of racial poison first seen in British Columbia when Chinese laborers were brought in to build the Canadian Pacific Railroad. Free trade can leave hard feelings: Japanese demand has pushed the price of salmon and timber beyond the reach of many Northwesterners, who feel they have a birthright to such products of their land.

"God forbid that the time should ever come when a state on the shore of the Pacific, with interest and tendencies of trade all looking toward the Asiatic nations of the east, shall add its jarring claims to our distracted and overburdened confederacy," said Daniel Webster, the American Senator of the midnineteenth century. Even as Webster thundered, the founders of Seattle and Portland and Victoria were plotting ways to get Asian ships to tie up in their ports, each calling itself the Gateway to the Pacific. Theodore Roosevelt, whose legacy has been astonishingly good for the Northwest, saw the Pacific Age as a coming tide of glory. "The Mediterranean era died with the discovery of America," he said at the turn of the century. "The Atlantic era has reached the height of its development. The Pacific era, destined to be the greatest, is just at dawn."

So, we have a Pacific Century, long predicted, that is finally coming of age, and one section of the North American continent primed to take full advantage of it. The prophecy of Winthrop may yet come to life in the polyglot future of the Pacific Rim. More than anything, what the Northwest meant to Winthrop was renewal—the promise of tomorrow that this continent has always held—a chance for his heart and mind to wander without the leash of the past. In the closing lines of his book, Winthrop said his tour through this land had cleansed him:

> And in all that period while I was so near Nature, the great lessons of the wilderness deepened into my heart day by day, the hedges of conventionalism withered away from my horizon, and all the pedantries of scholastic thought perished out of my mind forever.

In the near century and a half since Winthrop passed through the Pacific Northwest, the East has retained much of its dominance. The media centers are still there, as are government, and publishing, and finance, and most of the people. But everything Winthrop reveled in, the glaciers, the virgin forests, the green islands, the plump rivers, the fir-mantled volcanoes, the empty range of the high desert, Grandpa's trout streams, and the alpenglow, are here—a land that has yet to give up all its secrets.